Marcel Proust: His Life and Work

Léon Pierre-Quint   (Photo: Ilse F

MARCEL PROUST

His Life and Work

by

Léon Pierre-Quint

Translated by

Hamish and Sheila Miles
and Kurt Weinberg

With a Preface by

Germaine Brée

PETER LANG

New York · Berne · Frankfurt am Main

Publisher's Note: *Marcel Proust, Sa Vie, Son Oeuvre* was originally published in 1925 by Simon Kra in Paris. In 1927 Alfred A. Knopf published an English translation by Hamish and Sheila Miles in New York. Pierre-Quint augmented the French edition in 1928 and 1936, and this was published by the Editions du Sagittaire, who retain the French copyright. The present edition reprints the Miles translation together with the author's later additions, translated here for the first time by Kurt Weinberg, and a new preface by Germaine Brée, placing the biography in its historical context. An archive of Pierre-Quint's papers and books was established in 1981 at the Bibliothèque Nationale in Paris.

Library of Congress Cataloging-in-Publication Data

Pierre-Quint, Léon, 1895-1958.
Marcel Proust, His Life and Work.

Translation of: Marcel Proust, sa vie, son oeuvre.
1. Proust, Marcel, 1871-1922. 2. Novelists, French—
20th century—Biography. I. Title. II. Series.
PQ2631.R63Z82   1986   843'.912   85-31227
ISBN 0-8204-0330-X

CIP-Kurztitelaufnahme der Deutschen Bibliothek

Pierre-Quint, Léon:
Marcel Proust : His Life and Work / by Léon Pierre-Quint.
Transl. by Hamish and Sheila Miles and Kurt Weinberg.
With a pref. by Germaine Brée. — New York ; Berne ;
Frankfurt am Main : Lang, 1986.
Einheitssacht.: Marcel Proust [engl.]
ISBN 0-8204-0330-X

Printed by Weihert-Druck GmbH, Darmstadt (West Germany)

CONTENTS

PREFACE

by Germaine Brée

More than half a century after the publication of *Le temps retrouvé*, the last volume of *A la recherche du temps perdu*, why re-issue a volume of criticism which first came out in France in 1925, Léon Pierre-Quint's *Marcel Proust, His Life and Work*? Proust by now is a well-established literary figure. Since the fifties, *A la recherche du temps perdu* has taken its place among the major literary works of the Western world, a remarkably rapid consecration, no longer seriously contested. A vast critical edifice has attended this ascent. The Proustian corpus, besides, includes many texts unknown to readers in the Twenties: the unfinished early novel, *Jean Santeuil*, among them, and the fragments collected under the title *Contre Sainte-Beuve*. A multi-volume, carefully edited correspondence has come out. Critical editions complete with a host of variants are on the way; while ever more ingenious "readings" of ever more fragmented layers of Proust's text testify to its complexities.

This in fact is perhaps why it is particularly pleasing to step back from our late twentieth century critical sophistication to that candid era of the Twenties when Proust was "new"; an era in which the imaginative and critical realms of discourse had not parted company. Léon Pierre-Quint's *Marcel Proust* takes us back to that rare moment of "intoxication" when an unknown book, picked up by chance by a young reader, brings with it the feeling that, as Pierre-Quint puts it, one is "present at the birth of

v

a work of art such as we see only twice or thrice in a century." For Pierre-Quint, it turned out to be no temporary delusion. How, one often wonders, do new forms of art emerge, sort themselves out and find those first readers who act as mediators between the writer and the larger reading-public? Léon Pierre-Quint's bafflement at his first contact with *Du côté de chez Swann*, his sense that he was confronting a book written in a "foreign language" unintelligible to him while yet he felt its "magic," takes us to the heart of the process. His need to work out for himself and to communicate to others what attracted and moved him so deeply was all the more imperative because both author and critic were unknown at the time.

Léon Pierre-Quint was twenty-two in 1917 when, he tells us, he came upon a copy of *Du côté de chez Swann*. The name of the author was virtually unknown, except within a small coterie of Proust's intimate friends. It was some two years later that the then controversial award of the Goncourt Prize to Marcel Proust for the second part of *A la recherche du temps perdu* created a first flurry of interest in the work. A year *before* that first recognition, the young Pierre-Quint had sent Proust the manuscript of an unpublished novel asking for permission to dedicate it to him, an authorization Proust willingly gave. What he thought of the novel we do not know. It was entitled *Simplification amoureuse* (Amorous simplification) and was followed by a book of short stories *Déchéances aimables* (Pleasing depravations) and a brief disenchanted novella *La femme de paille* (the Straw-woman). Léon Pierre-Quint was not, it seems, destined to become a great fiction-writer. He was closer to the "fin de siècle" mannerisms of Proust's *Les Plaisirs et les jours* than to the more astringent and vaster vistas of *A la recherche du temps perdu*. But it was a writer's sensibility he brought to his reading of Proust, an enthusiasm for the very texture of a style which rebounded into the younger man's essay, with its underlying lyrical élan, semantic felicities and, sometimes, flamboyance.

In fact, his *Marcel Proust* was Pierre-Quint's first major work and seems to have been a turning point in his career as one of the more perspicacious critics of his time. He was never to be a one-author man, but his involvement in "Proust's universe" was neither casual, nor passing. In 1958, the year of his death, he was, typically, working on another article on "Proust's universe," for a special number of a Paris review *Le Point*. From the Twenties on, intermittently, he had lectured and written on various aspects of Proust's work. But the 1925 volume was not superseded. In 1928, and again "ten years later" in 1936, it was re-issued in France with, on each occasion, a new preface and new essays. An English translation of the original volume had come out with remarkable promptitude in 1927, no doubt a testimony to the growing interest in Proust's work shown by the literary English elite and sustained by the ongoing Scott-Moncrieff translation. The later prefaces and essays are included in translation for the first time in the present volume, a welcome addition, if only for the compelling account of the "last months of Proust's life" which ends the book. But they also open up new perspectives on the intellectual odyssey of critic and work in the changing atmosphere of the "entre-deux guerres."

The original three-part organization of the book obviously, cannot be considered as planned. Pierre-Quint did not revise his early, carefully developed essay. Rather, as critical commentaries began to accumulate, he filled in gaps in his early appraisal, sometimes candidly referring to its limitations. He casually admits, for instance, that he had overlooked the satiric-comic social dimensions of the Proustian narrative because, with the earnestness of the neophyte, he had focussed too narrowly on what intrigued him: the depth of the ethico-psychological analyses, the aesthetic values and the connections between the narrative and Proust's life. All in all nonetheless, the early essay remained the pivot of the book. Pierre-Quint never questioned the initial insight that motivated it. The imbalance of the three parts is thus understandable. In the French edition, the approximately 240 pages of the first part are followed by the 90-odd pages of the second and the fifty-odd pages of the third. The format becomes loose: "observations," "notes," "impressions," "remarks." As the circle of Proust's readers widened, Pierre-Quint carried on, in his new observations, an open dialogue with other commentators, while acquiring a more mature understanding of the complexities of Proustian writing. He was not hampered, as we may sometimes be, by what Milton Hindus described as "the tangled undergrowth of commentary which has grown up around Proust." By the 1930's he was not alone in his faith in Proust's "genius," as he was not afraid to call it. But it is surely he who more boldly than any other critic at the time disengaged the figure of Proust — "a writer of astonishing novelty" — from the image of the "fashionable amateur" and pampered aesthete which had dogged Proust from his adolescence to his death.

"To Marcel Proust, discoverer of a world of temptation, landscapes and love, with renewed gratitude." When he sent his novel to Proust with that dedication, Pierre-Quint was on the threshold of a brilliant career as a prominent "homme de lettres" in the versatile literary Paris of the Twenties. Proust, almost a complete recluse, obsessed by the urgent need to finish *A la recherche du temps perdu* was nearing the end of his. From our late twentieth century point of view he may seem strangely removed from the post-war era upon which Pierre-Quint was to leave his mark. To Pierre-Quint he seemed very much of it.

A young law student when he came upon *Du côté de chez Swann*, Léopold Léon Steindecker, the son of a Paris banker, had much in common with Proust. Like many in their social class, he had early tried his hand at writing. A delicate young man, he had been reluctant to take up a career in the family bank, much as Proust had side-stepped his father's suggestions as to a fitting profession. Because of his ill-health he developed a passion for literature which he considered, traditionally, as the transmission through aesthetic means, of fundamental truths about life, refracted through a unique experience and sensitivity. Like Proust a quarter of a century earlier, he had been drawn to the study of Bergson, to Bergson's exploration of non-intellectualized modes of consciousness. It was in 1918, a year after his discovery of the "universe" of Proust, that he adopted the pseudonym Léon Pierre-Quint, a sure sign that he was planning a literary career.

It was a propitious time for young writers. Young Europeans, tired of the constraints of the war years, were clamoring for something new. Literary circles were alive with iconoclastic new ideas, little reviews; young men, enamoured of scandal and easy contracts, exploited to their limit the "modernist" and "experimentalist" trends that had begun to surface in the pre-war days.

As Surrealism followed Dada, the new publishing houses indefatigably launched new collections, specialized anthologies, panoramas, introducing avant-garde and foreign writers to a bemused public. Pierre-Quint was one of the more knowledgeable of these. He had contacts in the publishing world and by 1923 was co-director of the "European collection" of The Editions du Sagittaire, the avant-garde publishing house which was to bring out his *Marcel Proust*. His associate in that task was Philippe Soupault, a writer well-known in most avant-garde circles of those years. One thinks of course of Proust's first ventures as contributor to the fin-de-siècle little reviews of his own generation. It was a milieu Pierre-Quint knew at first hand. He was able to gauge its importance in the development of the ambitious young Proust's early writing.

In the Twenties, after the hiatus of the war, and with four "generations" bursting into print, literary trends were harder to distinguish one from the other. Pierre-Quint was on friendly terms with the surrealists — André Breton, Artaud, Benjamin Péret — as with the maverick off-shoot of surrealism, the mystics of *Le Grand Jeu*. The terms he uses to characterize Proust's work, in that early dedication, suggest the connection he sensed between certain Proustian themes and the more militant "innovations" of the hour: "discovery, temptation, landscapes, love." The word "magic" is several times reiterated, with its variants "Proust the magician," the "wizard," the "fabulous necromancer." Proust here has acquired the enigmatic personality of "le bateleur," the magician of the Tarot cards, a favorite signifier for the artist and poet in surrealist imagery. For Pierre-Quint, to the very last, Proust would retain that aura.

X

Pierre-Quint's activities as discoverer of new texts, editor, launcher of reviews and critic slowed down when the 1931 economic crisis brought the publishing bonanza to an end. He was essentially a man of the Twenties, with an understanding of art rooted, as was the case with Proust and Gide, in the austere tradition of the poet and literary theoretician Mallarmé. For him, art lived in its own autonomous realm, answerable to others only in terms of an aesthetic integrity, which it was the critic's task to uncover. He was uncomfortable when confronting the ideological trends of the politicized Thirties when Proust's work was attacked for what was seen as its asocial irresponsibility and esotericism. Thence, in his later essays, his tussle with the question of the significance of the literary work, a question much debated in later years.

Pierre-Quint shared his surrealist friends' belief that the source of art lay in the deepest layers of the individual psyche, which, freed from rational constraints, disclosed inner desires and impulses that illuminated the basically unintelligible realities of human existence. The problem he set himself was to seek the key to the Proustian achievement through the careful observation of the patterns and contradictions manifested in his way of life; then as they were refracted in the themes and structures of the work that gave them and it their significance and "universality." Proust, of course, offered Pierre-Quint a particularly challenging topic of investigation, so eccentric was his way of life, even in a society where eccentrics were not rare. Pierre-Quint's admiration for the work oriented him toward a modern theme: the double transmutation of a life into a book; and of a book into that "étrange humain" as Proust himself put it, the writer, Marcel Proust. Thence his sensitive approach to the biographical elements, that, even now, are one of the fascinations of his essays. He does not "explain," condone nor blame. Because he does not separate man and work, he has no use for different systems of value — moral, socio-political, aesthetic — with which to evaluate the work as distinct from the man.

His portrait of Proust nonetheless is rich in anecdotal material, whether obtained at first hand or passed on through more intimate friends. He rightly refutes the accusation of hagiography. Proust's growing reputation was justification enough for the intensity of the portrayal. The sobriety and vividness of his descriptions of Proust's to us by now familiar way of life is one of the achievements of his book. Proust's passion for social intrigue, the lengths to which he went to find out who would introduce him to a brilliant hostess; and, in contrast, his reclusiveness; his "extreme amiability" and "impassioned taste for making gifts"; his kindness and cruelty; his "devouring ambition...." Already, at an early date he saw behind Proust's much debated "snobbery" and love of social "potins" (gossip) the drive of the "perpetual investigator," as he called Proust, to penetrate beneath the smooth surface of human relations to their true hidden meshings. The investigator in Proust, as he saw it, kept the magician in check: "His imagination sought to work only upon subject matters controlled by his own observation." The comment is perspicacious. It led Pierre-Quint to a quiet refutation of the criticisms of the "new generations" of the Thirties, and to the partial exploration of another theme he had overlooked, the social boundaries of Proust's universe. His approach to the questions is exemplary: first he notes that Proust's imagination takes in, besides the aristocracy, the "world of fashion and servants"; then that the society which Proust depicts was the "society *in which* he created his work," the depiction of the "upper classes" not being an end in itself. He raises the question of why the depiction in depth of one section of society would not be as revealing as any other. He was not, obviously, captivated by the dialectic certainties of neo-marxist aesthetics. In fact, the historical dimensions of Proust's text did not interest him, but those techniques whereby Proust introduced into his narrative the large discontinuous social frescoes which he discerned as part of the metaphysical structure of the book. They measured the passage of time in terms of changing bodies and social configurations. Proust's insights into the process of human aging and social change were, as Pierre-Quint saw, at the very heart of his concept of time and the question raised by the "recovery" through art of modes of being and feeling long since obliterated.

In 1928, only three of the seven parts of *A la recherche du temps perdu* had come out in print. True, letters had circulated, and lengthy dedications outlining anticipated developments. Fragments of future volumes had appeared in reviews which could signal what Proust was up to. There was, too, the over-all title with its counterpoint: the search for "time" lost ending in the final "time regained": for readers, even now, a title not without its ambiguity. But Proust's writing had already shown a disconcerting habit of overflowing announced developments, as volume followed volume. Pierre-Quint was thus taking a risk. Subsequent volumes might discredit his reading, as might new information concerning Proust's life. This happened, as he readily admits, when he found out, what he did not know in 1925 when he wrote his first essay on "Sodom and Gomorrha," that Proust had a first-hand knowledge of what he called that "Dantesque inferno." The young critic's ignorance, one feels, was not entirely to his disadvantage. For his sense of the violence and beauty, the unprecedented "audacity" of that depiction and of its sociopsychological implications was free of extraneous emotion.

The title of one of the later essays, "How I understood Proust," stresses the personal quality of his involvement as a critic. He was and remained an undogmatic reader with no axe to grind. His pleasure in the text is contagious in its spontaneity. Even today we understand his avowal of bafflement when he started to read "Combray" expecting a novel, like others, sequentially narrated and we sympathize with his decision to start reading anywhere in the middle of the volume; and we can share in his satisfaction when he finally grasped the inner organization of the narrative. We watch him struggling with that sticking point of Proust criticism: the uncertainty as to the identity of the first-person narrator; and with it of course the uncertainty as to the "genre." Autobiography? Fiction? A series of discontinuous "novels," or a coherently architectural whole? He wavers between those possibilities. He speaks of the "I" as "Proust"; of "Proust" (or his hero); of "Proust's hero"; and merges the worlds of autobiography and fiction: Bergotte, he informs us, delighted Proust in his youth; and he analyzes "Proust's" discussions with "Albertine" and his "agonizing passion" for that fictional young woman. But Proust himself, after all, sometimes did the same. Perhaps most indicative of things to come in the realm of criticism are his remarks on the "pathology of language" in Proust, an early prospection of a Freudian theme. All in all, *Marcel Proust, His Life and Work* is a remarkable achievement, which deserves to be re-edited and re-read.

MARCEL PROUST

INTRODUCTION

I N PUBLISHING an article on Marcel Proust a few
years ago in a review, I was obliged to make an arbitrary choice, from out of the whole of his work, of a
few particular aspects, and to neglect others which I
knew to be essential. I limited my subject. Since then I
have often been anxious to take up the theme again and
complete it with a second article. I waited. Each new
volume of Proust filled me with a new emotion, like
that which one experiences at the bends of a zigzag
road, as gradually a whole chain of mountains is disclosed to view. And my second article has become—a
volume of two or three hundred pages.

Nevertheless, I am not so presumptuous as to regard
it as complete. After reading already eleven volumes of
A la recherche du temps perdu, I am still filled with
impatience to know the secret of its continuation. Will
Madame Verdurin enter the aristocracy and become a
duchess or a princess? And on whom will the little Gilberte of the Champs Élysées bestow her hand? What
surprise does the new aspect of Saint-Loup hold in
store for me? I imagine that the end of this lengthy
modern epic, as impossible to forecast as life itself, may
oblige me, for my own part, to bring certain of my
judgments into a new focus. But I do not suppose that

it is likely to make me change anything of importance in my present study.

My principal object has been to make a general survey of the work of Proust as a whole, to envisage it as a self-contained structure, an organic whole. And although only about three quarters of this work have as yet appeared, my attempt does not seem premature. The main structure, with which we are acquainted, has reached a point of development far enough advanced for us to grasp the harmony of its vast proportions. We feel that everything is in place. We know that the obscure incidents of the beginning grow plain under the light of succeeding events. Without waiting for the publication of *Le temps retrouvé*, we can henceforward consider the work with one all-embracing view, as a visitor to a cathedral with uncompleted towers will move a few steps backward and take into his survey the united whole of the architectural conception.

I should say, however, as I feel bound to do, that my original thoughts were concerned only with the joy and the anguish which the books of Marcel Proust gave me. Reading, often enough, is no more than a distraction, a method of passing the time, or else only a duty which one imposes on oneself. But four or five times in my life, as with *Du côté de chez Swann*, for example, it has brought me one of those deep emotional experiences which leave a permanent impression behind them. With the successive appearance of the later volumes, I realized that this was the birth of a work of art such as we see only twice or thrice in a century, and at certain moments I felt, as it were, overwhelmed: I

4

could feel an inward tremor, an intoxication. It is to these sensations that I have sought to give expression.

After a short time I felt a desire to compare them with those of Proust's friends, in order to know better what kind of man he was. I enlarged my scope, and I was rewarded: this first-hand documentation only increased still further my admiration for this tragic genius.[1]

Accordingly, I have begun my study with the sketch of a biography. From this there emerges the same significance as from his work. On the one hand, I have brought out the trend, the meaning, of this magnificent life of his. On the other, I have retraced, from the testimony of his books, his *universe*. Here, then, we see Marcel Proust successively in the midst of the *"time past"* and of the *"time recovered,"* during his life in the heart of society, and then in his retreat, in art and in fame. And we learn to appreciate his ideas on the *"time past"* and on the *"time recovered,"* on the *salons,* on love, and on æsthetics.

Between these two parts, which balance and complete each other, I have inserted, in six chapters which are necessarily much more abstract, a study of the technical side of the work, explaining the fresh contributions

[1] I should like here to express my gratitude to Dr. Robert Proust, to the late Jacques Rivière, and to MM. Brunschwicg, Fernand Gregh, Henri de Régnier, Jacques-Émile Blanche, Frédéric de Madrazo, Albert Flament, Prince Antoine Bibesco, Reynaldo Hahn, René Blum, Robert de Flers, Constantin Ullmann, Jean Cocteau, Paul Morand, Edmond Jaloux, Paul Brach, Faure-Biguet, Georges de Traz, Jacques de Truelle, Jacques-Bénoît Méchin, Louis Serpeille de Gobineau, and to all others who have so readily furnished me with information and so greatly facilitated my work.

of the writer and the essential originality of his method. This is the keystone of my book.[2] I discuss the nature of Proust's composition, with its alternating themes, the rhythm of these themes, the themes of evolution and the unconscious, what the author says of sleep, dreams, and memories, his method of fathoming the depths of the mind, the appropriateness of his style to this method, the gradual ageing of his characters, and the way in which they display the problem of personality.

So my book divides itself naturally into three parts: the life, the work, and the universe of Marcel Proust. As appendix, I have reproduced a few of the documents of which I have made use and which I was not able to introduce into the body of my work, some fragments of the still unpublished correspondence of Marcel Proust, and a bibliographical note.

L. P.-Q.

---

[2] However, for readers who are visiting Paris in seven days and Venice in three, a special Baedeker would advise them, if they are too much pressed for time or find it too exhausting, to skip this central part and go straight on to the next one.

PART ONE

THE LIFE OF MARCEL PROUST

CHAPTER I

THE TREND OF A LIFE

THE life of Marcel Proust holds a lesson. From his
earliest childhood upwards, he used to write; at
every stage he was gathering material for that future
work which never for one moment forsook his thoughts.
But from his early days he had known suffering, and
by the age of thirty-five he was a chronic invalid.
With that, he took his leave of society and fashion, and
devoted all the vitality that was left to him to the
Remembrance of Things Past.

It would be fallacious to distinguish two completely
opposed phases in the life of Marcel Proust: a span of
youth given over to pleasure, and then an ascetic withdrawal from the world, during which the writer was
never again to look up from his note-books. It was thus
that Pascal, after his famous night of conversion, renounced the world and abandoned himself with tears of
joy to God. But Proust did not need to become converted to a religion. His life, it is true, has the appearance of being marked out in various stages, but it was
not touched by any great spiritual crisis. Quite imperceptibly, rather, throughout a decade or so, he gradually began to drift away from the *salons* and the
fashionable gatherings which so long had held him in

their spell, though without any definite resolution never to return to them.

It was a renunciation which was certainly acutely painful to him; illness overshadowed him, continually stabbing, ineluctable. His whole desire was to create, to bring his work into the light. Would there be time to finish it? In his very young days he had enjoyed the most exclusive of welcomes, and tasted of the flattery of success. At fifteen he had been the faithful little attendant of Madame Straus in her *salon*, sitting at her feet on a great plush footstool. Illustrious personages of the Third Republic came to pay their respects to the lady of the house; nor did they forget to spare a moment or two of attention for the young favourite. They used to compare him to the exquisite Italian princess of Paul Bourget's stories. At home his looking-glass was lined all round with notes of invitation. Once a famous courtesan sent him a book bound in the silk of her petticoat. And very soon he came to understand with a peculiar intimacy the society of his generation. The friends he chose from its midst had to be either intelligent, devoted, or of noble birth. And he was not hampered by lack of fortune from shaping for himself an existence in accordance with his taste, nor from indulging the cravings and promptings of his soul.

Already, however, he recognized the threadbare values of such pleasures for what they were worth. He knew that human life must needs reach out towards happiness, but that every enjoyment which mankind brings to light by its activity is transient and illusory. The distinctions imposed by society, the honours it confers, are no more than relative blessings, which cannot alter those who receive them. They are satisfactions which lie on the surface; how can they allay the despair that lurks in the very depths of our being? It would be absurd to deny pleasure, but we must rest content to seek it without marvelling that it should never attain consummation, that our longings become tempered before they reach fulfilment, and that in the unheeding flow of time we can grasp only that which is perishable.

External existence is like a garment flung over our bodies—yet in each one of us there burns a more essential life. And art is surely the kindling of this flame? Proust knew well what this meant. For him art brought the means of escape from an empty universe towards the ideal, and the promise of a joy which very nearly touched the absolute.

When he came within sight of forty, he gave up his entire being to it. He spent the last years of his life, years in which he knew himself to be in the presence of death, revising and completing his manuscripts, a task which only the attacks of his asthma, ever more lasting and more distressing, could interrupt.

If he did sometimes on very rare occasions go once more into the fashionable gatherings he had deserted, it was to confirm some particular detail bearing upon his work. He might wish perhaps to see with his own eyes that the manner of the Comtesse d'Haussonville's greetings was one and the same as the Courvoisiers'. Perhaps, too, the object of his social relationships had been none other than to help him in the construction of this book, and he had been an indefatigable frequenter of the *salons* just in order to glean all the information he could. "It is true," he says, "that I attach infinitely more importance to the book which has absorbed the best of my thought, of my life even, than to anything else I have accomplished hitherto, which is as nothing compared with it." [1]

It will be seen that the same teaching makes itself felt in his book as in his life. A world of people, of passions, and of emotions springs forth from it. The only treasure which cannot be exhausted lies within our own memories, the impressions drawn out from the depths of our being, through the medium of art; and these perhaps are life's sole realities.

Once the work was written down, though still uncompleted, Proust had only one thought—to see it published before death should overtake him. "It is only asking now for a tomb which may be completed ere my own be tenanted." [1] To a friend who had thought him neglectful he wrote: "In all that concerns my work, I have the foresight of a bee, a foresight reaching beyond the grave itself, which most likely is not very distant from me." [1] But in spite of all his exertions the war prevented him from seeing the complete publication of his work; and he himself helped to delay the appearance of the later volumes by endlessly correcting and adding to them.

Yet there was still time for him to know fame, a fame of the rarest kind: first the admiration of a select

---

[1] Unpublished correspondence.

few, then spreading little by little to the whole reading public. It penetrated beyond the boundaries of his own land. His novels were translated into English. Socialistic intellectuals began to discuss the jealousies of Swann, and the foibles of M. de Charlus. And so his last days were suffused in the glow of a radiant dawn.

It was only a short time before his death that he reproached himself once more for having infused too little of himself into his books. To the dying Bergotte "there appeared a pair of heavenly scales. In one pan lay his own life, while the other contained that little piece of projecting wall so admirably painted in yellow [in one of Vermeer's finest pictures]. He felt that he had imprudently exchanged the first of these for the second."—The last scruple of an unbounded devotion to art!

CHAPTER TWO

REMEMBRANCE

MARCEL PROUST was born in Paris on July 10th, 1871. His childhood was very happy, but all too brief: only until he was nine years old could he taste the joys of sunshine; and then one side of the universe was barred to him. One day, as he was coming home from a walk in the Bois de Boulogne with his parents and some friends, he was suddenly seized with a terrible fit of suffocation. His father, Professor Proust, was panic-stricken, fearing that he must succumb to such an attack. It was the first manifestation of chronic asthma, that intermittent agony which was never again to leave him. The open country air, the aroma of trees, the perfume of flowers, nearly suffocated him, and to breathe became a torture.

His mother, who was of Jewish blood, had been a Mlle Weil before her marriage to Proust's father, a Catholic, and a native of Chartres. People have tried to find the key to certain of Proust's mental characteristics in the fact of his Jewish heredity, but such deductions can only be quite theoretical, and throw no light whatever on the subject. The Jewish mind has begotten many contradictory schools of thought, many conflicting systems of philosophy. We find on the one hand, for example, the intellectualism of a Spinoza; on the other, Bergson's theories of intuition. A race does not produce only one type of thought. Perhaps most characteristic of Proust was his amazing fight against suffering and death. And it is just that which is the only really Jewish characteristic that comes out in Swann, whom Proust portrays as being, like himself, entirely assimilated.

Baptism, catechism, first communion—none of these left any trace of religion in Proust's mind. His parents were very careful not to let any questions of belief come up between them. Their child went on maintaining this indifference. He has neither faith nor hostility. God is left out of his work, forgotten.

His mother it was who taught him to abhor falsehood, to be scrupulous in all things, to deny himself willingly; but above all he derived from her contact an all-embracing goodness of heart. M. André Berge [1] has discovered and published an album of confessions in which a group of friends is asked to submit itself to a uniform list of questions. In answer to the question "What is your favourite saying?" Proust wrote, at the age of fourteen: "One which cannot be set down, because in its simplest form it holds all that is noble, beautiful, and *good* in nature." And in answer to "What is your pet aversion?" he replied: "People who have no feeling for the good, who pay no heed to the delights of friendship." And once more: "What is your idea of wretchedness?"—"To be parted from Mamma." This fragile and sensitive boy responded to his mother's unbounded love with an impassioned and gentle ten-

---

[1] *Les Cahiers du mois* (December 1st, 1924).

derness. Those years of his childhood were wrapped in his memory by the gentle atmosphere his mother created around him, in her endeavour to soften the continual attacks of nervous trouble which beset him. It seemed to him that the azure seraphim, of which the children in the Tales of Hans Andersen dream, must have chosen his mother from amongst all the mothers in the world for her goodness, placing a blessed halo upon her fair and comely forehead. We are made aware of this atmosphere of felicity and anguish in the first chapter of *Du côté de chez Swann;* and when in the following volumes he is describing the hero's ever restless passion for his grandmother, it is again of his own mother that he is thinking.

During those years his sensibilities were abnormally acute. Such violence of the emotions contrasted strangely with the frailty of his body. His sentimental effusions found their outlet in gestures of adoration, or in tears of despair. "Do not weep so much, Master Alexis"—so opens *Les Plaisirs et les jours.* Little Alexis could not face a visit to his dying uncle. "He felt he had not the strength to endure the pain of seeing him.—'But what shall I do if he speaks of it [his death]?' 'You will tell him he is mistaken in thinking that he is going to die.'— 'And if I should weep?' 'You have wept so long this morning already that you will not do so while you are with him.'—'But, if I do not weep,' exclaimed Alexis in despair, 'he will surely think I feel no sorrow, that I do not love my dear uncle.' And he burst into a flood of tears."

Every year Proust and his parents used to spend the

summer months with his uncle at Illiers. It was a large estate, not far from Chartres, midway between the regions of the Beauce and the Perche. Before long, however, his health made it necessary to forgo these holidays in the country, for the sake of the more invigorating air of the seaside. Thus it was that while he was still in his early childhood he discovered the eglantine flowers he loved so much, yonder amidst the untamed thickets over by Méséglise. The true wild roses, which are still blooming and which only lately were plucked in reverence at Combray, by Americans come thither on pious pilgrimage.

Combray does not take its colour only from Illiers, but also from the country-house at Auteuil which belonged to M. Weil, a great-uncle on his mother's side. One can never find infallible clues in the novels of Marcel Proust. The writer is merely searching among divine realities, in *various* localities, in *various* individuals, for those *chosen* peculiarities out of which to mould one single imaginary country-side, Combray; one single individual, Swann; one single sonata, the sonata of Vinteuil.

About the years 1885–95, Auteuil was in relation to Paris what Saint-Cloud or Ville-d'Avray are to-day. There, amidst noble parks, certain rare spirits lived all the year through, self-exiled; Dr. Blanche, father of the painter Jacques-Émile Blanche, was one; later on there came Fernand Gregh, and, for the sake of her dogs, the Comtesse Potocka, to whom the Comte Gabriel de la Rochefoucauld remarked the first time he undertook this pilgrimage: "It is quite charming. . . . Is there

anything to been seen in the neighbourhood?" [2] Each
spring, when attacks of asthma did not threaten him,
Marcel Proust and his parents went to live at his uncle's
house in the Rue La Fontaine. The furnishing of the
house was quite bereft of taste. Its dining-room was
hung with imitation tapestries, their subjects borrowed
from Teniers. Often the young Proust would gather
strawberries in the great garden, which has since been
cut in two by the Avenue Mozart [3] being driven through
it; and here he would have his friends to share in
rustic picnics. In this circle it was that he met the friend
who was first in revealing Musset to him, and who was
afterwards to serve as a model for Bloch. Here too he
could study Jewish families, and the way in which they
formed themselves into impenetrable groups.

In spite of his delicate health, Proust entered the
Lycée Condorcet. At that time Jules Ferry was putting
the reforms of secular instruction into force. To the
great astonishment of the pupils, the professors no longer
wore cassocks, nor were the children obliged to say
prayers. Proust was not able to attend the classes regu-
larly. Owing to his attacks of asthma, he had often to
report himself absent, and to miss "essay days." That he
gained excellent marks in spite of this handicap was due
to his extraordinary intelligence, to his prodigious memory, and to his tireless curiosity. But he was inevitably
an irregular pupil, and as such did not win any prizes
at the end of the school year. He followed Jaliffier's

[2] *Le Salon de la Comtesse Potocka,* by "Horatio" (an article contributed
by Proust to the *Figaro*).
[3] Marcel Proust's preface to *De David à Degas* by J.-É. Blanche.

courses of history with passionate enthusiasm; the court
of Louis XIV dazzled him, as did the past history of all
the illustrious names which later he tried to find again
in the Faubourg Saint-Germain. In his comrades' eyes
he excelled in nothing so much as in natural history.
It left an enduring impression upon him. Abundant are
the parallels he draws between mankind and certain rare
species of plants and birds and fruits. Does not the very
title of *Within a Budding Grove* suggest his taste for
botanical things? In a certain sense Marcel Proust is
a naturalist dealing in human values; his work is to lay
bare the countless vanities of individual types, together
with their emotional peculiarities.

After school hours, on half-holidays and Sundays,
young Marcel went to play in the Champs Élysées.
Between the summer concert of the Alcazar, which
has since been turned into a miniature golf-course, the
wooden horses, the woman who sells marbles and sweets,
and the great lawn of the Avenue Gabriel, stretches the
pathway where the schoolboy used to meet his friends:
Léon Brunschwicg, a schoolfellow, who to-day is a
member of the Institute, Robert Dreyfus, Paul Leclerq,
Louis de La Salle, killed in Champagne during the war,
Jean de Tinan, who died when he was only twenty-four,
and a host of others. . . . As a rule he liked talking
better than games, at which he was rather clumsy; he
amazed his young followers by the vivacity of his
mind, and the way in which he was able to sound the
depths of general ideas. He used to recite innumerable
verses by heart, lines from Mallarmé, whom in this way
he revealed to his companions, or poems by Baudelaire,

19

of whom he used to say: "He has a feeling for the value of gestures. It is as fine as Bossuet." Leconte de Lisle filled him with enthusiasm, and when he told his companions of David Copperfield, of the death of Dora, and the death of the little dog, he was deeply moved.

In those days the theatre enjoyed a dazzling prestige, which nowadays is a little difficult to understand. The kiosks, brilliant with posters of every hue, blazoned forth heroic names—Sarah Bernhardt, Mounet-Sully, Got, Delaunay. All these are merged and personified into the genius of Berma. The Comédie Française seemed like a temple of the gods. The plays of Augier were performed there, and those of Dumas *fils*. Arthur Meyer contributed a series of notices to the *Gaulois*, while Sarcey reigned supreme on the *Temps*. Young Proust showed an overwhelming enthusiasm for this life of the boulevards, and he was as intoxicated by his enthusiasm as by a passion.

A few little girls too belonged to the group of playmates in the Champs Élysées. Proust had his favourites amongst them. In their presence he did not indulge in passionate conversation; novels and poetry were laid aside. To them he had to confide the tumult of his thoughts, and the stormy vicissitudes of his soul. Already he experienced the need to give, and to give himself fully. There stirred within him the first tremors of love. He implored Gilberte, fashioned out of these young girls, to enter with him upon a new friendship, pure and indissoluble, which was to begin on a certain New Year's Day then close at hand. He learned to understand that love demands the sacrifice of all that one is and has, and that in return for a few brief moments, moments which constitute those rare sublimities which in themselves alone make life worth living, there follow long months of suffering.

.   .   .   .

The year 1889 saw the last of voluntary service in France. When Proust was eighteen years old, and had passed his *baccalauréat*, he anticipated the summons and joined the 76th regiment of infantry. He was exempted from hard tasks and long marches on account of his delicate health, and Colonel Arvers, commandant at Orléans, watched over him with friendly interest. The young man set out to fathom this new world into which he was thus transplanted; his earnest intelligence, which could not look at anything superficially, turned its interest upon strategy. We can trace these interests in *Le côté de Guermantes*, where the hero and his friend Saint-Loup are considering problems in tactics which the great generals of history have had to face.

Immediately upon his discharge Proust had to turn his thoughts towards the choice of a permanent career. Literature attracted him heart and soul as nothing else did. Already he had written a few essays, and some poems—*Les Portraits de peintres*. At fifteen he had written that passage so characteristic of his future style, in which he analyses the powerful impression left upon his mind by the three church-towers of Martinville. He was to reproduce it without any touching-up in *Du côté de chez Swann* and also in *Pastiches et mélanges*. He knew beyond a doubt that in his head lay a book waiting to be written, though he knew nothing of the plan or the form of it. But one thing he knew for certain, that it must in its essence spring from that voyage of exploration into his consciousness which he must make in order to recapture his most precious memories. One day as he was walking in the neighbourhood of Méséglise while he was still a child, the quickening of a landscape after a storm of wind and rain made a deep impression upon him. "And seeing that a ravishing smile from the water and from the face of the wall answered to the smile of the sky, I cried out in my enthusiasm, all the time brandishing my closed umbrella: 'Zut, zut, zut, zut! . . .' But at the same time I felt that my *duty* was not to stop short at these opaque words, but to try to see more clearly into my delight." To seek out the obscurest sensations that they might be brought under the scrutiny of the mind, and to understand the most secret springs of one's being—those were the intellectual and sentimental functions which Proust regarded as his foremost obligation towards himself. Each time that he had let the moment slip by without making an effort to lay captive an emotion by submitting it to analysis, thus giving it a larger significance, an emotion which he knew was irrevocably lost, he would blame himself for this laziness as for some grievous fault, nor did he forgive himself. In these moods of inspiration, these moments of apprehension, he was made aware that his vocation was to write.

Rarely in a bourgeois *milieu* is the profession of art looked upon as a legitimate one. Marcel Proust was not understood by his father. Professor Adrien Proust, who was a hospital physician, was at the height of his career.

He was an imposing figure, tall, with a beard that was just turning grey, clothed all in black. Having entered the Civil Service, he very quickly became Inspector of Public Hygiene in France. He it was who organized *"cordons sanitaires"* as a protection against cholera and the plague, and who invented that expression for them. It was he too who first held the chair of hygiene in the Faculty of Medicine, and he was already speaking of the campaign against tuberculosis. The pince-nez which he was perpetually waving in the air seemed to be the symbol of an extremely busy life, which was spent almost entirely away from home, in great activity and always bustling.

The irony of the contrast is clear indication of the divergence which estranged the son from his father, when one thinks of the life that Marcel Proust was going to lead in after years, of his room, through whose windows no breath of air should ever find its way; of his habit of staying up all night and sleeping all day; of his horror of doctors—a life lived in veritable defiance of hygiene. "The tragedy of family differences," wrote Marcel Proust,[4] "is that it is just those very qualities, that very analogy of one's tastes with those of one's relations which, in order to manifest and assert themselves, come into conflict with their own." And just these qualities which Proust had in common with his father were a sense of duty and a feeling for work, the sense of a lofty ambition consecrating a prolonged and disinterested labour. But in his love of action Professor Proust was not able to esteem a purely intellectual

---

[4] Preface to *De David à Degas* (already cited).

23

activity as in any way the equivalent of the tasks he himself was accomplishing.

The son gave in. He did not prepare for a diplomatic career, as his father had wished. His frail health was the excuse. He entered the Sorbonne in the Faculty of Law and the École des Sciences Politiques. At one time he thought of entering the Cour des Comptes as a "secondary profession" which would leave him a relative amount of freedom to follow his own intellectual interests. He considered every possible profession. "Is not the magistracy too greatly discredited?" Proust asks in a letter to his friend Robert de Billy. "What remains for me, given that I can be neither a barrister, nor a doctor, nor a priest . . . ?" One day he was wanting to buy a notary's practice; the next he went into a solicitor's office, to leave it a month later. His examinations tided him over for a while, as they do for many another vacillating young man, until the time when he must make a definite choice.

Proust found little to interest him in his lectures. It was philosophy that attracted him most in his law studies. At the Lycée Condorcet he had acquired a taste for the great systems of philosophy through the lucid teaching of Darlu, his classical master. He was fascinated by the prestige of Boutroux, and Lachelier, and Ravaisson, who led him little by little to a comprehension of Bergson. Whilst he was at the Sorbonne, Proust came to know this philosopher, whose influence was to dominate his thought. Bergson's thesis, *Les Données Immédiates de la conscience,* had just appeared (1889). Soon after that he became a relative of Marcel Proust by his marriage to Mlle Neuburger. And so the great metaphysician's hold over the young novelist became strengthened through their personal relationships. There are certain ideas which dominate the mind and the work of Proust: the flow of time; the perpetual evolution of personality in its duration; the unsuspected riches of the unconscious, which we can only recapture through intuition; memory, or associations which are involuntary, but which it is only possible to express with the help of the intelligence; the intelligence, which alone is capable of grasping life; art, the sole reality in the world, through which we are to recover life in its fullest depth —all these ideas find their inspiration in Bergson. Proust seems himself to have lived, felt, and tested the Bergsonian psychology.

Examinations and the necessity of deciding upon a career did not hinder him from becoming daily more and more aware that there dwelt in him a being, an artist, who must inevitably one day attain to self-expression. It was towards this period that he made his first appearance in the world of letters. "The simplest way to enter noiselessly upon a literary life is to found a review," wrote Fernand Divoire in his *Stratégié littéraire*. "Nothing could be easier . . . one seeks out a few companions . . . each pays his monthly subscription. When the subscriptions cease to come in, the review breathes it last."

Le Banquet was founded by Marcel Proust, together with a few friends, in the *salon* of Madame Straus: they were Fernand Gregh, Robert Dreyfus, Daniel Halévy, Robert de Flers, and Henri Barbusse. The rate of sub-

scription stood at ten francs a month. It became necessary, according to the collaborators' budget, to reduce
the extent of the impression of the second number sub-
stantially; this issue is quite unprocurable. The review
met with considerable success. Léon Blum, to-day the
president of the socialist group in the Chamber of Dep-
uties, addressed in it some pleasing quatrains to the moon.
Most of the collaborators in the *Banquet* are now famous
men. How many reviews started by a rising generation
can boast of so many names which since have risen out
of obscurity?

What is most striking in looking through a collection
of the *Banquet* is the freshness of its interest to-day.
The greater number of its articles make interesting reading still. Daniel Halévy translates an act of one of
Ibsen's early plays; and he writes in collaboration with
Fernand Gregh, who prefaces *La Maison de l'enfance*, a
study of Nietzsche, who was little known in those days.
Numerous articles are devoted to Schopenhauer, Ros-
setti, and Swinburne. Proust, in the over-florid style
which he then had, draws portraits in outline of great
ladies and of courtesans, sketches miniature pictures,
land and sea, and sometimes writes what to-day we
should call "notes" on books which have recently been
published, notes which towards some are excessively
lenient and eulogistic, often ironically so. Always he
comes forward with the concerns of moralist and judge.

It is just that social, political, historical, and intellectual curiosity which was characteristic of those young
men. They were not afraid of seeming dogmatic because
they took an interest in general ideas, or of being

thought dull because they had a regard for philosophers. It is easy enough to understand how such a generation could become excitedly eager over an event like the Dreyfus Case. Quite outside any considerations of "school," indifferent alike to the symbolist movement as a movement and to the anarchic leanings of *La Revue Blanche*, they held their seniors in respect, nor did they want to assert themselves against the Parnassians, or against the aged Hugo. They sought quietly to build up a work which might have in it the potentiality of numbering with the classics. In this way individualistic temperaments tacitly, nobly even, proclaimed themselves; and their goal was not an easy one to reach, because there was nothing to bring it immediately under the public notice.

Marcel Proust was ignorant of all literary stratagem, even more so than any of his friends. The attitude he adopted in making his début in the world of letters was later to hamper him for a long time; it was to be a stumbling-block to him in the eyes of publishers, and one of the reasons why success was so slow in coming to him. Even though he founded a review, which was certainly the "first step" towards making a name for himself, he did not know how to make use of these advantages to impress himself upon his "colleagues," or to carry out the wise counsels which M. Fernand Divoire gave for preparing a reputation before actually publishing a book.

He did not even seem afraid, out of exaggerated sincerity, of putting himself into a false position. In *La Revue Blanche*, the stronghold of symbolism, in which Henri de Régnier, Maeterlinck, Gustave Kahn, and Mallarmé collaborated, an article appeared entitled *"Contre l'obscurité,"* which opened thus: " 'Do you belong to the younger school?' is the question which every twenty-year-old student who dabbles in literature asks every elderly gentleman of fifty who does not. For my own part I confess I cannot understand this; one has to be initiated. Moreover, there has never been so much talent as now; nearly everyone possesses some talent nowadays."

There is no doubt that Marcel Proust laid stress on an idea which he constantly repeated, that all works of art of any real value shock the public by their very quality of newness, and that time alone can make them comprehensible. "The paradoxes of to-day become the prejudices of to-morrow." In this article too he sets himself to define a few of his conceptions of style: "Every word . . . wields over the imagination an evocative force quite as great as its capacity for strict definition." In the act of criticizing a system of deliberate obscureness, he gives the impression (quite a false one) that he is making an attack upon symbolism, he who admired so much the poetry of Francis Jammes, and so ran the risk of appearing to be, contrary to what he really was, a back number. Although in his social relationships he linked himself with most of the celebrated men of letters out of every group, he fell into a state of literary isolation. Misunderstandings concerning his talents began to spring up; he was taken for an amateur, a reactionary, and a *"boulevardier."* Later on, when he published a series of articles in the *Figaro* on the

28

salons, his estrangement from all who were concerned in literature became even more complete. How powerful must have been the leaven of freshness in his work that, twenty years afterwards, the most advanced groups should bow down before a writer then forty years old! As far back as 1896, Lucien Muhlfelds dubs him *"mondain."* He had indeed seen Proust's article before it appeared in print, and had followed it up with a long refutation of his own called *"Pour la clarté."* It was a piece of bravado, full of verve, in which he tried to make out that he was the champion of the younger generation against the *salons.* Proust was to take his revenge later on.

During the same year, 1896, two books of his made their appearance: through *Le Menestrel,* a slim volume entitled *Portraits de peintres,* together with four pieces for the piano by Reynaldo Hahn, and a few months later *Les Plaisirs et les jours,* published by Calmann-Lévy, with illustrations by Madeleine Lemaire, "as famous across the seas as in Paris itself." Anatole France wrote a signed preface to this work. The book was merely a collection of reprints from portraits, studies, sketches, and stories which Proust had contributed to *Le Banquet* and to *La Revue Blanche,* together with a few unpublished pieces, and as such did not help to dispel the legend of fashionable dilettantism which had grown up around him.

Léon Blum showed great shrewdness of perception in a criticism which he made: "I am impatiently waiting for his next book . . ." he writes; "when a man possesses the gift of style, and the subtlety of thought

29

which this too self-conscious and too precious book contains, he has gifts which cannot be allowed to run to seed." The style of *Les Plaisirs et les jours* is occasionally admirable, but at times it verges on the finical. Contrast that too abstract terminology, those too puristic epithets, those too symbolic images, with the magnificent form of *A la recherche du temps perdu!* *Les Plaisirs et les jours* is infinitely precious to us: by means of it we can follow the author through his adolescent years, and contemplate, whilst they are yet in bud, some of those blossoms which he will offer us later on, in the full bloom of maturity. But in spite of everything there is a big gap between this book and the next one: it took Marcel Proust nearly twenty years longer to acquire that prodigious sharpness of observation, that power of penetrating into thought itself, that audacity of portraiture of the kind which Oscar Wilde has said makes even the most intrepid draw back aghast.

. . . .

Marcel Proust could not be wholly satisfied by the publication of *Les Plaisirs et les jours*. He was too much engrossed by a mundane life, and over-anxious to infuse into his art a love of refinement, an affability and amiability which were merely a part of his external life. He had not yet withdrawn into his cell. He would need many "days" yet before he could renounce the "pleasures."

He came to realize little by little that his asthma could never be cured. At twenty he still had faith in all the remedies as yet untried. No sooner did he hear of a fresh doctor than he wrote to his friends for information. "This autumn I ought to try (and I think I shall try) a cure of the Dubois [5] variety. If after it, as they promise, I can lead . . . a normal life, I hope that without being in your way I shall see a great deal of you." [6] But he could never make up his mind to start. When he wrote: "I ought to try (and I think I shall try) . . ." he was really writing: "I don't think I shall try . . ." Before very long he gave up all hope of cure, unless it were by some hidden chance, some gigantic good fortune—a miracle, in fact.

The sense of how short was his existence haunted him. An adolescent will sometimes contemplate suicide, but he rarely thinks of the nearness of death. But Proust, so ardently in love with life, was obsessed by the thought of his end. When he was twenty-two years old, two of his friends, delightful striplings both of them, disappeared. One of them was Edgard Aubert, a Swiss; the other, Willie Heath, an Englishman, to whose memory Proust dedicated *Les Plaisirs et les jours*. Speaking of the former, he wrote to Robert de Billy: *"I feel that he was still expecting much from life,* that he still thought it full of promises, and this makes it all the more heartbreaking." Each time Proust called up this memory, his grief came back to him afresh. A voice, "intimate and far-away," reminded him of his duty as an author; every moment of time he had wasted, time so short, so precious, made him suffer. In his dedication to Willie Heath he says: "Though it [death] may release us from

[5] A Swiss psychiatrist.
[6] Unpublished correspondence.

31

the pledges we have made towards life, it does not release us from those we have made towards ourselves, more especially from the foremost of them, which is to live so that our lives become things of value and deserving of praise."

The first sacrifice Proust made for the sake of the work he knew he had within him was to give up all ideas of a regular profession for the sake of literature. How much rather would he have liked to devote one part of his life at least to action, had illness not curtailed his activity! His mother's kindness made this decision easy for him. At an age when most young men leave their families, Proust went on living in the room which had been his as a child, in the apartment in which he was born, near the Madeleine, in the Boulevard Malesherbes. In *Le côté de Guermantes* he reconstructs the arrangement of this first-floor apartment at the end of a large interior courtyard, most of whose windows looked out on to another street (the Rue de Suresnes). He lived in such perfect harmony with his parents that he remained with them until they died.

Proust used to sleep a part of the day. Most of his social engagements were at night, and he preferred doing any intellectual work at that time, partly in the belief that at night his attacks of asthma occurred less frequently. Bernard Shaw declares that life is the possession of those who rise early; but Proust belied this assertion. He got up so late that he had lunch alone, after his family had finished. It was his mother's habit to sit beside him whilst he was at his meals, her heart filled with love and admiration. Madame Proust was a woman of gentle manners, with hair like ebony, and great lustrous dark eyes, alert and shining with kindness. Her son had inherited her wonderful eyes. She watched over him with solicitous care, forgiving his whims even before he had been guilty of them, and overlooking those nonchalant habits to which he so readily gave way. Proust had not even finished dressing by the time coffee was served after lunch. It took him an incredible time to button his boots; indeed they were not properly fastened up until he had reached the front door and was ready to go out. Between whiles he spent his time in writing letters, or in hunting for his mislaid cuff-links, or a lost shirt-front. Proust saw little of his father, who left early in the morning. He was allowed to lie in bed and let the hour when the servants come down slip by unnoticed, nor did anyone attempt to rouse him. His mother sheltered him against interference. Thus it was that society and the external world became subordinated to his own mode of living. He sought greater enjoyment for himself in the freedom which this mode of life gave him—but the seeds of a discipline lay concealed in this lack of constraint.

Proust received his share of the family fortune when his father died, in 1903, which freed him from financial cares and made it possible for him to give up all his time to literature. About this time too he had to give up all hope of foreign travel. Yet this was something that he adored, something of which he had often dreamed. It was one more pledge to life that he was sacrificing. The only journey abroad that he undertook, apart from a few days spent at Geneva or in Belgium, was a short stay at Venice with his mother and Reynaldo Hahn. In his novel we shall find the immense hopes, the emotions, the false starts, the happiness, succeeded by the usual disappointment, inspired in him by the city where so many writers have loved and suffered. After 1900, except for the summers spent at Trouville or Cabourg, he no longer left Paris. During the next few years he just managed to visit the cathedrals and historic places so dear to him. Some friends got him with difficulty as far as Senlis or Amiens. These were highly complicated changes of scene: he was afraid of being late in the morning, so he remained up all the night before. In order to ward off any possible attacks of his sickness he subjected himself to fumigations before going out. None the less he was capable of short and sharp physical efforts, which gave evidence of a strong vitality: during an expedition to the Château de Coucy, he climbed, in spite of his fatigue, up to the platform of the great tower, leaning on the arm of his friend Bertrand de Fénelon, "who, in order to encourage him, sang *sotto voce* the *Enchantment* of Good Friday. It was, in fact, a Good Friday, with the fruit-trees in blossom under the first springtime sun."

These were Proust's last travels, but travels of study rather than pleasure. The suffering which the slightest change of scene inevitably caused him he imposed on himself for the sake of better knowledge of the churches he wished to describe. He had at that time determined to translate and annotate Ruskin, that "powerful brain" which had laid its spell upon him. He was delighted at having found a task which would bring him the discipline he desired, without binding him to that immense effort of the whole being demanded by original creation. After 1900 he published in the *Mercure de France* his essay on "Ruskin at Notre-Dame d'Amiens." His translation of *The Bible of Amiens* did not appear until 1914, and that of *Sesame and Lilies* in 1906. Each was accompanied by a preface which would have made a volume in itself. His knowledge of English was poor, and he worked with the help of dictionaries. For six years he was absorbed in Ruskin. The enormous task counteracted his idleness. "Ruskin has gone to my head a little," he then confessed to a friend; "and archæology too."

There remained one last sacrifice for him to accomplish: the abandonment of the fashionable life which he loved to distraction. Many years passed before he shut himself up completely in the Boulevard Haussmann, in his famous cork-lined room. It was a cruel separation. "I cannot be alone!" exclaims Dominique in *Les Plaisirs et les jours*. And a stranger answers him: "Soon you will have killed me, and yet you *owed* me more than you owed others . . . I am your soul; I am yourself." And Proust might have been able to add: "I am the work that is within you." For it is this work, in spite of all, that will be victorious. Through the pleasures which he longs for always, in the suffering which he hates, but which is the one and only road towards the highest happiness, he will end by finding himself. To appreciate the significance of this supreme renunciation we shall see how much Proust was attached to this world which he forsook with such heart-break.

CHAPTER THREE

RANK AND FASHION

THAT world was for Proust the centre of pleasures, the scene of a life staged upon another plane, wherein discoveries were illimitable. From his adolescence until the day of his death, and even after the time of his isolation, his thought turned naturally back to concern itself with the habitants of this world of rank and fashion. The *salons*, the "sets," the little heroes of each of those groups, held an almost exclusive place in his conversation. He seemed to be more passionately enamoured of it all than they themselves. He was amazed that one of his friends did not put himself up for the Jockey Club. "You," he used to say, "you, whose father has a highly privileged position in Paris! Why aren't you a member of that club? It would give you so many advantages!"

His curiosity regarding the social usages went into such endless details that it seemed to complicate still further the thousand and one real shades of etiquette and refinements of courtesy. "But really, madame," he asked the close friends who lent him their protection, "tell me— Will you put Monsieur A—— in the same company with Monsieur D——? Now, is the place at your table of guests so, or so . . . ? But, madame, in taking seats . . . ? In greeting, would one . . . ?"

He never ended with his process of self-instruction, and the questions that he put with such art were inexhaustible. The manner of a handshake, and genealogical trees, assumed the importance of grave problems. Prince Bibesco had given a luncheon party at which the guests were so chosen that the Comtesse G——, notwithstanding her many high-born connexions, found herself seated at the foot of the table: etiquette had demanded that precedence should be given to the other guests. This apparent error, in conformity nevertheless with the strictest rules, this mundane paradox, like all combinations of this sort, surpassed in his eyes the limits of an amusing notion, and excited his lively imagination as much as some grave political event.

His passion for the *monde* was of such intensity that it was merged, during his adolescence, with the passion of love. He was enamoured, without having any personal acquaintance, with one of the most elegant ladies of the aristocracy, and to see her go by, passing up the Avenue de Marigny, he concealed himself with beating heart in the doorway of Émile-Paul's book-shop. And similarly, in his novel, we find his hero, "the earthworm in love with a star," clinging to the footsteps of the Duchesse de Guermantes.

But this intense love of the world of rank and fashion was not blind. The writer knew how to extract the rare metal from the dross of his dissipations. The Empire and royalty had barely disappeared. Certain *salons* were conducted only from hopes of the re-establishment of the old régime and all its privileges, above all things justifying the idleness of the nobility. Other *salons*, after

1870, considered themselves shrunken, and desired to appear almost inaccessible. Nevertheless, a part of the intellectual elect, a few of the greatest artists and the greatest savants, found their way into this society: and Proust at that time considered it as the centre of all values, as the only choice of the country, as the equivalent of the court under Louis XIV. The names of La Trémoille or of La Rochefoucauld evoked the history of France before him. He found pleasure in moving back through a family to reach its ancestors—Turenne, Condé, Richelieu, Noailles, or sometimes Napoleon. He was delighted when, in contemporary personages, in their courtesy or greetings or speech, he could detect the customs of bygone centuries which heredity and tradition had planted deep within them. The profound poetry of these names, no doubt, names of estates or regions, would not rise in his heart when he was set face to face in a drawing-room with the man of flesh and blood whose title had so deeply moved him in his childhood. There supervened the failure of the dream under the light of reality. But there was a wonderful richness of impressions for a psychologist such as he, in this power of searching in a human being for the origin of his every movement, of discovering the springs from which his passions were fed, of illuminating through the past his shape and form of the present. "Every social condition has its own interest, and it is perhaps no less curious for the artist to show forth the ceremony of a queen than the customs of a dressmaker." [1]

In latter years he would bring a more severe judg-

[1] Articles of Marcel Proust in the *Figaro*.

ment to bear upon the people of the *monde*, while still interesting himself in them in no less degree. How often he would say: "Ah, what fools they are!" Never, at no single moment, was he their dupe. A few lingering timidities had to be vanquished to please and conquer them. He amused himself with exercising over them an incomparable power of seduction. Everyone was desirous of giving her *salon* the splendour of the old régime. The *Figaro* published reports of resplendent parties, and those of which it made no mention must be of still greater elegance. By this fever of brillance, Proust was intoxicated.

．　　．　　．　　．　　．　　．　　．　　．

In a series of articles appearing between 1900 and 1905, the writer described some of the *salons* that he frequented. It was at the Princesse Mathilde's that Proust came to know the imperial nobility. Hearing the princely names of Moskowa or Essling, the young man could conjure up an epic. The ceremonial of the Princesse Mathilde was in his eyes historic. She received seated in a red fauteuil, and at her side were her ladies-in-waiting, Mlles Rasponi and Mme Espinasse. When the guests began to arrive, she rose for each of them, made response to their reverences, smiled as they touched her hand with their lips, and embraced the members of her own family. The writer drew inspiration from this scene for his pictures of the receptions of the Princesse de Guermantes and the Princesse de Parme.

At Coppet, with the Comte d'Haussonville, Proust discovered with delight the furniture that belonged to Madame de Staël and Madame Récamier, the family heirlooms of the great liberal conservative. Under the roof of the Princesse Edmond de Polignac, he met the Comtesse Greffühle, passing across the drawing-room "in the charmed and murmurous wake which her entrance drew out behind her." In that mansion of the Rue Cortambert the name which most fascinated his imagination was that of the Prince de Polignac, son of the reactionary minister of Charles X who signed the famous ordinances of 1830, and he took pleasure in picking out in him the characteristics of his race. "His face," wrote Proust, "had remained that of his lineage, something anterior to his individual self. And I remember how, on the mournful day of his burial, in the church where the great black hangings bore in scarlet the closed crown, the only initial was *P*. His individuality was effaced. He had returned into his family. He was nothing now but a Polignac." [2]

"The court of lilacs and the studio of roses"—that was Proust's description of the *salon* of Madeleine Lemaire. No ceremony. In the small studio where she worked, this artist, "who, after God, had created the greatest number of roses," used to receive a company of extreme elegance, so numerous that many people did not find room to sit down, and others, unable to gain admittance, had to stay in the garden. A small stage was set up at one end: Mounet-Sully declaimed, Massenet or Saint-Saëns sat down at the piano; Reynaldo Hahn sang a couplet to his own accompaniment; or perhaps Réjane and Coquelin and Bartet played a *saynète*.

[2] Articles by Marcel Proust in the *Figaro*.

The younger Dumas was the particular star of Madame Aubernon's *salon*. The setting changed; it became literary and bourgeois. Madame Aubernon and her niece Madame de Nerville were so Republican in sentiment that they were nicknamed *"les précieuses radicales"!* Conversation had to be general and bore upon serious topics. Each person spoke in turn; the interrupter was called to order by the mistress of the house tinkling a porcelain bell. Not many women came to this house. "I entertain for conversation," she used to say. "I don't entertain for love." We are reminded here of the stern dogmatism of Madame Verdurin, of the atmosphere of her "Wednesdays," at which Swann, the frequenter of the Faubourg Saint-Germain, felt so ill at ease. But these "tiresome *salons*" were often of service to letters: it was at Madame Aubernon's that the first performances took place of Becque's *La Parisienne* and Ibsen's *Doll's House*.

Proust did not often appear at the *salon* of Madame de Loynes. His pro-Dreyfus sympathies kept him away from there, as also from other circles of a political tinge. On the other hand, he was often to be found in the Avenue Hoche, at Madame Arman de Caillavet's. There he saw Anatole France, the master of the scene. But he was specially fond of meeting France alone, apart from the famous "Sundays," reception days, at which there was a procession of so many persons from the most varied circles.

The *salon* in which he really found himself, in which he passed a great part of his youth, was that of Madame Straus-Bizet, one of the most brilliant of its time, and

that in which he made the acquaintance of most of the
men of letters and men of fashion. He owed his introduction to his school friend Jacques Bizet, son of the
musician and the mistress of the house. It was there,
crouched at the feet of ladies and raising towards them
his splendid eyes, ablaze with intelligence, that Proust
tasted his first success. It was from there that the spoilt
child set out for the conquest of a whole society.

. . . .

Marcel Proust at twenty: large, black, brilliant eyes,
with heavy eyelids that drooped slightly to one side; a
look of extreme gentleness, fastening a long time on the
object it fell upon; a voice still more gentle, breathless
a little, and somewhat drawling, verging on affectation
yet always avoiding it. Long hair, black and thick,
falling sometimes over his forehead, hair that was never
to have a white thread amongst it. But it was to the eyes
that one always turned back, immense eyes ringed with
mauve, weary, wistful, of extreme mobility, eyes that
seemed to leave their orbits to follow the secret thoughts
of the speaker. A continual smile, amused and inviting,
hesitated and then fixed itself motionless on his lips.
His complexion was dull, but then fresh and pink, and
in spite of his fine black moustache he gave one the
impression of an overgrown child, indolent and over-
observant.

How fascinating he was in his youth! He had the
studied refinement of the dandy, tempered already with
a loose carelessness as of an old mediæval scholar, a
resemblance of which we are later to be reminded. An
exquisite turn-out—but a button was missing on his

overcoat. Under his turned-over collar he wore badly
tied cravats, or large silk shirt-fronts from Charvet's,
of a creamy pink, the tint of which he had long sought
to find.[3] He was thin enough to allow himself a double-
breasted waistcoat. A rose or an orchid in the button-
hole of his frock-coat, tightly waisted yet flowing. He
was heart-broken when this rose of his came from a
garden and not from a florist, who wrapped its stem
in silver paper. Very light-coloured gloves with black
points, often soiled and crumpled, and bought at the
"Trois Quartiers" because Robert de Montesquiou dealt
there. A tall hat with flat brim. (This, when a call was
paid, was placed on the floor beside the chair.) A cane
completed the elegance of this somewhat wild Brummell.

Such was the fascination of every aspect of the life
of pleasure for Proust that he braved the fresh air,
which was almost forbidden him from the age of nine,
to appear about midday in the Avenue du Bois, the
rendezvous of the young men, and of the old men of
fashion with "their square monocles with large black
cords." [4] The Prince de Sagan wore a grey top-hat. The
Prince of Wales drew "all hearts after him." The ladies
in their victorias, moving at a walking pace, slowly
distributed their greetings with calculated smiles. They
blazoned the fashions of Doucet or Virot. Caran d'Ache
scribbled a caricature on his cuff, the handsome Helleu
saw dry-points and composed pastels. In June, between
the varnishing day of the annual exhibition of the
"Épatant," and the opening of the water-colour painters

---

[3] Cf. his portrait by Jacques-Émile Blanche.
[4] Articles of Marcel Proust in the *Figaro*.

at Georges Petit's the Fête des Fleurs was a kind of saturnalia at which the decorated equipages of the great *cocottes* and those of the Faubourg Saint-Germain appeared in open rivalry. Marcel Proust met his friends again in this setting, among others the Marquis d'Albufera and the Comte Bertrand de Fénelon, who probably, along with other young men, gave him the inspiration for the charming Saint-Loup.

It was likewise in the Bois that he often saw Laure Heyman, whose grace and elegance were to help him in forming some traits of the figure of Odette de Crécy. She was noted, it was said, for her skill in the education of princes. Like Odette de Crécy, she received in her house in the Rue Bassano men of the best society, many of them belonging to an older generation. She was closely allied with some writers of fame. Paul Bourget wrote a story for her entitled "Gladys Harvey," one of his *Pastels de femmes*. Proust was an admirer, and liked to salute this woman, with her magnificent clothes and dazzling vivacity, as she passed on horseback, or to accompany her when she took her walk.[5]

---

[5] Madame Laure Heyman is still living to-day, in retirement. She has disclosed a charming gift for sculpture. When Proust's novel appeared, she was told by friends that she had served as the model for Odette de Crécy. She began to read the books which the author had sent her, and, furious at what she took to be her portrait, she sent Marcel Proust a letter of lively reproaches. He replied with long explanations which reassured her somewhat. What these explanations were may be guessed from the letter he wrote to Gabriel de la Rochefoucauld (*"Souvenirs et aperçus,"* *Nouvelle Revue Française,* January 1st, 1923):

"Alas, when, being irritated at having people say to me: 'Don't defend yourself, the Duchesse de Guermantes is Madame G.' (when the Duchesse de Guermantes, who is everybody and nobody, is in any case the exact contrary of Madame G.), I wrote in the *Œuvres libres* that people have

As often as not, Proust's day began only in the afternoon, yet always with a delay which during the whole of his life he was never able to catch up. He had lingered too long over his calls, or a number of catastrophic incidents had held him up without his being able to foresee them. He "dressed" almost every evening, and every time it was a complex and difficult operation. Most often he dined at home when he was invited out. Even when he received guests for dinner at his parents', he took a meal alone beforehand, so as to be able to talk more freely. As the result of an accidental movement he made a huge stain on his spotless white shirt-front. He was forced to change his shirt hurriedly. He donned another suit. To get on the trousers he was forced to take off his shoes. So here he was, driven to starting all over again the interminable operation of the morning, buttoning them up. His new clothes were too big, and had the appearance of being ready-made. The drama played out between reality and himself was one much more serious than that of the troublesome and ill-intentioned objects which avenge themselves on mankind, the pencil that disappears when it is looked for, the

---

so little idea of artistic creation that they imagine that one brings a person into a book just as he is, I did not know that one woman . . . would claim to recognize herself in Odette de Crécy, who is her exact opposite, etc., etc. These ridiculous assimilations annoy me. *If, in a totally opposed character, memory suggests a trait, this is what inevitably happens.* Thus, the Duc de Guermantes has nothing of the late Marquis de L. in him, but it was with a recollection of the latter that I made him shave in front of his window. . . ."

For this reason, all the keys I have given and shall give in the course of this work will, I repeat with emphasis, be no more than indications always reduced to one single aspect of character, essentially partial resemblances.

monocle that cracks, the theatre ticket that is left at
home. It was not distraction that delayed him and prevented him from behaving like everyone else: it was
the particular vision of his mind, which proceeded by
a process of development, and which, like field-glasses,
brought objects nearer him and allowed him to discover
them in all their complexity. In a human face he saw
only a portion of the cheek, but he saw it with all its
pores and furrows and wrinkles, details invisible to
everyone else.

At last he was ready. He put on, even on the warmest
days of summer, that heavy pelisse which, to all who
knew him, had become legendary. His hay-fever made
him extremely susceptible to cold. He sent for a cab—or,
to be more exact, a cab had been waiting for him since
luncheon. Dinner, of course, had begun, and Proust's
excuses were unending. At evening receptions he often
arrived when most of the guests had already gone.
Before being announced on these occasions, he used to
have the servant ask whether his appearance were not
inconvenient, or permission to keep on his cloak. In
the drawing-room, during his passage from the door
over to the mistress of the house, whom he was going
to greet, he was diverted by countless distractions in
the room itself: he noticed a new picture, or a vase that
had had its position changed, or perhaps he still kept
proffering apologies.

The last guests formed a circle around him upon his
arrival. For several hours he was dazzling. Under the
interrogatory form so familiar to him, he recounted the
dinner-party of the previous evening: "Do you know

46

whether the Duc de —— stayed on in the boudoir with Madame Z.? Could you explain the kiss he gave her, in the very middle of the ball? Did someone see through the door. . . ?" Keen-edged irony showed through the accumulation of his courtesies and polite attentions. A tang of sarcasm, which later was to broaden out, lay hidden behind the futilities that he recounted, trifles to which his intelligence lent a generalized meaning, and which his astounding memory allowed him to report with the same precision of detail after several years. And yet there was never anything in his words that could shock, or wound, or displease. He was listened to with delight. One by one the candles went out. The footmen yawned and fell asleep. The hostess herself was tired. Marcel Proust was talking.

After the party he took back a friend as far as his door, but could not contrive to leave him. He got down from the carriage and paced up and down in front of the house. Suddenly, feeling fatigued, he asked to be accompanied home. The cab had been waiting, and he paid the driver the fare for the journey in advance. In front of his own home the same pacing up and down began again. He made excuses to the cabman for making him wait, and paid him a second time, and the price of the return trip too, so that the cab could take back his friend, a price which he doubled and trebled from fear of its being insufficient. At last he begged his companion to come up with him. He had a morbid fear of solitude. When the friend saw the dawn break and left him, he rounded off the suspended conversation next day with his valet. In his books he has frequently made mention of the painful depression which he experienced after the excitement of a party or a restaurant meal. It was during these moments that he felt in his heart the limitations of those intoxicating pleasures, which, in spite of their vanity, he still continued to desire, with all the ardour of his unsatisfied being. His features became drawn: fatigue showed suddenly in that too fragile frame. He knew that in his room he would not be able to sleep. He went to find his night attire—several knitted garments and a long night-shirt. He took them from the kitchen, where he found them hanging, according to his orders, above the stove, where they were warming. His nerves would not let him bear the touch of cold linen. As he had come back so late, the knitted things, of course, had had time to singe: their burnt sleeves had that splendid and venerable appearance which so many objects, as time went on, came to assume around this strange being.

Nevertheless, in some other drawing-room, the next day would see him starting again on this life of enchantment, with more zeal than ever. His inexhaustible curiosity made him desire to widen and renew his social relationships. When he noticed a new face, he would ask: "Who is that? Do you know him?"—with, as it were, the professional curiosity of the man of fashion.

For some his friendships were passionate, and lasted three months. When anyone was mentioned to him whom he had never seen, he immediately desired him to be brought to him, and he contrived endless devices to bring about the meeting. He saw his new friend assiduously until the day when, having exhausted his possibilities, he turned back in weariness to his old intimates. In a drawing-room he seemed unhappy at not being in every group at once; all the more so since, on his entrance, he had seen all the members of the party from the door. However, he knew how to take his seat by the side of the most renowned writer or of a Highness. He astonished Caro, the fashionable philosopher, by the highly individual form of his mind. At Madame Daudet's, Edmond de Goncourt foretold his future. He was the attendant page of the Princesse Mathilde, and the Baronne Alphonse de Rothschild. He accompanied them to the dressmakers' on their visits, and heaped ruinous flowers upon them.

"Do you not think, madame, that your portrait is really ravishing? Do you know how dreadfully I should be pained if you did not agree with me?"

Nothing was lacking to his prestige. This boy might have ended by never being taken seriously, so exaggerated were his homages. But he had had his duel. On the point of honour he was most sensitive, and too intelligent not to conform with all the proper usages. Jean Lorrain published an article in the *Écho de Paris* which he thought offensive to himself, and two shots were exchanged, without result. For a few days he became a hero.

Capricious though they were, the inhabitants of the *monde* resisted none of his desires or whims. They came to his house. In his parents' flat, furnished in true bourgeois style, in that dining-room with the large, traditional sideboard and its Second Empire furnishings, he gave dinners of the utmost brilliance. Anatole France was a guest, and the Comtesse de Noailles, who recited her first poems. Montesquiou declaimed some unpublished sonnet. He relished in advance the pleasure of bringing together a writer and dukes, people who did not know each other. He prepared each of his guests for the unwonted encounter by a lengthy description of the new friend he was expecting, whom he depicted in a glowing light. His taste for bringing together persons unknown to each other afforded him a kind of anxiety which put him into a state of high delight. After dinner, according to custom, poems were recited by Mlle Cora Laparcerie, the rising star of the Odéon, or some other actress.

His parents were rarely present at these festivities. Madame Proust, who was of a retiring disposition, stood aside. His father, Dr. Proust, could not understand his son's success. "Is he really so fascinating?" he asked a lady on terms of friendship with Marcel. "Why is he asked out so much?" [6]

In spite of his prejudices he contemplated, with a pride which he did not admit, this brilliant son of his who was so much sought after. He did not refuse him money for his pleasures. Proust made liberal use of this paternal generosity. He had never been able to keep count of money. For his friends nothing was too beautiful or too good. It was always to the most expensive restaurant that he took them. He might have declared,

---

[6] And if he regretted his lack of occupation, he could no doubt console himself with the thought of his other son, Robert, who was almost the same age as Marcel. The future Dr. Robert Proust passed his examination with brilliance and gave his father every sort of professional satisfaction.

in order to make you accept an invitation without hesitation, that he wanted to go to some more modest place, but he ended by taking you to Larue's. The *maître d'hôtel,* who knew him, offered him some dishes which were not marked on the menu, the preparation of which must necessarily have been very costly. He ordered old wines, rare fruits, but did not eat, as he had already taken his meal. His pleasure was entirely cerebral, and he found it in the atmosphere of the evening, in the dinner he was giving, in the gift of himself.

When he visited the theatre, he frequently went on to Weber's. He discussed in detail the piece he had just seen, to the great astonishment of the friend accompanying him. For, during the whole performance, he had done nothing but look at the audience, the boxes, the people, the Grand Duchess Vladimir's new robe, the unexpected presence of Porto-Riche with Madame ———. He had seemed to be listening to everything except what was going forward on the stage, and yet he had heard everything.

This mundane existence was endless and exhausting, much as a regular profession might have been. In the summer, at Trouville, it continued, either at the Hôtel des Roches Noires,[7] or at the Frémond with the Baignières.

What a ceaseless effort in his zeal to please! There was a victory to be won every day! And what force there was then in his "imitations"! He knew how amusing these were to his friends in the *monde,* and with his

---

[7] This hotel, along with the Grand Hôtel at Cabourg, helped him in the creation of the Grand Hôtel at Balbec.

in-born taste for pastiche, he pushed the gift to perfection. In the drawing-rooms he was giving the dress rehearsal of the portraits which he was later to bring on to the stage in his work.

The character he knew best, the one which he rendered with a kind of genius, was that of Montesquiou, "Count Robert," as he was called, an extraordinary character, who fully deserved the intensely curious interest which Marcel Proust bestowed on him. Montesquiou's original tastes, his voice, which seemed always to be breaking and rose to the shrillest notes, his insane susceptibility, his quarrels, his ostracisms, his reconciliations, his immense pride in his noble birth, his vexed tone, his airs of reproach, his precosity and impertinence, his unbridled snobbery, if the word can still be applied to a kind of delirium of grandeur—all these traits had made a unique personality of him, round which there grew up some coteries who naïvely believed in his immortality. Over a small group of society, of which Charles Haas [8] and some others formed part, he exercised a veritable tyranny. Some personages of society, his friends only yesterday, became in his furious and sudden hatred "Monsieur Pipi" or "Madame Caca." One day, in the drawing-room of José-Maria de Hérédia,

---

[8] Charles Haas, ". . . shy because he was a Jew, was the only one of his race who was poor, the friend of all women, petted in the drawing-rooms, esteemed by men of worth. He belonged to that category of witty and useless idlers who formed, as it were, a luxury of the society of those days, and whose principal merit consisted in gossiping before dinner at the Jockey Club or at the Duchesse de Trémoille's." Thus writes the Marquis Boni de Castellane in *Comment j'ai découvert l'Amérique*. Marcel Proust had in mind the astonishing social success of Charles Haas when he built up the character of Swann.

before the usual assembly at those "Saturdays," Montesquiou was reciting one of his poems, none of which had then been published. Hérédia expressed admiration of his technique.

"You ought to publish these verses," he told him.

"What good could that do?" answered the great seigneur, throwing back his chest. "My reputation as a writer, if ever I acquire one, will not prevent me from ever being anything but a Montesquiou-beast!"

This maniac of pride, this censor who gave lessons to a whole society, was a wonderful object for the sarcastic fire of Marcel Proust. So completely had the writer assimilated his nervous tricks that no one knew whether they were still part of the parody or whether they had become his own. The irascible nobleman was annoyed by these imitations, which he held to be lacking in respect. He did not suspect that Proust would later produce, in the principal character of his book, a very different imitation, more grave and more terrible, a kind of fantastic pastiche, an enormous and magnificent caricature, a hero so great that he transcends the fame of an ordinary novel and assumes the epic proportions of a contemporary Don Quixote. If there is no real key to be found in the work of Marcel Proust, if all the characters are formed from different alloys, Palamède, Baron de Charlus, is the sole exception. In the early volumes, no doubt, Charlus is still an amalgam. One may trace in him certain peculiarities of the Baron X. (whom Proust had met in the *salon* of Madame Straus), his stoutness, for instance, and his coarse, powdered face. But gradually he became a living and irrefutable portrait, recognised unhesitatingly by everyone. Moreover, it was not the first time that Montesquiou had served as a model: Huysmans, in *A rebours,* had already found inspiration in him for the character of des Esseintes.

It should be added that Montesquiou's own memoirs throw a curious light on certain chapters in Proust's novel. The story of Montesquiou and the musician Delafosse reminds one of that of Charlus and the musician Morel. It is for Morel that Charlus gives a party at Madame Verdurin's. It was "to bring forward our young artist" that Montesquiou organized a great fête. These fêtes, moreover, are for him the object of his life, pleasures more intoxicating than travel or love, more beautiful than the masterpieces of antiquity or the Renaissance; and indeed, they called forth no less of his time and money, tears and disappointments, patience and determination and talents. That which he gave on Delafosse's behalf took place in Sarah Bernhardt's garden. The elevation of a theatre was built for one day, entitled the Ephemeral. Sarah "of the golden voice" and Bartet, although rivals, and Reichenberg, recited together the *Ode à Versailles* of André Chénier. Then Delafosse took his place at the piano. Like Charlus, of course, he issued his invitations with an arbitrary exclusion of numerous personages fully worthy of figuring at such a function.

Shortly afterwards he informs us that he "executed" the musician. And some of his friends tell how, to avenge himself on his former protégé, he hung his portrait in the lavatories of his flat. The very style of the memoirs of Montesquiou recalls the style of the diatribes of the Baron de Charlus. Strange irony of fate! These memories, which Montesquiou wrote in self-justification, to put an end to all kinds of legends that had grown up round him, are changed in meaning when they are set alongside Marcel Proust's novel. We can never know what the effects of a posthumous work may be.

.   .   .   .

Passions of the heart, griefs and pleasures, the joy of being handsome and being loved, a mirage endlessly renewed—the life of Marcel Proust, between the Étoile and the Faubourg Saint-Germain, was one bewildering flux, an unceasing movement on the same axis, *"le temps perdu"*! Sometimes he was chilled by a fearful remorse: he had rejected all careers for the sake of writing, and he was doing nothing! A work was there within him, so vast and so imposing that in alarm he kept postponing the moment of starting on it.

None the less, he was studying his material, whilst considering his time to be entirely dissipated, and he did not let his impressions fade. Every four or five days, on scraps of loose paper, cards of invitation, visiting cards, telegrams, he set down the result of his investigations. Occasionally a friend would cast a glance over this work of documentation, expecting to find therein thoughts or reflections with some intrinsic significance. But, soon undeceived, he would fling down these incomprehensible notes, in which were recorded the gesture of so-and-so, the glance of such-and-such, the probable motive of a refusal or a laugh, the explanation of facts of the most minute importance with their entangled causes. For this work which he had in mind, one of complete novelty, Proust was amassing material which no one else could make any use of.

His friends asked him why he did not write. Sometimes he would make up his mind to read to one or two intimates a few pages in which he had made his first attempts at laying the foundations of his future novel. He read at great speed, frequently breaking off to give explanations, and adding to the parentheses and subordinate propositions of his sentences commentaries which took their place like critical notes amongst critical notes. Already difficult to follow in reading, his style became incomprehensible when read out loud. Nevertheless, when one of his friends managed to catch hold of something, he thought he was finding only the portrait of someone he knew. Proust confirmed this impression. He explained who were the real personages he had thought of. It was still impossible to comprehend the construction of the work, the original contribution of its creator.

"Marcel can never be anything but a man-about-town," his friends passed the word round, "simply the *Figaro's* Horatio." And the misunderstanding which separated him in literature from men of letters, likewise isolated the writer in his own circle of acquaintances.

In 1905 his mother died. This was the greatest blow of his life. Reciprocal love, the cherished words of the being who loves you, seemed to him to be almost unrealized dreams. But he adored his mother. For her he had the most violent and the most tender passion. It was she who called him "My little silly! My little stupid!"—and now, until his dying day, he felt himself solitary. And with her memory, following the "intermissions of the heart," he was to live, now at a distance, now as closely present as an apparition. Ten years later he said to a friend, in that voice that was like a gentle moan: "Come and look at the portrait of Mamma," pronouncing her name, which came dying from his lips, as if she were still alive.

And does she not still live in his work? For it was this immense grief of his which the writer strove to keep, so as the better to understand and immortalize it. It was this grief which brought him to withdraw little by little from the social world. Sickness also encroached step by step upon his active life. The time was approaching when his long, unconscious meditation, pursued throughout the whole period of his mundane activities, was to reach maturity. He left the empty flat where he was born and went to shut himself up in the Boulevard Haussmann. It was there that he was to fill his twenty enormous note-books.

CHAPTER FOUR

RETREAT

A N apartment with the air of being uninhabited, as if the masters of the house were away travelling. In a large drawing-room, easy-chairs, and sofas in gilded wood or upholstered, the furniture of Monsieur and Madame Proust crowded together. A portrait of a young dandy of an epoch that now has a distant air—Marcel Proust at the age of twenty, by Jacques-Émile Blanche; as pendant to it on the other side—an infanta of Velasquez, haycock-shape.

A room entirely lined with cork, so that no outside sound can penetrate. This cork was meant to be covered with some stuff, but—delays? obstacles?—the upholsterer had never managed to come. The window was always shut. Marcel Proust could not, without terrible attacks of suffocation, let the scent of the chestnut-trees reach him from the Boulevard Haussmann. But he adored them none the less, lived with them in imagination, and as he slept by day and never saw them, he used to ask people in springtime to talk to him of their blossom.

A single lamp on the ceiling cast a feeble glow, its light absorbed by the dull brown cork. In one corner an immense and cumbersome grand piano. On the chairs some beautiful books lay about, and photographs. A dressing-room, its door left open, was encumbered with large chests of silver plate, a legacy of his parents. As no one ever managed to arrange them, they were left standing on the floor.

The man who lived shut up in this buttoned-in room, dreary and void of personality, had no eyes for his apartment. Background, in his life as in the books that he wrote, did not play an important part. He lived now and henceforward in the souls of the numerous characters with whom he was peopling an original world. And there he lived entirely, having turned his back for good on the real world.

Sickness had wrought a deep change on him. The face had gone pale, the moustaches drooped unevenly. The nose was pinched, the cheeks thicker, the eyes more brilliant. He received you, when he was not in bed, in a dark-brown dressing-gown. More sensitive than ever to cold, he wore a pad of cotton-wool over his shirt-collar, and he had floss silk gloves on his hands, knitted woollen shoes on his feet. He dreaded the air, covered himself as much as he could. Fumigating apparatus gave off a suffocating odour. He seemed, in this laboratory of his, like some fabulous necromancer: the dead whom he evoked were the people he had known, and in his work he was bringing them back to life.

"My dear friend," Marcel would murmur, "never have I been so ill: I shall keep you only a moment."

Three hours later one was still there with him. On a gilt bronze clock one read the hour—two o'clock in the morning. Talking had reanimated him: he was seeking to provide documentation for himself through conversation. Suddenly he would break off.

"My dear friend," he would say, "I beg you: shall I be causing you much convenience if I ask you to take the handkerchief out of your jacket? You know how I can't bear any perfume. . . ."

And he gave three rings on the bell, out of habit, as if in his parents' house.

"Céleste, take the gentleman's handkerchief and put it in another room.—My dear friend, the last time you were so good as to come and see me—for nobody comes any more to see the wretched invalid that I am—I was obliged to take the chair you sat in and keep it out in the courtyard for three days: it was impregnated with scent. . . ."

This same friend told him once about a *demi-mondaine* who gave evening parties that ended up "orgiastically." Proust saw the opportunity for finding documentation for his book, and asked to be taken there. He passed a night of festivity at this lady's house. The place was filled with flowers, but he did not seem to pay any heed to them. His friend expressed astonishment.

"For three whole weeks," answered the writer, "the attacks I had as a result of that expedition prevented me from rising at all. . . ."

His sensibility had such extremities of refinement in suffering that he was not taken seriously. Seized sometimes with a desire to have a glimpse once more of the hawthorns or the water-lilies, he would have himself driven into the country in an hermetically closed car-

riage, and contented himself with gazing at the woods
and meadows through the window-panes. His friends
thought they were accompanying an imaginary invalid.
Until the day of his death his complaints were not
believed in.

In the summer he went to Cabourg. From the time
of his first onset of asthma, after he was able to leave
Paris, he could go only to the sea. At the Grand Hôtel
there, he engaged the four rooms adjoining his own,
above, below, and on either side, and left them unoccupied: the slightest noise caused him real pain. Moreover, he was for ever changing his room, for the aspect
of the one he had, or the view from its windows, never
suited him. He was known as the gentleman with the
parasol, whose worst enemy was the sun. The regular
frequenters of the hotel (better perhaps than those who
were in close touch with him) felt instinctively that
there was something more than mere eccentricity in
these habits of his: they had a certain grandeur, and
even the waiters unsmilingly respected them.

He was aware of how his condition, this kind of
hypertrophy of the nervous-system, impossible of full
diagnosis, aroused the scepticism of his best friends.
"Say nothing further about the gravity of my condition," he wrote, "for if, after that, you live for some
time longer, it is never forgiven you. I can recall people
who have 'dragged on' for years. People seemed to suppose that they had been acting a comedy. As with
Gautier, who delayed so long in setting out for Spain
that people used to say to him: 'Ah, you've got back?'
so they will be saying of me that I have been reincar-

nated; they won't be able to admit that I am not dead." [1]

.   .   .   .

"I can only move with such difficulty," we find him writing again. Moreover, almost every time he ventured out anywhere, it was with a definite object which dominated his whole life: to complete and determine exactly his investigation of the world, the outside world, and the psychology of its beings. He had become a perpetual investigator. He no longer entered those *salons* which once he had loved, except to provide himself with material.

One evening Proust rose. He was seen, to the astonishment of everyone, at a great reception. But the fact was that he wanted to have a clear idea of just how the Prince de Sagan wore a monocle at the present day, and if he could take him as a model for one of his characters. When he had compared his memory with a new reality, he went back to bed again for several weeks.

The smallest mundane episode interested him passionately. He made people tell him all possible stories. He harvested the same anecdote in several tellings. The special gilded skin of Oriane's shoes, Albertine's kimono, the parasol of Madame Elstir, the style in which the Princesse de Guermantes's hair was dressed at the Opéra —these questions of fashion were for him (he no longer visited the dressmaking establishments) the object of attentive cares and endless, touching precautions.

"Tell me, madame," he asked one of his old friends, who had managed to gain admittance to his room, "what

---

[1] Unpublished correspondence.

is the name for that stuff that a girl might throw over her shoulders when she is in evening dress?"

"*Crêpe?*"

"That's a horrible word, and the girl in my book is charming!"

"A veil?"

"Impossible."

"A stole?"

"No!"

"A fur? A scarf? A foulard?"

"Something else," Marcel besought, "something else. . . !"

He had two young men brought to his apartment one day, two brothers, solely because he wanted to ask them for some information regarding armorial bearings. By cunning transitions he had worked the conversation round to this subject, but his visitors, with polite fears of becoming boring, immediately spoke of something else. Proust returned with an effort to his question, and they, out of politeness, made the same effort to escape it. In the end the writer, having proved unable to extract what he wanted from them, broke off the conversation and refused ever to see them again.

His capacity of investigation had no limits. He conducted his inquiries into love as into everything else. The private life of people interested him prodigiously. "Now tell me," he used to say to some intimate friends, "do you love each other? Do you love? Are you loved?" And he listened to the replies with the naïve gaze of a child, as if this domain were one unknown to him.

His imagination sought to work only upon subject-matter controlled by his own observation. At one o'clock in the morning Marcel asked leave to go up and see Madame de C——.

"My dear lady," he said, "nothing could give me greater pleasure than to have a glimpse again of the little hat with Parma violets that you wore at the time when I lost my heart to you, when the young man I once was admired you—and the man I am admires you still—when he saw you passing down the Avenue Marigny. . . ."

"Dear Marcel! That's a hat of twenty years ago—I no longer have it!"

"That can't be, madame! You simply don't want to show me it. You have it, and you want to spite me: you will pain me sorely!"

"But, my poor Marcel, I don't keep my old hats. Come into my room. Here is my wardrobe. Look for yourself . . . In this drawer? . . . Look. In that box? Nothing . . . No, I can't call my maid to unpack all my things for you: she's gone to bed."

"Madame Daudet kept all her hats," murmured the writer, still incredulous. "I have seen them."

"It's a charming idea. But I don't keep any such museum."

When he had not secured his information, he wrote: "Who is it who was with you six months ago. . . ? It is through her that I can get to know this man I spoke to you about, and so I can find out . . . My dear friend, bring this person to see me. You cannot imagine how much this matter interests me . . ." The letter was eight pages long.

His two great sources of evidence were the world of fashion and servants. From the point of view of observation these opposite settings were in the writer's eyes of equal interest, and from the point of view of human nature he put these extremes on one and the same plane. He loved to gather information from his inferiors. His vision of the great *salons* never seemed to him complete unless it were supplemented by the servants' hall. He spoke in terms of familiarity to waiters at the café, or footmen, and picked up valuable information from them. He would stay for two or three hours talking with Hector, the *maître d'hôtel* of the Reservoirs at Versailles, with Charles of the Weber, with Olivier of the Ritz.

This last-named hotel became practically the only place he went to when he went out. It was the only one where he felt himself at his ease. There he had set up his head-quarters of investigation. He arrived about nine or ten o'clock at night, in dinner-jacket or full dress, with a badly tied bow. Almost always he was alone, and he did not leave again until one or two o'clock in the morning. His slender, bony hands contrasted with his puffed-out chest, exaggeratedly developed by his asthma. His eyes lit up the whole of his face.

"I have had nothing to eat for three days," he declared to Olivier. "I have never stopped writing. My black coffee last Sunday wasn't strong enough. Get them to make me first of all a really strong black coffee, one that is as good as two. And remember, don't be afraid to put down two on my bill."

When he was with his friends, he dined in a private

room. But after the clock had marked a certain time, he would desire to be left alone. When the waiters had finished serving, he began to talk with them at great length.

"Look behind you first," he used to say, "and see that there is nobody listening to us.—Right. Now tell me: those two ladies who were dining just now in that corner over there—who are they? I must know which is the younger. She is very like a character in my book about whom I am thinking a great deal. As for the other, I think I know her. If you had ever seen her in my day! Women were very different then: sheathed in their corsets, their busts and bustles gave them a charming outline."

And as the waiters laughed: "Life is finished for me," he went on. "And I don't expect anything further of it. But tell me: I heard steps in the passage!"

"You must be mistaken, sir."

"No, no, I'm not. Go and look what's happening."

His extraordinarily developed sense of hearing had not deceived him, it was a chambermaid on her way to bed who had let a door bang.

. . . .

When once his information had been gathered, he enjoyed in his memory a wonderful instrument for its conservation. In reality his data did not remain unchangeable, but ripened and were amplified by all the richness of his extraordinarily complex mind. To the acts of men he attributed innumerable and complicated motive forces, linking up one with another as the series worked its way downward. One got the impression that he was drawing them from his own consciousness, and applied them to others with a hazardous boldness which almost always turned out successfully. These constructions of probabilities were of necessity true. Even if the reasons for an action which he attributed to a person were more numerous than those which that person found in himself, these reasons became true by the very fact of his discovery of them. His vision of a person constituted one of the aspects of that person's individuality, and the latter was enriched by the very creation of the psychologist that Proust was.

But this spontaneous faculty for the decomposition of all the acts of life became a source of extreme difficulties in the natural organization of his own time. These difficulties were added to the countless precautions imposed on him by illness, the delicacy of his heart, his inborn nonchalance, and they ended in making practical action almost impossible to him. The fixing of a rendezvous became a great undertaking. Or more exactly, he was incapable of arranging a rendezvous. He would declare that he was always in ignorance of the moment when his painful crises would keep him helpless in bed. When he was well, he would send Céleste in the middle of the night to call on the friend whom he wanted to see and asked to come. If the latter were not at home, Céleste returned the next day, and so on, until it happened that their two spaces of free time coincided. The letters he sent in connexion with meeting anyone were as innumerable as they were interminable.

He wrote four long pages, full of parentheses as in his books, to ask the favour of some service to which

67

he attached the utmost importance. He gave a thousand details. He insisted. But at the bottom on the very last page he would discover a postscript of a couple of lines: "I have just been reflecting: it would be better if you did nothing in the matter. Consider my letter as unsent." And he sent it off just the same.

He was obsessed by a fear of the post office's losing his letters. The envelopes themselves seemed long recitals:

"To Monsieur Faure-Biguet, Editorial Staff of the Écho de Paris, *care of the* Écho de Paris, *Place de l'Opéra, 3, Paris (2nd and 9th arrondissements).—If this letter should not be delivered to its addressee, kindly return it to M. Marcel Proust, man of letters, 102, Boulevard Haussmann, Paris."*

Moreover, he most often had his letters delivered by a page-boy from the Ritz or one of the hotel waiters. In the day-time it was Céleste who went out with them. Her husband, Odilon Albarret, a taxi-cab driver, put his vehicle at Proust's disposal from ten o'clock at night at the ordinary price. At night it was he who acted as messenger: he was frequently instructed to arouse some concierge and give him, together with a twenty-franc note, the message which such-and-such a person, according to Proust's wish, was to receive the next morning.

If the writer had invited a friend to his house, free at the same time as himself, he was always obliged to improvise a dinner. Odilon set off with his taxi to fetch a chicken from the Ritz (the only place in Paris, according to Proust's ideas, where one could really obtain one's provisions), and beer from a *brasserie* on the other side of the river, and cakes from Rumpelmeyer's. In his anxiety to give his guest the best he could, no doubt, he was willing to order only the finest dishes. But none the less, each dish was not a speciality, and it would have been quite possible to buy them elsewhere than in diametrically opposite corners of the town. But simplicity in action was unknown to him.

When some subject was occupying his attention, it filled the whole of his brain. It presented itself to him in all its complexity, like those elaborately articulated marionettes, each movement of which is the outcome of the moving of several strings. His mind refused to neglect any single thread, and in everyday life he was no longer capable of accomplishing the action which his analysis had too deeply dissected.

Nothing was less of an affectation than this absence of spontaneity in everyday activities. A move of any distance seemed in his eyes to be encumbered with such a vast accumulation of details that the mere idea gave him real pain. In this way he was continually postponing his projects, using his ill health as a pretext, until the moment when extreme necessity sometimes forced him to take final action. "At the moment," he wrote to me, "when I imagined that nothing could possibly be added further to the annoyances and physical sufferings which are actually overwhelming me, I find myself obliged at short notice to look for an unfurnished house. . . . My landlord in fact has sold the house where I live to a banker, and he is turning out all the tenants, myself included, in consequence. At the same time my publisher returns from America, his printers are demobilized, with

the result that I am suddenly going to have the proofs
I have been awaiting for years, and, for their correction,
I have hardly any eyesight left, mine having deteriorated
without my general condition permitting me to go and
consult an oculist. . . ." This tone of lamentation was
habitual with him.

Jacques Rivière told him one day that he would have
to go for treatment to a sanatorium near Bruges. At the
mention of this project Proust began to commiserate
with him deeply. How did he dare to set off on such a
distant journey? Was he not alarmed at the prospect?
Proust used all his strength in insisting that he should
give up such a dangerous adventure, and even went so
far as to offer him money so that he might receive the
treatment in Paris.

This invalid was still less capable of making any move
when he was impelled only by his taste for pleasure. He
might speak of an exhibition or a play or a concert, to
which he wished to go, but he knew that these wishes
would never be realized. With every day that passed,
his isolation became closer. If he worked now, in the
silence of the night, he had not yet attained renown.
His friends, when they came to visit this "midnight
sun," grew tired sometimes of the vigil. Many of them
were prevented by the demands of their own active
and different lives. On account of the peculiar disposition of his time, Proust was bound of necessity to lose
sight of them. It was with difficulty that he replaced
them: "I hope very much to know you," he wrote,
"when I have a roof over my head," or else: "I oscillate
generally between a fever of 100° and 103.8°, which

does not make correspondence, or even the slightest movement, very easy. All the same I have days of calm and I hope I shall be able to make your acquaintance. . . ."

·   ·   ·   ·   ·   ·   ·   ·

The more the complications of his character and his ill health kept him shut up with his work in his apartment, the more his personality, freed from the egotism of pleasures, opened out into kindness of heart. It was on this that his whole morality, detached from God, was laid. It was this which welled up from the most obscure recesses of his unconscious, as if it had been deposited in him in some previous life: for in this life, where the wicked are rewarded and the good punished, what could be the reason for its existence? In spite of everything, his kindness spoke to him as an instinct, and appeared to him as the most elementary, and the foremost, of his duties. In this sensibility to the prolonged inward echoes his kindness assumed the most varied forms, from simple pity to a complete sacrifice of self.

On leaving one of the most elegant of aristocratic ladies one morning about two o'clock, he found, seated on the landing, a very young servant-girl, who had arrived that same day from Pau for his friend's service. The child had not dared to go up alone to her sixth storey, but had waited for the departure of the unusual visitor.

"My poor child," murmured Proust, when he saw her crouching on the first step of the staircase, "come along with me.—You aren't going to sleep under the roof there all alone: you would feel much too lonely. Get into

my carriage, my poor girl: it is waiting here. Céleste
will get a bed ready for you at my house: she will look
after you. . . ."

Proust knew well the pain of coming away from home
to strange places, and has spoken much of it in his books.
And all the sufferings which his complex spirit had invented were felt by him in others no less acutely than
in himself.

"I was very frightened that night," the poor little Pau
girl confided later in her mistress. "I was not surprised
to see a gentleman staying with madame until two in
the morning. I had been told so many stories about Paris.
But when the gentleman wanted to take me back to his
house, I was very frightened then!"

It is perhaps among inferiors that the sufferings of
others affected Proust most immediately. His old servant
brought him once some lime-flower tea, barely tepid,
which he had to drink very hot. He reproached his faithful Céleste, who protested her constant care and scolded
him rather sharply for being always discontented.

"You are quite right, Céleste," murmured Proust,
deeply moved to think that he had hurt her feelings.
"This tea is excellent like that. I did not know what I
was saying. It isn't too cold. It's you who are right. It
ought to be taken tepid."

Céleste smiled. It was ten o'clock at night. Proust rose.
Céleste passed him his vest, put on his tie. He had to be
helped to dress like a child. And like a child too, he had
kept a certain need for caresses. As he could not give the
expression in outward tokens, it was his mind that gave
the caresses.

He knew that when your desires find realization, it is never "either at the time or in the circumstances where they would have given extreme pleasure." [2] Accordingly he was never more attentive to anything than to the manner of his gifts. If he had heard one of his friends say: "I should like to have such-and-such . . ." he would procure it without delay. He did not restrain his eagerness until Christmas, or to the distant prospect of a birthday, before making the gift. He wanted joy to arrive immediately, like a roast quail fallen from the heavens. He remembered always that a pleasure for which one waits is a pleasure lost.

When he asked a friend to dinner, he asked him what persons he would like to meet. "I shall ask you with Léon Daudet, Morand, Robert de Billy, in fact whomever you like. . . ." Proust did not seem to put any value on his own presence, and with an almost systematic humility he was eager that a friend should draw his satisfaction at being with him solely from the other guests, from the excellence of the dishes, from everything that was not *himself*. His extreme amiability and his desire to overwhelm had to some extent their origin in that quasi-mystical forgetfulness of self.

His touching letters, full of distracted gratitude, his immense remorse, if he had borrowed some money from a friend for a night, returning it next day with eight pages bewildering in their gratitude, the very exaggeration of his courtesy—these were all the masks of a certain disdain, were a manner of protecting himself in relation to society, of stopping it short at the entry to one's per-

[2] La Bruyère: "Of the Heart."

73

sonal life, of preserving a complete independence without giving offence. But at the same time Proust felt a kind of wild joy at letting himself be taken at his own game, at counting himself of no worth. "The publication of your beautiful book with the *Mercure de France*," he wrote to me, "has given me much more pleasure than my Prix Goncourt." [3] He abandoned himself to this strange need for self-abasement, rather as certain believers, intoxicated in the divine ecstacy, seek to debase themselves, or as the lover, rejoicing in his humiliation, delivers himself a bondslave at the feet of his mistress.

In his perpetual desire to render service, nothing gave him more pleasure than to facilitate the meeting of two persons who were trying to make each other's acquaintance. He was delighted to act as go-between, and to be present at the different movements of a scene between two beings who were discovering each other. It was always one more occasion for him to forget himself before grateful friends. Thus his notion of kindness considered as a moral obligation, his continual fear of causing suffering, was mingled with this curious mysticism which brought him, in contempt of himself, to make the sacrifice of all that he was, of all that he possessed.

"I do not know at the moment what I shall be able to give you . . ." he wrote, in beginning an admirable letter to Edmond Jaloux. "I feel a desire, almost a need, of making you a present. . . ." Prompted by this kind of sentimental effusion, which had nervous roots, he had an

---

[3] Unpublished correspondence.

impassioned taste for making gifts. To Walter Berry, who had invited him to dinner, he sent a sumptuous sheaf of flowers. Louis Serpeille once sent him an unpublished essay of his grandfather Gobineau on the war of 1870, and to thank the young man Proust wanted to send him five hundred francs. Serpeille did not accept them, and Proust thereupon gave him a brilliant set in a tie-pin.

Paul Morand told him once in the course of a conversation that he was probably going to consult a certain doctor. Next day he received a thousand francs, ten times the cost of the consultation. He wanted to refuse, but he received imperious and threatening letters. Proust declared that he would be very annoyed if he did not keep the money: already his complex nature was searching out the endless possible reasons for a refusal, which he would genuinely have regarded as an unfriendly act. Later Morand managed to return the loan, but only piece by piece and by dint of bringing into play all his great diplomatic talents; each hundred-franc note was sent, returned, sent again. The struggle for this restitution went on until Proust's dying day.

The generosity of his tips has become a legend. No American millionaire would have given more grandiosely. When he had paid forty or fifty francs over and above the price registered by a taxi, he would say: "I am so terribly afraid it isn't enough." No doubt he calculated the sum of a normal gratuity and then, in dread of its being insufficient, he multiplied it by two, by three, by four. He experienced a sort of sadistic joy in regarding himself as so wretched a creature that he was bound to make a much greater return than anyone else for the least thing done for him, the smallest inconvenience he had caused. And how fine a sensibility of heart was linked with this humility! He gave, and did so with the greatest delicacy, seeking a pretext on every occasion. "You have taken a lot of trouble for me," he said to an hotel waiter who had brought him a letter. "Here's fifty francs. Oh, but I have kept you talking till one o'clock in the morning. You've no longer got any means of getting home. Here's another two hundred francs. . . . And then, did you not tell me that your mother was on a visit to Paris? You will be wanting to go out with her. That will lead you into various expenses. . . ." A gesture like this, though it seemed at first sight exaggerated and incomprehensible, was not astonishing as coming from him. It was only the culmination of his wonderful kindness of heart.

Frequently his friends were led to protest. When he dined with them in some new restaurant (although that was certainly exceptional), they would say to him: "But you will *spoil* this place! We shan't dare to come back here after you if you are so insanely generous!"

"All the same," murmured Marcel, "I can see a waiter over there, standing in that corner, who has not had anything from us. He can't remain the only one not to get any rewards."

"But, my dear Marcel, at no single moment has that waiter been serving at our table. You are just encouraging idleness."

"Oh, but did you not notice how sad his eyes were when he was watching what we gave to the others?" . . .

He may have kept a cab all night long, he may have given magnificent dinner-parties, he may have entertained the whole hotel at Cabourg, he may have made endless gifts—but on himself strictly he spent almost nothing. He kept a suit for three years, and always the same dressing-gown. In spite of his fortune he was for ever bemoaning his lack of money. It is always possible for the richest man to regard himself quite sincerely as poor.

"My dear friend," he said to Constanin Ullmann, "here is a financial catastrophe added to all my other disasters. I am losing a fortune on De Beers, and my broker won't let me hold on. I beg you, go and see this Monsieur Léon, tell him to have patience, and that if he sells out, I am ruined."

When inquiries were made, the catastrophe was reduced to an insignificant loss. The boon of happiness seemed complete in Proust's eyes only when it rested on the basis of some grief, even an imaginary one. His nervous system, more and more exacerbated, made him live in a purely intellectual world, where he invented, whilst fathoming it, his sensibility. It was the world in which he created his work.

He worked in his bed, over which the loose sheets of paper were scattered like a rain of enormous confetti. This strained and inconvenient position increased his fever. He naturally had difficulties in turning back on the written page to correct or re-read it. His sentences, though they correspond to the complexity of his brain, were also moulded by the complicated position in which he placed himself when setting them on paper.

During the long years when he was writing, from 1906 until about 1912, he spoke little of his work. At the time of his life in the *"temps perdu,"* he had sometimes felt the need of reading his attempts to some of his friends, as if to calm his remorse. Now he was less perturbed about himself: "What this book brings," he wrote, "is real and impassioned, very different from what you know of me, and, I think, infinitely less bad, and does not any longer deserve the epithet of 'delicate' or 'fine,' but is rather something living and true (which does not mean 'realist,' I think)." [4]

If he felt the surging power of his novel, he still dreaded the criticism of those who "put taste before everything." Taste is a reactionary element in art. "I can scarcely hope that the book will sell, at least before the public has grown gradually accustomed to it." [5] He knew, since evolution was one of his main ideas, with what hostility every new work of art is met, and how slowly it penetrates and makes its impression.

Another agonizing reflection obsessed him. He was afraid that in the first volume (he then anticipated two volumes of 650 pages each) the composition of the general structure of the book did not emerge in sharp enough outline.

"It is so complex," he wrote, "that it becomes manifest only very late in the day, when all the themes have

---

[4] Unpublished correspondence.
[5] Unpublished correspondence.

begun to coalesce"—a prophecy which, alas! was to be
realized very exactly.

Then here we find anxiety seizing him in another
guise. "In the first part," he wrote to the same friend,
"there are . . . certain very indecent pages . . . and
in the second . . . others even more so. But the character of the work is so weighty and the presentation so
literary that that cannot be an obstacle." Here he is
estimating the true greatness of his boldness. He knows
that in introducing a theme almost unknown in literature, he can only be enriching it. And finally he discovers in his fears the object of a new torture: "When
Monsieur de Charlus appears," he groans, "you will see
that everyone will turn their backs on me, and the
English especially. Now, although I have not left my
bed for a week, I am still invited out a great deal. Open
that drawer there, opposite you. You will find an invitation from the Duchesse de C—— there: I scarcely
know her at all. (I show you these almost confiden-
tially.) But to-morrow no one will invite me any more.
I shall be banned everywhere, by the 'Charluses,' who
will recognize themselves depicted under the most horrible traits, and by the others, who will find my book
a matter of scandal. For having judged them dispassionately, I shall have made myself a black sheep."

And a long time afterwards, as it turned out, after
the appearance of *Sodome et Gomorrhe*, Proust related
with a laughing voice, putting his gloved hand over his
mouth, how a certain writer had come to see him and
had said: "You take *them* down terribly." But by that

time he found this anecdote prodigiously comical: fame had reached him.

. . . .

When one considers the immensity of the effort which he had to give to attain fame, after his book was written, one is left stupefied with admiration. "Our craft in itself seems easy to us, but to bring a book out, to obtain what one wants of a publisher—these seem to be crushing tasks. It seems so easy to write the volumes, and in their very difficulty more agreeable still. But how difficult it will be to get them printed." [6]

He had, moreover, everything against him. The situation he was in was worse than that of somebody unknown.[7] He had published, fifteen years ago and without any success, two books and some translations.[8] Both in literary circles and in the drawing-rooms he was looked upon as a fashionable amateur in authorship. The enormous work he had done on Ruskin and his wonderful prefaces had not succeeded in modifying this preconceived opinion. The work he had written seemed already something of a monstrosity simply on account of its physical bulk: a subject without action, entering into no definable genre—and he himself hesitated to call it either a novel or a work of memoirs. He was determined to publish it not only without division into chapters, but even without paragraphs, in crowded and

---

[6] Correspondence with Louis de Robert: *Revue de France,* January 1st, 1925.

[7] "When readers write to me at the *Figaro* (a rare occurrence) after some article, they send their letters to Marcel Prévost, my name seeming to be merely a printer's error for his."

[8] A small volume at the *Ménestrel,* and *Les Plaisirs et les jours.*

compact pages. "That makes the conversation enter more fully into the continuity of the text," he declared.

He was in an impasse. But time was pressing. The idea of death haunted him. Towards the end of 1911 he had finished and corrected the first seven hundred pages, "entirely ready for press." He was unwilling to wait longer: while they were coming out, he would go over the rest again.

In spite of his incapacity for action he had a profound sense of reality for all that concerned his work. But it was mingled with a complete ignorance of the practical details of realization. From the depths of his bed he sought a publisher. Calmann-Lévy he put aside at once, judging the book to be too free in tone for him. He thought of the *Nouvelle Revue Française*, the review which he found "the most intelligent, the only readable." He meant "the least stupid"; he was continually in disagreement with it all the same. He could not understand what it was doing with Péguy and so many other great men. No matter! "A purely literary publisher will have more chance of finding readers for a book which, to tell the truth, has no resemblance to the classic novel." [9] His friends tried to help him. Prince Antoine Bibesco invited him to dinner with André Gide, who was then, along with Jean Schlumberger and Jacques Copeau, editor of the *Nouvelle Revue Française*. And it was likewise to André Gide that Jacques-Émile Blanche spoke of Marcel Proust. The question was asked: "Proust? Proust? Isn't that the man who writes articles in the *Figaro*? An amateur? A *boulevardier?*"

[9] Correspondence with Louis de Robert.

The manuscript was declined. Perhaps it was not even read. Proust recalled that he had formerly published his two translations of Ruskin with the *Mercure de France*. Of its editor he retained "charming and grateful memories," and he sent him *Du côté de chez Swann*. The manuscript was again declined. No doubt it had not been read any more than on the first occasion. The enormous size of the text was enough to cause it to be laid on one side.

Time was passing. Proust could rise only at eleven o'clock at night. He grew desperate. Once more he had recourse to his friends. He wrote to ask advice of Louis de Robert, one of the few people who then admired his gifts. "There are moments like that," he told him, "when I dash myself against what seems to be insurmountable obstacles." In the end Louis de Robert and Gaston Calmette both recommended him to Fasquelle. Proust waited for a reply for a long time. He trembled at the idea that adjustments and cuts would be asked of him, and that "different titles for each volume would be imposed, and an interval between their publication." The manuscript, however, was declined. In contrast with what had happened before, some notice was taken of it this time. But it was too massive, and too "different from what the public is in the habit of reading."

After that Proust wanted to bring out the book at his own expense: he would be free to dispose of it according to his own ideas. But he was persuaded out of this by his friends, who declared that it would lower his repute as a writer. Proust was obstinate. He stuck to his idea. But in the end he yielded. Louis de Robert warmly recommended the work in offering it to his own publisher, Ollendorf.

Once again Proust waited. He was afraid of being summoned at some hour when he could not rise. But Humblot, the head of Ollendorf's, replied to Louis de Robert in these terms:

"My dear friend,

"I am perhaps very dense, but I cannot understand how any-one can use thirty pages in describing how he turns over and over in his bed before getting off to sleep. In vain I take my head be-tween my hands. . . ."

These successive checks brought no bitterness into Proust's soul. Of these judgments passed on his work he made himself the judge in his turn. That of Fasquelle he found "false," that of Ollendorf, "absolutely stupid." He preserved the same serene confidence in the worth of what he had written, but he despaired of ever winning the comprehension of his contemporaries. The stupidity of men did not surprise his philosophy: "I have seen articles of France's, celebrated though he then was, rejected by the *Temps* as unreadable . . . and the *Revue des deux mondes* found his *Thaïs* so extremely ill written that they asked his permission to suspend its publication, and could not in any case leave it in the usual position of the serial. . . . What I have told you briefly of France, I could tell you with almost burlesque details of Régnier, of Barrès, and of many others." Nevertheless, "it is a duty of every writer, and especially of a writer who is ill, to transfer his ideas from a fragile brain into pages which may perhaps be fugitive, but are at least independent of the destruction of the living body." [10]

This time he decided to have the publication carried and at author's expense, and he asked his friend René Blum, an acquaintance of Grasset's, to take the manuscript to the latter. Would Grasset refuse? He would then take it to *Vers et prose,* and then, if he had no better success, he would look for a printer "whose particular line might be the printing of books for people who cannot find a publisher." But Grasset accepted. At last Proust received his first proofs. He corrected, crossed out, endlessly. Half of *Du côté de chez Swann* was rewritten four times. He shortened his text in accordance with the advice of friends, hesitated a long time, but in the end took out a quarter, not without regrets. He had conceived his book in the beginning as one in two volumes; but would it run now to three, or four, or five? The choice of a definite title also obsessed him. He liked a title to be "quite simple, quite colourless."

At last, in 1913, after the struggle that had lasted for two years, this book to which he had given so many years of his life, which is indeed his life, this work, as he himself modestly said, "long meditated, loyally written with no '*trompe l'œil,*' with no prettiness," appeared under the worst circumstances, in an atmosphere, as it were, of mistrust. The silence with which the writer had enveloped himself in real life seemed to cling likewise to his production. The general body of criticism remained silent: a silence that was even more terrible than the refusals of publishers. The latter had to judge

[10] Correspondence with Louis de Robert.

the work from the point of view of its immediate success, and Proust himself had no belief in that. But the complete absence of interest in a book so extraordinarily new as this is evidence of the inadequate culture, the lack of taste, the log-rolling, and enviousness, and intriguing spirit of the most of the critics of the press and the reviews.

One exception was Paul Souday. He devoted a whole article to the book in the *Temps*. He reproached it with its lack of composition and its faults of style, but he was the first to consecrate what in a few years was to become a kind of revelation.[11] As for Proust's friends, a few devoted articles to him: Jacques-Émile Blanche the first, in the *Écho de Paris*, Lucien Daudet in the *Figaro*, Maurice Rostand in *Comœdia*—— They hailed a genius. But people were distrustful. It is the opinion of a few fashionable people, they said, on one of themselves. The hyperbolical tone of these articles, which at the present day does not strike us as exaggerated, weakened their force completely.

Lying in his bed, Proust greeted every line that was written with the utmost attention. The newspaper *Excelsior* asked for a portrait, twenty lines deep. He was delighted. But no writer's vanity possessed him. Formerly he had been a stranger to every literary group and every intrigue, and now he took count of the judgments of others upon himself only to confront it with his own. A certain sense of shame, as it were, forbade

---

11 Similarly, a few weeks after the appearance of *Du côté de chez Swann,* one of the most authoritative and clear-sighted critics, in the midst of the over-abundance of novels, discovered his book, to which his attention had not in any way been drawn.

him to read criticisms that were too laudatory. But
when, in the midst of the general indifference and the
dogged stupidity of fools, he saw that he had been understood by a friend—what joy it gave him! "Truly un-
speakable!" he exclaimed. Louis de Robert, and Grasset
likewise, were very anxious to put up his book for the
Prix Goncourt. Proust yielded to the idea solely because
he considered that his primary duty was to undertake
any measure that could make the book be read. He
realized now that the isolation in which he had lived
was weighing heavily upon the fortunes of his novel.
He desired a few more readers: might there not possibly be some "friend of his thought" to be found there?
How pained he was by the spirit of cabals. He was told
that his private fortune might possibly prove an obstacle to the members of the Académie Goncourt who
awarded the prize. "Alas!" he murmured, "when I am,
not completely, but to a great extent, a ruined man!
Alas! In heaven's name, do not let that argument have
any weight! All that I could do (if I had this prize)
would be . . . not to accept the money." [12]

But contrary to his hopes, the book was not even
discussed by the jury. None the less, in the January
1914 issue of the *Nouvelle Revue Française*, Henri
Ghéon published a somewhat short notice of *Du côté
de chez Swann,* making reservations, but classing the
book amongst the works characteristic of the younger
literature. At the same time Ghéon was recommending
it to his friends. Jacques Rivière read it and felt the
advent of a great work. But he was then only the

[12] Correspondence with Louis de Robert.

secretary of the *Revue*. It was, however, thanks to his influence that the group of the *N.R.F.*—not without lively resistance—consented to recognize in the once-disdained man about town one of those neglected writers famous twenty years too late. The *Revue* then published, in two numbers (June and July, 1914), a fragment extracted from *Le côté de Guermantes*. Slowly and discreetly the book filtered through the choice few, that "aristocracy without patent," and amongst the lettered, those rare persons who, as Valéry Larbaud has said, "read for the sole pleasure of reading and seek out this pleasure with ardour." It was at this period that I came one evening upon *Du côté de chez Swann,* a stout volume with a yellow cover, on the bed-table of a friend of mine. "It is very intelligent," he said to me, "but extremely hard to read. It seems that the author is a neurasthenic: he lives shut up in a room with cork walls."

On the strength of this somewhat disquieting information, but with keen curiosity, I took the novel away with me, and as soon as I got home, opened it. But I admit that soon, like Humblot, the director of Ollendorf's, I could not get over the boredom of the third page. I began then to run through the pages, but I found no chapter divisions and felt my courage failing still further. At last, tired of it, I resumed my reading, starting at random, in the middle of a sentence. I was actually at the Verdurins' with Swann and Odette de Crécy. Then all was enchantment. The story of this passion, of this jealousy, the *salon* of Madame de Saint-Euverte, the Vinteuil sonata—a new universe was opening out before me. I went back to the beginning of the book; I was already accustomed to the intricate style of Proust, which struck me as almost easy and amusing, like those elaborately patterned keys with which one opens without any effort the heavy lid of a coffer. I did not, of course, return the borrowed book, but lent it to other friends—with all the fervour of proselytizing! But how many times the volume was returned to me, with the despair which corresponded to that of my own, and Humblot's, first impression. But I insisted, I explained, I defended my discovery. And doubtless there were many other Proustian neophytes then preaching the same gospel as I did.[13]

In a short time M. Gallimard, who had become director of the publications of the *Nouvelle Revue Française*, offered Marcel Proust the full repentance of the firm. At the same time, with Maurice Rostand as intermediary, Fasquelle asked to be allowed to publish the future volumes. The elect—"the poor elect with the incomprehensible secret," as Larbaud says, "an elect with no temporal authority, insignificant in numbers, and divided into tiny groups"—had in spite of everything succeeded in altering the opinions of the publishers, who were converted in advance of the critics. Grasset in his turn proposed to Proust a contract worthy of his

[13] M. Vandérem indicates an analogous method for the pleasurable reading of Proust. "You begin the first week with reading a score of pages a day. . . . Apart from this, the absolute rule is never to force oneself. . . . You continue for a week, at the end of which you increase by five pages a day . . . and you will reach the end in a relatively short lapse of time, and your pleasure is always more lively and more penetrating."— *La Miroir des lettres: 5e série.*

talent. With a "skilful delicacy," he left him free to go elsewhere, and Proust, "vanquished by this procedure," remained "in the cradle." The writer was now kept waiting no longer. He could hope at last to reach the wider public which he hoped to conquer. The first proofs of *A l'ombre des jeunes filles en fleurs* were printed—when the war broke upon France.

. . . .

There could no longer be any question of issuing the continuation of his work. In every country not only men, but intellectual forces also, were mobilized. During five years the only books that came out were "war books." Thought was silent, in suffering and oppression.

Marcel Proust had never been a nationalist. "At bottom, politics are all one to me," he wrote in 1905. "What is the good of wasting our time on things with which only the demon of perversity can induce us to occupy ourselves, for they are no part of our real temperament. . . ." [14] But he was irritated by the attitude of certain of the former Dreyfusards, who imagined they were being logical with themselves and continuing the struggle by pursuing a policy of anti-clericalism or anti-militarism. This sort of politics seemed to him poor in ideas, petty and stupid. Under the Combes ministry, the expulsion of the religious orders revolted his feelings: "I admit," he said, "that I prefer to find in a monastery members of an order re-establishing Benedictine music than a liquidator destroying everything. I like there to be workmen in factories, sailors on ships, and monks in

[14] Unpublished correspondence.

monasteries." [15] And later on, when Briand brought about the voting of the separation of Church and State, Marcel Proust, although urged neither by clerical doctrine nor by political passion, felt before Barrès "the great pity of the churches of France," and published in the *Figaro* an article on "the murdered churches." [16] It was the man in him, or rather the artist, who protested, the friend, that is to say, of the lowly church-towers no less than of the great cathedrals. During the Russo-Japanese war he denounced those of his friends who seemed delighted at seeing the Russians beaten. "In counting the Japanese aggression as excellent," he wrote, "we shall have made morally possible the aggression of Germany. . . . In belittling an ally at pleasure, we run the risk of seeing our neighbour rise up against us." [17] Of war he had a conception analogous to that of the duel. No doubt he had no belief in the absolute value of the point of honour, but he thought that a European country, like a man of standing if he is to make himself respected by others, a condition essential to social life, is under an obligation to defend its dignity with all possible scrupulousness. At the time of the Agadir crisis he wrote to Robert de Billy: "As a good *human*, one cannot desire recourse to the lot of arms, but as a good *Frenchman* one may well wonder whether it would be unfavourable to us."

Never did his isolation and ill health seem so cruel to him as during the war of 1914. He would have been

---

[15] Unpublished correspondence.
[16] *Les Églises assassinées.*
[17] Unpublished correspondence.

eager to take part in this activity, the thought of which tortured him in his sealed chamber. But his trouble only went from bad to worse. Frequently his throat was seized; he was afraid lest his almost chronic angina should be transformed into a fluxion. His suffering and his taste for suffering grew more and more complex.

When the government were seeking men of every age, he was filled with a dread of being summoned to appear before the medical board at some hour in the day when he could not rise from bed. Immediately he got his friends to make approaches to the military authorities concerned; he used all his connexions to secure a preliminary notice of the day on which he would have to appear. As a matter of fact, he was really so ill that it would have been enough for a military doctor to come to his flat and report on his condition. At last, however, he received his summons, and read "3 o'clock in the morning." It was the only time at which he was up. He was relieved of his anxiety. At the appointed time he proceeded to the Invalides. On his arrival he was stupefied to find not a light burning, the doors shut, nobody there. The "3" had been badly written—it should have read "8"!

He was no longer capable of adapting himself to the habits of everyday life. His retreat had become more strict, his appearances in the outside world more irregular. During these terrible years he was completely dominated by the idea of the war. He followed the armies in his thoughts. When Amiens was threatened, he wrote to a friend: "My dear friend, I am not going

to speak to you about the only thing of which everybody is thinking, of the only thing of which I, like
everyone, am thinking. . . . But I know that these
subjects are illicit in correspondence." [18] During his
waking and his sleeping hours, he saw young men struck
down, others sick, or mutilated, or blind. Within himself he heard the unending shock of these stricken
bodies. He was the first to arrive at the side of families,
even though he knew them only slightly, half an hour
after the tragic news, knowing well how solitude aggra-
vates a grief, just as expectation will kill pleasure. In
his presence one felt him so capable of suffering all that
was being suffered by those whom bereavement had
just struck, so open to the pains of separation and
death, that he brought relief even to strangers. To Paul
Morand he wrote the finest words that I know upon
the war. "It is, for me, less an object in the philosophic
sense of the word than a substance interposed between
myself and external objects. *As men loved in God, so
do I live in the war.*"

. . . .

Du côté de chez Swann continued to be read by the
few. The guiding spirits and the collaborators of the
Nouvelle Revue Française gave token to the author of
their admiration. André Gide had discovered in Proust's
style "a lake of delights." Jacques Rivière, in his German prison-camp, had this novel with him and preferred it to any. The most tempting offers were made
to him by the *Nouvelle Revue Française*. It seemed to

[18] Unpublished correspondence.

Proust that if he accepted them, his book, like a child, would be deserting the foster-mother with whom it had been boarded out, and returning to its true parents to find affection and love awaiting it.

Nowadays authors will often abandon their first publisher in a very offhand way. Let some rival make a commercial advance of terms to them, and that will be enough to decide them. Marcel Proust, however, changed his publisher "for reasons of pure literature." "I add further," he wrote, "that I shall not accept from the *Nouvelle Revue Française* conditions that are one centime better than those of Grasset (which in any case, after the first volume, had become good)." A touching scruple, an anachronism, especially if one remembers that Proust always thought that he was half ruined.[19] First of all, he was anxious to free himself from Grasset. And it was René Blum, to whom he appealed once more, who undid the marriage, to the great regret of Grasset, who realized too late the loss

[19] "I told him [Grasset] one day, rather in light-heartedness (*although it was true and most vexing*), in the postscript of a letter, that I had just been ruined. That same day (and very nicely, I must say) Grasset had to telephone to me. I could make nothing of his pitying tone or his circumlocutions, and in the end, fearing that something was troubling him, I asked him what was the matter. He answered me, still on the telephone (and I think it charming and retain my sympathy for him although he imagines, I think, that I am prejudiced against him): "It's—it's what you wrote to me. . . ." I could not recall what I had written to him, but at last, having forced him to say something specific, I realized that his condolences had reference to my financial troubles. I thanked him effusively for his interest in the matter, and begged him not to alarm himself more than I did myself—and had not the courage to add: and not to make them any worse by not paying enough attention to the sales."—Unpublished correspondence.

that was befalling him. Proust then hoped that his work could appear in its entirety at one time. He anticipated four volumes in all, appearing simultaneously. The proof of the first, *A l'ombre des jeunes filles en fleurs,* were corrected during the war. Alas, the book was put on sale, isolated, after the armistice, and with four years' delay.

Little by little his new publishers dissipated his legend of the fashionable amateur. But the welcome of the general body of criticism remained cool. Yet some magnificent articles appeared—*Une Rentrée sensationnelle,* by Robert Dreyfus in the *Figaro,* and a dithyramb of eulogy by Léon Daudet in the *Action Française.* For the third time a book of Proust's was put up for the Prix Goncourt. On this occasion time had allowed the realization of the astonishing novelty of this genius. A few of his friends, Robert de Flers, Reynaldo Hahn, Lucien Daudet, were eager to secure a brilliant revenge for him. With an almost unbounded zeal they resolved to secure the award for him. It is generally given, as is well known, only to a candidate whose "patrons" have laid a long plan of campaign on his behalf. But the members of the Académie are hesitating, apprehensive, drawn this way and that. What hosts of difficulties, objections, stubborn prejudices! Proust is too rich, or not young enough: too fashionable, too——!

Nevertheless, in November, 1919, Léon Daudet wrenched six votes from his colleagues in the Académie. The other four went to Roland Dorgelès' fine novel, *Les Croix de bois.* Friendship, gratitude, and merit triumphed over intrigue. Never perhaps had the Prix Goncourt been awarded with so great a measure of justice; never did it consecrate in so useful a way a difficult writer. This happy choice, with all its fruitful consequences, reconciles one to some extent to literary prizes.

In the majority of the newspapers the flood-gates of wrath, irony, sarcasm, and envy were opened. The more restrained sheets were content with a prejudicial analysis of the book. Further, the worst arguments were resumed: "This time," said one press cutting, quoted by Valéry Larbaud, "the Académie Goncourt has given its prize to a truly unknown author. He is not young: but unknown he certainly is, and will remain so . . ." and so on! The new recipient was even reproached with not having been mobilized, and with having stolen the prize from a combatant. It was indecent, it was said, that the shadows of the "budding grove" should take pride of place over the shadows of dead heroes.[20] None the less, the Académie Goncourt had for four years been crowning books about the war, the majority of which, it is true, were inferior to that of Dorgelès. "Mourning is out of fashion," [20] they added, as if Marcel Proust's novel were not one of the most painful that ever was. And the Académie Goncourt became a target for abuse.

A few of its members, however, defended their selection with becoming dignity. A very fine article by J. H. Rosny the elder appeared in *Comœdia*. Proust no

[20] Robert de Montesquiou, *Mémoires.*

longer had need of defenders. Rarely had the award of the Prix Goncourt given such sudden notoriety to an author. Snobbery was about to follow the elect, and the wider public would follow snobbery. Marcel Proust's era of fame was opening. He was forty-eight, and had three years to live.

CHAPTER V

FAME

EIGHT hundred and seventy letters of congratula-
tion—"too kind"—reached him from every part of
the world. How was he to make acknowledgment? His
gratitude surpassed the powers at his disposition. He
gave evidence of his extreme thankfulness in the splendid dinners which he gave at the Ritz to those who
awarded him the Prix Goncourt, or helped him to that
award. As in former days at his house, he invited men
of letters, academicians and critics along with some
personalities of the fashionable world.

His nervous attacks left him always in uncertainty
as to the morrow, and so he named his guests only at
the last moment. Dinner was ordered for fifteen persons. In a private room, at the head of an immense
table, laid and decorated with odourless flowers, Marcel
Proust waited. In the end he remained alone with two
guests in all, the only ones who happened to be free
that evening. Then he renewed his invitations. The gra-
tuities which he gave to the waiters were more generous
than ever. In the intoxication of his generosity he spent
the five thousand francs of his prize in a few nights.

The prize had drawn many new friends towards him.
He particularly cherished these late arrivals, who had
loved the writer before they had known the man.

Many young men were among them. This fervour of the youngest generation was the homage which moved him most, and the reward of his profound and sincere effort as an artist. What, indeed, could the others, the elders, bring him? "I do not understand his work," said Anatole France. "I have made efforts and I have not succeeded. One understands only one's contemporaries, perhaps also those of the generation immediately following one. After that, all is over." [1]

The people of fashion, with whom he could not speak of art, he kept at a distance, and above all did not suffer them to meet the others. His friends were skilfully classed into different categories. Between the rival groups a spirit of emulation and rivalry was set up. The new-comers were accused of wanting to profit from the scraps of the author's celebrity, the older friends of not having believed in him. Proust found the utmost amusement in these paltry quarrels which his person had so tardily aroused.

He savoured his renown with delight. Formerly he had not believed in it, although having faith in himself; but now he was stupefied, intoxicated by his success. At his flat he gave audiences, like a king. As the publication of his works proceeded, people had hopes of recognizing themselves in certain characters depicted, yet trembled at the same time lest they should find themselves therein. "Marcel cannot have forgotten me," thought his friends of childhood's days. "Yes, but his art is a cruel one: how has he painted me?" A few persons who thought they discovered themselves protested

---

[1] See *Anatole France à la Béchellerie,* by Marcel Le Goff.

furiously. The pretensions of these fools delighted the writer. He reassured them gently. With some of his intimates he gave violent expression to his contempt for so many of his fashionable admirers who had not even read his books. Sometimes, in his letters or in a dedication, he openly and severely taxed such a woman, claiming to be his friend, with indifference. His celebrity had given him increased strength. Little by little all his other passions weakened in the face of this dominating passion of fame. His customary preoccupations fell to a secondary place: he thought of the duration of his work, his work which would live on after him in time and space.

From abroad likewise came a flow of tributes. An American and his wife came to France solely with the object of paying their respects to Proust. They selected the Hôtel Majestic as their stopping-place, close to his flat, so as to see him more easily. During a whole winter the American lady called at Proust's door. Céleste received her in the dark ante-room and gave the invariable reply that monsieur was too ill to see any visitors. Rebuffed but unwearying, the couple sent the author enormous bunches of roses. Proust was told of these flowers being in his flat, and, afraid of succumbing under an avalanche of sneezes, he had them thrown outside as quickly as possible. The Americans were on the point of returning to their country without having had one single glimpse of this man of mystery for whose sake they had made the journey, when at midnight, on the eve of their departure, Proust went up to them at the Majestic, wrapped in his enormous black pelisse, and appeared for a moment, he announced, a moment which, to the child-like delight of his hosts, was prolonged until dawn.

In every direction the renown of Marcel Proust had transcended the frontiers of his own country. The elect of other nations had followed the elect of France. In England, Arnold Bennett, Joseph Conrad, Virginia Woolf, had discovered his genius. Mr. Scott Moncrieff translated his works. In Germany, Curtius was one of the first to speak of him. At Stockholm, the Academy of Nine made his work known. The newspapers of Holland, Spain, Italy, Jugo-Slavia, and Persia discussed him. He was compared to Saint-Simon, to Balzac, to Jean-Jacques Rousseau, to Henry James. *The Nation* and *The Times* allowed him to be a great writer. The approval of the foreigner is doubtless the true sanction of renown to the artist: and now the renown of Marcel Proust was consummated.

.   .   .   .

What a contrast to this splendour was offered by his private life during these last years! Turned out of the Boulevard Haussmann by his landlord, he became a pitiable migrant. He passed a few months in the Rue Laurent-Pinchat in the house of Réjane, now belonging to Jacques Porel, and was stranded at number 44, Rue Hamelin, on the fourth floor, a very gloomy furnished apartment, "costing 16,000 francs and looking rather like a servant's room." [2] He had hopes, of course, of not remaining there, and left all his property in store—which meant fresh expenditure. But the worst thing was the noise of this bustling house: there were children

---

[2] Unpublished correspondence.

who stamped about in the apartment above his, and to them Proust made presents of felt slippers.

He hoped shortly to move. He pitched his camp. But he was fated never to leave this strange and hostile lodging, where the sense of homelessness—one of his greatest sufferings—contributed to hasten on his death. He was deprived of all the objects most dear to him. He wanted to have his books brought out of store, but he never took the decision. In the *salon* the chairs were covered with dust-sheets. In the middle of the room a lustre was laid on the carpet. His periods in bed became always more prolonged, and his bed was never made. Potions and empty phials lay alongside the piled-up papers. Newspapers strewed the floor. In this frightful disorder the note-books containing the conclusion of his work lay heaped on a table.

Céleste, his housekeeper, assumed a growing authority. She held the immense power of guarding the door of her master's room. She had brought to her side not only her husband, Odilon Albarret, but also her niece and her sister.[3] Proust also sheltered a young Swiss who acted as his secretary. About 1920 he was anxious to get rid of him by finding him a position in a bank. He applied, as always when he had a favour to ask, to several of his friends, to Robert de Rothschild, to Gans, to Horace Finaly. He told them: "I ought, no doubt, to tell you confidently that this young man is rather idle, and I should add that he has no great liking for figures, but . . ." In spite of this discouraging recommendation

---

[3] From these two women Proust borrowed a few traits in creating the character of Françoise's daughter.

Proust succeeded in having him admitted to the Bank of France.

The irony of the writer had taken on a tone of greater frankness. He felt himself at once so clearly superior to the majority of men he had mixed with, and yet so near to death. After an existence composed of pleasures and agonies and struggles, his art had raised him up even to those mountain peaks of joy of which Nietzsche speaks. And now, like a child, he had moments of free and ingenuous gaiety. He took pleasure in teasing Céleste, that housekeeper as amazing as her master. From her daily association with Proust she had acquired some of his qualities, incommunicable though they seemed to be. She had an unrivalled memory and could retain almost word for word, with all the incidental propositions which Proust added to his phrases, the verbal commissions with which she had been entrusted on his behalf. Céleste spoke in the plaintive tones of her master. Like Proust himself in former days, she gave mimicking imitations of his friends. Proust, who was greatly amused by this, asked her not to hide her talent, but in public Céleste needed a great deal of asking, and as often as not refused to "make an exhibition of herself." Proust insisted, but, as in all his disputes with her, he always had the worst of it, and yielded. In the evening he made her come in with Odilon and her sister and niece, and he gave the assembled family a course of French history which was attentively listened to.[4] The presence of these unusual pupils, their questions, and the way in which they received their instruction,

---

[4] See *Sodome et Gomorrhe.*

put him into a state of pleasant excitement. His instinct for kindness was satisfied by his efforts for their instruction, and when Céleste had resisted one of his caprices, he could think of no more severe punishment for her than to deprive her of the evening lesson.

He organized his life, as in his youth; but it was no longer for the pleasure of the fashionable world, it was rather for these innocent pleasures of the sage. His illness had grown worse and he was now scarcely ever free from fever. Sleep escaped him and he had recourse to all kinds of narcotics. By dint of veronal he slept for three days on end. To make up for this abuse he kept awake for three days without a break, sustained by the aid of stimulants which helped him to work.

When he woke up, generally in the middle of the night, and did not want to be left alone, he would send off Odilon with his taxi to one of his friends. The friend had gone out, or was perhaps asleep. As there was no means of seeing Proust otherwise than at these difficult hours, one had to submit, rise, and allow oneself to be driven to his address.

He was in bed, of course, with a scarf round his neck. When one arrived, he often got out fully clothed from his blankets, with gloves of black or white cotton, several pairs of stockings, and his ruffled, white shirt-front.

"Wait a moment or two before you speak to me," he said in faint tones. "The caffeine I've just taken to waken me up has not yet taken effect: I'm incapable of opening my mouth. But I can feel the moment coming: I shall be better. . . ."

He smiled. The admirable light of his brilliant eyes gained the mastery little by little over his face, badly shaven and puffed-up with fatigue. This man who had just been absenting himself from life, who had just vanished for several days into sleep, was coming back to life. To the stupefaction of the friend, he had read the newspapers, replied to a large number of correspondents with his own astonishing letters, in a rapid, burning handwriting, with their postscripts longer than the main part of the letter itself. He knew the latest books that had appeared. It sufficed him to cut a few pages of a novel to be able to speak of it better than any critic; he would retain whole sentences out of it, which he would quote in writing to thank the author.[5] From his closed chamber he took an interest in the youngest writers, in the Dada movement, in the finds of Giraudoux, the music of Darius Milhaud, the drawings of Picasso. His conversation was an enchantment. He returned often to his favourite classics. He recited by heart, as in his youth, whole pages of Balzac, Saint-Simon, Anatole France.[6] After a long and unhalting recital he would complain of his bad memory. He discussed the poor manuals of literature. In style he cared only for the precise term, the unique and exact expression, from which he derived a profound joy. His conversation

[5] In running through the manuscript of my novel *La Femme de paille,* which I had sent him, he had had the time to notice that in a phrase from *Du côté de chez Swann* which I had placed as a motto at the head of a chapter, the word *lui* had a capital L instead of a small one, and he begged me to correct this printer's error.

[6] He knew hundreds of anecdotes of Anatole France, and with all his admiration of him, he foresaw that it would be possible to write a most amusing work on him, like those of Nicholas Ségur, Le Goff, or Roujon.

passed from art to finance, from finance to politics, to return to the world of fashion.

No one knew how the news of the day had penetrated his walls and reached into the obscurity of this apartment. If there had been a boom on the Bourse whilst he was asleep, he was informed of it on his awakening. But he took pleasure in feigning ignorance. "My dear friend," he would say in colourless tones, "I found just now in a drawer that I haven't opened for fifteen years some old share certificates I did not know I possessed. Perhaps you will be able to tell me what you think about them. In spite of their Germanic and princely name they have nothing either German or aristocratic about them: they are, I believe, Royal Dutch . . ." Well, a few hours previously that same day, the Royal Dutch had leapt up to 60,000 francs in a miraculous bound. Attentive to the current prices of the Bourse, he was trying to find out, in spite of his air of innocence, whether the opportune moment for selling had yet arrived.

He had renounced practically all the pleasures of the outside world—museums, concerts, nature. He no longer went anywhere save to the Ritz, where he was to be seen up to within the last six months of his life. There he had become so much at home that he felt better there than in his own flat. In the room where he dined, he knew how to manipulate the electric switches, and when a friend came to see him after midnight, he himself lit up all the lustres in fine style. If he deserted the Ritz, in a few brief infidelities with the Carlton or Ciro's, for instance, it was because he wanted some information which he could not have found elsewhere. One evening he dined at the *Bœuf sur le Toit,* because, perpetually curious concerning new forms of life, he was anxious to observe the dances, the couples, the Negro bands. His taste for investigation, too often thwarted by sickness, had been quickened. The completion and perfection of his work were his obsession.

. . . .

Since attaining renown Proust had set about working over the whole of his book again. His last years were taken up in the completion of this novel which lived as he lived and was developed by time. To the pages already written he ceaselessly added, pasting the sheets to each other, and then folding them fanwise and inserting the whole between the pages. The correction of proofs was a crushing task for him. His eyesight was failing; he had never found the time to visit the famous oculist of whom he spoke so frequently. So much did he suffer from the effort he had to make that sometimes, too impatient to remain in bed, he was to be seen bending over his paper in the porter's box at the Ritz, a glass cage, well heated, where the coming and going of the people of the hotel, which he could observe, gave a favourable stimulus to his mind. On the proofs he began once more the same task of amplification as he had undertaken on his manuscript. And on the revise proofs he added still more. The publisher was obliged to tear them from his hands.[7]

At the same time the slowness of others aroused his

[7] The work as it now stands is nearly three times as long as the manuscript in 1913.

irritation. He could feel the approach of death. Formerly he was anxious at any price to see his work come out as one piece. To appear, he used to say, this work needed himself. He complained bitterly of the continued delays of his new publisher, sometimes to the point of regretting Grasset.

Bonds of deep affection joined him with Jacques Rivière, but he took a playful pleasure in speaking somewhat freely of the *Nouvelle Revue Française*. One of the most serious griefs that befell him in this last period of his life was a purely intellectual disagreement, relating to the publication of a fragment of *Le côté de Guermantes* in an issue of the review. Rivière had firmly insisted on giving only a grouping of extracts of psychological analyses, taken from a chapter of the work, cutting out the descriptions of the *monde* which were closely interwoven with the rest. When this "slight sketch of the pain caused by a separation" was published, Proust showed consternation at seeing this portion of his work mutilated: he explained that he exposed his psychology on different planes, from different points of view, which were complementary to each other, were all of equivalent force, and could none of them be suppressed. Later, when other parts of his novel appeared in the review, it was he himself who indicated the cuts to be made. He endeavoured to stimulate curiosity, and give a foretaste of the next volume. His work was, as it were, his own flesh: if a stranger made a cut in it he was tortured like a wretch condemned to the rack.

At last *Le côtè de Guermantes* appeared, in two volumes, in 1920 and 1921. At the beginning of the year 1922, *Sodome et Gomorrhe,* one of the most audacious books in all literature, was issued in three volumes. But he realized that he should never see the publication of the subsequent books. Proust was endowed with an almost miraculous art of divining the motives of men, often unsuspected by themselves, and the thoughts which they might want to hide from him, but of which, by a mysterious gift, he was immediately warned. And with this he was too finely endowed not to be forewarned, by ethereal, invisible antennæ, of the arrival of approaching death. To several friends, to whom he wrote a month before his death, he said that he was definitely about to disappear. And this, he added, would then be in all reality *"le temps retrouvé."*

Already his thoughts were cast forward, over beyond the days that he still had left to him. He was much concerned by the announcement of the memoirs of Robert de Montesquiou. It had been vaguely reported to him that the great man had therein put down a number of extremely unpleasant things concerning many people, including Proust.

"I am going to die," he said. "It would be much better that my name should not appear, as I shall not be able to answer."

Friends reassured him: the memoirs would not be put before the public without modifications and suppressions.[8] Since the summer, following a cold which de-

---

[8] M. Edmond Jaloux, at that time literary adviser of the firm of Grasset, which was to publish these memoirs, gave Proust many assurances in this matter.

veloped into an attack of influenza, he had never been free from fever. Proust believed that he was the only person who was capable of understanding his state of health. He lived in a cold room, because he was afraid that central heating stirred up a dust that was harmful to his asthma. He had forbidden Céleste to clean the house or do any dusting. The air was unbreathable, redolent of confinement, but he made it still more close with his endless fumigations. Remembering with a kind of superstitious adoration his mother and her methods of treating herself, he put himself under rules of diet: he already ate very little, and now took nothing more than a little coffee with milk. In this enfeebled organism of his, unbalanced by excess of narcotic and stimulant drugs, the ground was ready for every aggravation of disease. Pneumonia set in. But he still refused to see doctors: if the very few friends now about him insisted, he threatened in terrible outbursts of anger to fling himself out of the window. Even his own brother, Dr. Robert Proust, was unable to approach him. In an attempt to save him, he forced a passage in, but met with the frightful violence of the invalid. It was only in the last few days that doctors were able to gain admittance. It was too late.

Up to the last moment, amid terrible sufferings, he kept complete consciousness. On the last night he dictated notes, his impressions on the approach of death. They were intended to complete the fine pages he had written on the death of Bergotte. He died on November 18th, 1922. At his side, blackened by the overturned bottle of one of his countless medicines, was found a scrap of paper, on which was decipherable, among some illegible words, the name of Forcheville, one of the characters of the second stage of his book.

PART TWO

THE WORK OF MARCEL PROUST

CHAPTER I

THE FATHOMING OF DEPTH

IN the course of the biography I have just sketched, there is continual evidence of a close connexion between the man and his work. I am now able to proceed to set forth with greater amplitude the ideas and images which the work of Proust contains.[1] But before that, I should like to enter into the technique of the writer, and to examine how much he brings us that is essentially new, and wherein lies the fundamental originality of his book.

When *Du côté de chez Swann* first appeared, the work was held to be confused, full of digressions, overluxuriant, burdened with too great detail. Its true significance was not apparent. Proust had set himself an immense task of the fathoming of depths. What was to him an exploration in the interior of beings and things seemed to others to be no more than minute descriptions. And some time was necessary before the sense of his method could be appreciated.

This method is first and foremost a painful, almost agonized, effort to penetrate to the very bottom of nature and of men. It is directed to the prizing open of secrets, and it lays bare unsuspected treasures. And

---

[1] Such will be the aim of the third part of the present work. Cf. *Introduction.*

in this way it comes in the end to certain great laws: a law of movement, a law of evolution, a law of the unconscious.

There are certain devotees in the East who contemplate with their heads turned up towards the sky, and, that they may not be distracted in their contemplation, cut off their eyebrows and throw them as an offering to the god of their adoration. On the spot where they fall, two stems rise from the earth and break into flower. The work of Marcel Proust seems to be born of a sacrifice akin to that of these believers. In order to see reality better, the artist has torn off his eyelids. His gaze is free. Nothing can stop him any longer. He can create in freedom.

The psychology of Marcel Proust is something that surpasses the quality of mere observation. The analysis is based upon the personal impressions of the writer. His novel, as he himself said, is real, because nothing is more real than the contents of one's ego. But it is not realist. Indeed, the novelists who have styled themselves realists have never achieved a living creation except by abandoning their note-books. It is only when Émile Zola turns to romanticism, that is to say when he plunges into his inward vision, that he can bring to life before the eyes of his readers a mine, a city, or a war.

"I have tried," wrote Proust, "to envelop my first chapter in impressions of one's half-wakening state . . . which I have pushed as far as my powers of penetration, alas, so modest, have enabled me; to reach right into that furthest recess wherein lies truth, the real uni-

verse, our authentic impression." [2] And this, in consequence, calls for exactitude of expression.

This method of the fathoming of depth has affinities
with the intuition of the Bergsonian method, if we consider that, with Bergson, intuition is instinct which, by
turning back upon itself, by reflecting upon itself, becomes reflection.

Having caught a glimpse of three trees, the sight of
which causes in him a kind of inward shock, Marcel
Proust describes the actual process of his search as an
artist. He would like first of all to isolate himself. But
he is in a carriage with friends whom he cannot leave:
"I placed my hand in front of my eyes," he says, "so as
to be able to close them without Madame de Villeparisis
noticing. I remained thus without thinking of anything,
and then, with my thought gathered up, held again with
greater strength, I leaped further forward in the direction of the trees, or rather in that inward direction at
the end of which, within myself, I saw them." But an
obstacle holds him up; those trees are covered with something on which his mind has no hold: they are like objects placed too far away, objects "of which our strain-
ing fingers, at the end of an outstretched arm, can only
for an instant brush the envelope, without managing
to catch hold of anything." Are those the trees he has
already seen in his childhood at Combray? Was it only
in dream that he saw them? Or are they an outcome of
tired eyesight? This time he does not succeed in finding
his impression. When he does succeed, and is then able
to translate it into words, his work seems to put him

---

[2] Correspondence with Louis de Robert.

into a state of trance, mysterious and almost mystical. But to arrive at this kind of communion with nature he is obliged to engage in a veritable struggle with himself. I cannot insist too strongly upon its importance. He thinks then that he hears the trees saying to him: "A whole part of yourself which we were bringing to you will fall for ever into the void." And he adds: "I was sad, sad as if I had just lost a friend, or died within myself, gainsaid one who was dead, or overlooked a god." The whole of the Proustian philosophy, in effect, rests upon the idea of this obscure travail of the superior beings who succeed in recovering, in those emotions hidden away in their most secret recesses, the very essence of life and of things. And the first Proustian moral imposes upon us, as a supreme duty, the search for these profound impressions: a duty so lofty that it contains within it the duties of goodness and of love, procuring the most exalted joys, and, for those who have not faith, standing as an equivalent of religious ecstasy.

And thus from this method of exploration there emerges a Proustian æsthetic. It is art itself which we find at the end of this mysterious quest. The obstacle of which Proust speaks, the envelope which prevents him from catching hold of the three trees, is composed of a tissue of ready-made visions; it corresponds to a disposition which is interested, active, practical, mechanical, idle, centrifugal, which is that of our mind. And it is precisely beneath this envelope that all objects and all sentiments, even the most trivial, are objects or sentiments of artistic worth.

At the same time the deep impressions are the only

realities of the external world. This search into our own breasts will lead us to a metaphysical vision; those envelopes, those obstacles which fetter the onrush of our spirit at the very moment when we strive to reach the secrets of our soul, are no more than a world of appearances, with no more real foundation than the legends of early peoples. It is behind these illusions that there lie, merged and blended, reality and art and joy.

CHAPTER II

STYLE

WHEN, by insensible effort, a writer has obtained a hold on the fugitive moods of the mind, he seeks, with the aid of the stern and rigid processes of logic, to express these by language. It is a pursuit of reflection after our emotions: a reflection seeking to analyse our emotions in their ephemerality, to reconstitute them before they have already perished. And from this comes our surprise, on a first reading, at Proust's sentences, sometimes so long, overburdened with parentheses and conjunctions, and yet always correct. The reader, who undergoes a kind of anguish in the midst of the midst of their labyrinths, is left with the impression that the mystery enveloping life has been finally penetrated. When he has reached the end of a passage, he discovers a psychological truth, small in appearance, but precious as the pearls brought up from deep waters by a breathless diver. The style of Proust reveals his extraordinary undertaking: to reach by intuition and to express by intelligence the most fleeting sensations of the inner life.

In order to appreciate the boldness of this task it is enough to recall that phrase of Bergson's: "Intelligence is characterized by a natural incomprehension of life";

or again, that line of Rimbaud's: *"Ah! Songer est in-digne—puisque c'est pure perte."*

The undertaking of Marcel Proust calls for a new style.[1] The language is so original that it is necessary to learn it, as if it were a kind of foreign tongue, all the words of which would be already known to us. The reason is at first rebuffed by the lengthy and en-tangling sentences, as a pupil is by exercises in diction or solfeggio, but then he grows accustomed to the diffi-culties and is astonished to find that his reading has be-come easy. Every new form of art calls for this process of accustoming oneself. The style of Proust resumes and refashions the traditional style of the seventeenth and eighteenth centuries, and surprises us because it differs so widely from the impressionist form of our own day.

If Proust was obliged to transform, as if for his per-sonal use, the style of the classic epoch, the reason is that in the seventeenth century the writers were princi-pally engaged in the handling of general ideas, while Proust on the other hand was devoting himself to catch-ing the fleeting shades of sensibility. He was obliged to dismember the classic period, to cut it up, and, like a conjurer drawing out hundreds of coils from one single ribbon, to bring out of it a multiplicity of in-cidents, in order to be able to interweave, and enclose in each of them, some or other subtle particles of our consciousness. Thus, if the sentence of Proust is not made up of immediate clarity and logic, it is because our psychological life is confused, and because intelli-

---

[1] Speaking of his own style, Proust said sometimes that he had "the thread of Ariadne"—alluding to the last words of his preface to Paul Morand's *Tendres Stocks.*

gence can penetrate only by dark corridors with numerous windings.

It is curious to come upon the very frequent *que* of the seventeenth century, replaced in Proust by *soit que* or *peut-être que*. The *que* in seventeenth-century rules subordinates propositions following each other as in a plain enumeration. The *soit que* of Proust, on the contrary, explains almost always the different and often contradictory motives of an action or an attitude. A gesture or a sentiment which our language expresses with a single word is in reality the effect of a multiplicity of desires and thoughts. Each *soit* of Proust's writing represents one of these desires; and from the converging whole of these *soits* emerges a state of consciousness, or a decision, somewhat as from several simple elements, oxygen and hydrogen, comes a single compound substance—water. Let us choose an example at random: on the first evening that Swann possessed Odette, he began by leaning over her bosom to arrange the flowers in her corsage. And ever afterwards, each time his desire for her returns, he makes use of this same pretext, "either [*soit*] from fear of ruffling her, or [*soit*] from fear of appearing in retrospect to have lied, or [*soit*] from lack of boldness to formulate a need greater than that (which he could indeed renew, as it had not vexed Odette on the first occasion)."

The numerous adverbs are generally the starting-point of one incidental proposition, which, inserted into the general unity of an abstract phrase, brings us back suddenly for an instant to a point of the narrative which long developments might possibly have made us forget.

The *tandis que* ("while they [*tandis qu'elles*] were slowly coming forward" or "while [*tandis que*] I passed beside the dark one") serves to recall to us opportunely, in the midst of the long analysis of the meeting of the hero with the *jeunes filles en fleur* that they are strolling and that the young man meets them as they walk. Subordinate propositions, beginning with *si, peut-être que,* allow us to leave for an instant the scene in which we are engaged, and to make a rapid incursion into the past, into our memory, allow us to escape from reality through the vision of a hope. Present participles also attach to the sentence an idea capable of completing it. Proust indeed is attempting to enclose within one single period, not only a moment of the life of our consciousness, but further to enclose within it the *milieu* or the landscape, the characters near to us, our occupation in that moment, our ego seen from within and from without at one and the same time.

It happens thus that the direct complement is often thrown back to the very end, like the verb in German.[2] We are obliged to wait a long time for it; numerous adverbs (*par, après avoir, à la fois,* etc.) make ready for its arrival, breathlessly sustaining our curiosity and impatience, like those secondary characters who at the theatre occupy the stage before the entrance of the hero.

How astounding is the variety of the Proustian sentence! Brief and light, like a bridge made of a single

---

[2] In a letter to the critic Curtius, professor at the University of Heidelberg, Proust writes that he considers German to be the modern language which has kept a syntax that is not only the richest, but the most closely akin to the Greek syntax.

span, or splendid and complex, built up as it were on heavy piles, it recalls by its opposing graces the most noble Wagnerian phrases.[3] Verbs in general abound: Proust sees things in their aspect of movement. Epithets are rare. But when, in the description of a flower, a woman, a landscape, the author suddenly keeps up several lines of qualifying words, an unexpected poetry shoots forth like a ray of sunlight darting from the moving clouds.

To obviate further the possibility of his form's becoming too intellectual in nature, Proust makes constant use of the image (not the symbol). Almost at every line we find comparatives such as *comme, tel que,* or *de même,* without making mention of comparisons brought directly into the sentence. Proust, in fact, proceeds instinctively like certain philosophers who work in the realm of the abstract and feel the need to return to the concrete world. Their idea is in this way to prove that abstractions have a life as real as the life of external objects. They hope to make themselves more comprehensible. They realize that the image completes their thought by its suggestion and that their analysis would in spite of everything be incapable of giving it full expression.[4]

And how great is Proust's art in the development of

---

[3] In the celebrated passage that describes the sleep of Albertine, we have an example of the short phrase. Here, like someone walking on tiptoe in the room of a sleeping child, the phrase of Proust suddenly changes its measure; it marks a stop every two or three lines; it becomes pure, soft-winged.

[4] It is worthy of note that Proust very often draws his comparisons from art, pictures, pieces of music or architecture, tragedies: from the rhythms of Wagner, for instance, or from Racine's mode of writing.

an image! It appears, it takes to flight, like a stream running now underground, and now in the open. Faithful,
invisible, it follows the sentence through all its meanderings, suddenly to reveal itself in an epithet, further
on in a verb, and at last broadening out into a delta and
filling a whole subordinate proposition. The writer, for
instance, is depicting a sunset over Lisieux, seen from a
height. First of all we are told that it is the hour of
sundown, and two lines further on we notice "the *blood-
red* basin of the sun." A little later the vanished image
reappears transformed, in the *"wounded* houses," and
in "the tall *empurpled*" chimneys.

There we have a parallel development of several impressions of absolutely different kinds, one defining the
moment of the day, another the place, and a third the
odours and savours that are in our consciousness, or
again our expectation of some pleasure, our regret, or
our impatience. All these conditions alternate in the
same sentence, at first without reciprocal influence on
each other, but then they mingle, and supplement each
other. Each receives from its neighbour a significance
that intensifies its own. A number of images are mixed
together and lie across each other. In the midst of this
flood a parenthesis abruptly brings a complementary
sense to one among them, a light from without, as if
from another world, independent of the unity of the
system in which we were. Here is a simple example.
Proust is travelling by motor-car and has just visited
several churches. In a short time the images suggested
to him by the vehicle become linked into the images of
architecture. The driver, putting on his driving-helmet

resembles, as it were, "a nun of speed." The hum of the engine is like a certain "stop" of the organ. "But for most of the time the driver only held in his hand his wheel—his steering-wheel—not unlike those crosses of consecration held by the apostles who stand with their backs against the columns of the choir of the Sainte-Chapelle in Paris; like the cross of St. Benedict, and in general like all the stylized forms of the wheel in the art of the Middle Ages. He did not seem to make use of it, so motionless did he remain, but held it as he would have held an emblem by which he should properly be accompanied."

Frequently Proust develops one scene with the aid of elements borrowed from another, although this second one has in itself no logical connexion with the first. They simply find themselves, one and the other, fused together in his consciousness. Thus it is that he quotes lines of Racine drawn from the rôle of a king; and, twisting the natural sense and giving them an interpretation in accordance with his thought at the moment, applies them to a valet or a cook of whom he is speaking in his novel. These alliances of a grave with a vulgar tone engender effects that are irresistibly comical. Whatever may be the nobility of the form, the sentiments of a valet or a king are seen by him on one identical plane.

Sometimes he will compare concrete objects to feelings that are purely abstract: these are perhaps his most beautiful images. Thus, arriving at Lisieux, in a motor-car in front of his parents' house Proust hears "the driver sound his horn." At this sound an emotion takes shape: "In my parents' hearts [the sound] has resounded gladly *like an unhoped-for word* . . . They rise and light a candle . . . while there, at the foot of the park, the horn, of which they can no longer mistake the sound as it becomes joyous, *almost human,* continues uninterruptedly to give forth its uniform call *like the fixed idea of their imminent gladness,* urgent and repeated like their growing anxiety. And I reflected that in *Tristan and Isolde* . . . it is to the repetition of two notes, strident, indefinite, and increasingly rapid . . . that Wagner entrusted the expression of the most prodigious expectation of felicity that ever filled the human soul." In this passage the uncertain sound of a horn seems at first to hesitate, and then leaps forward, is associated with feelings of gladness and anxiety, and then, by a new association, evokes the music of one of the greatest artists. The image is thus the development of an inward emotion long probed to its depths.

And so the multiple images, abstract or concrete, brief or developed, alternating or interwoven, insinuate themselves into the phrases, hurrying on with them, close up or farther away, and bespangling them with their reflections. To the books of Marcel Proust they lend a poetry that is very strange—though scarcely lyrical. About these marvellous studies of intelligence they form a veil of sensibility.

In order to appreciate to what depths they penetrate, it is enough to compare the style of that first work, *Les Plaisirs et les jours,* with that of *A la recherche du temps perdu.* In the former, there is not yet a personality in the phrase, which is pretty and neat, agreeable and full of careful charm. In the latter, the writer has reached the inner goal towards which he was moving. In the process of search into his emotions he has succeeded in finding always the exact, the unique, expression. It is precisely the opposite of the style of a Péguy, "a kind of indolence in the course of which one word makes us imagine another, and where one has not the courage to sacrifice one's gropings." [5]

[5] Unpublished correspondence.

CHAPTER III

THE RÔLE OF THE UNCONSCIOUS

WRITING to Louis de Robert, Marcel Proust said: "My concern is only in that which seems to me to unfold (in a sense analogous to that of the carrier-pigeon) some general laws." And so this distracted quest after the most fleeting sentiments of our consciousness leads the writer to the discovery of certain great ideas. An artist first and foremost, he has not sought to develop them. No work is less of a thesis than his. A certain world has imposed itself upon him. He knows that by courageously penetrating it to a sufficient depth a spontaneous philosophy will be set free. "Every great artist," he wrote, "who voluntarily leaves reality to expand in his books forgoes the appearance in these of an intelligence, a critical judgment which he holds inferior to his genius." [1]

But to the attentive reader there emerges first and foremost this great idea, that our inward life is not intelligible. If Proust dissects and reconstructs states of consciousness by means of the logical processes of language, it is only to tell us that logic does not apply thereto. The passages which, from a literary point of

[1] "Concerning the 'style' of Flaubert," in the *Nouvelle Revue Française*, January 1st, 1920.

view, are the most remarkable of the novel lead us to this conclusion: that the emotional life has its own particular laws differing altogether from those of the intelligence. There exist an association and a memory of sentiments, which are not the association and memory of ideas. Their obscure workings are hidden under the unconscious, which itself forms the most essential part of our ego.

Marcel Proust reaches the same ultimate conclusions as the modern philosophers. By these it is stated at the present day that the conscious is only one lighted point on the vast, dark expanses of the unconscious. Some, such as Freud, declare that the unconscious is so vast that its deepest parts remain always obscure, always suppressed, and are visited only occasionally by the troubled light of our dreams.

This is just what Proust realized. And this is why sleep, the great manifestation of the unconscious, interests him so much. A frequent subject of his is the entrance into sleep, "as into a second room that we might have," or, on the other hand, of the awakening from sleep, which makes us lose "the memory of the slightly filtered light in which our intelligence lay at rest as in the opaline depth of the water." Further, there are many kinds of awakenings, those which end a night of deep sleep, those of insomnia, or those which surprise one in an arm-chair after having fallen asleep for a few minutes that seem like centuries. Often Proust will imagine a dream in order to define the precise shade of an emotion such as the dream of his grandmother experienced by the hero, ending with the words: "deer, deer, Francis Jammes, fork." [2] A psychological impression, such as that of the three trees, which slips away into the unconscious, will immediately excite the attention of the author. He is not attached by the play of a difficult conquest, but by the abrupt disclosure which can be revealed to the observer by the flight of an emotion into this unconscious region of ourself. Also, it is from out of this unconscious, as from a hiding-place, that Proust draws forth the wonderful treasures which he proceeds to analyse in the light of intelligence. Dreaming and sleeping make up one of the great sources from which the novel gradually emerges.

One of these treasures is the emotional memory. We know the example of the author (or his hero), who one day dips a little cake, a *madeleine,* in a cup of tea. The taste of this cake brings back to him after an effort another little *madeleine* dipped in another cup of tea, in the house of his aunt Léonie when he was a child. And then the whole of a past, with all its power of evoking emotion, rises up from this impression, and serves as a starting-point for one entire part of the book. "The flowers of our garden," writes Proust, "and those of M. Swann's park, and the water-lilies of the Vivonne, and the good people of the village and their little dwelling, and the church, and the whole of Combray, all that takes on form and solidity, has emerged, town and garden, from my cup of tea." The memory pertaining to the

[2] Or likewise the dream at Venice of a Gothic city bathed in the greenish waters of the sea.

intelligence would have been able to give him only information about the past, but would have emptied it of all emotional content, which is yielded to him by the association of the two savours.

Baudelaire was perhaps the first to demonstrate the poetic charm of odours and tastes. Proust explains the part which they play in the mechanism of the unconscious. The perceptions of each of his senses remain, for him, linked with emotional memories. The noise of the hot-water radiator recalls to him the days spent at Doncières; the catch of the elevator as it passes the floor on which his rooms are is enough to evoke the women who have been impatiently awaited and have not come. The Vinteuil sonata, suddenly heard again in the midst of an evening party, brings to Swann the memory of the time when Odette, nowadays indifferent and coquettish, loved him, and tried to please him by playing for his especial benefit this piece of music of which he was so fond. "All his memories of the time when Odette was in love with him, which up to that day he had succeeded in keeping invisible in the depths of his being, had been awakened, beguiled by this sudden gleam from the days of love which they thought had returned, and had risen on hurrying wings to sing passionately to him, with no pity for his present sad lot, the forgotten refrain of happiness. . . . Instead of the abstract expressions 'the time when I was happy,' or 'the time when I was loved,' which hitherto he had so often uttered, and without overmuch pain, for his intelligence had enclosed therein only pretended extracts from the past which preserved nothing of it at all, he now met with everything which had fixed for ever the specific and volatile essence of his lost happiness; everything he saw once more, the sensitive petals of the chrysanthemum which she had flung to him from her corsage . . ." etc. (And here follows a page of the love-tokens of Odette at the beginning of their liaison.)

In this resuscitation of emotions, so beautiful that, instead of continuing this work, I would willingly quote the complete passage, Marcel Proust always reaches the conclusion that the intelligence is incapable of recalling to us the reality of our joys and sorrows. And it is no less impotent to bring back to life our beloved dead. The love we bear them lies hidden in the unconscious, and the unconscious alone is capable of awakening them. In *Les Intermittences du cœur* Proust explains how, a year after the death of his grandmother, he returned to Balbec, where she had accompanied him the year before and watched beside him when he was in suffering. And now, on the first evening of his return, as he is suffering from "a crisis of heart fatigue" and bends down "with slowness and prudence" to take off his shoes, he is suddenly overwhelmed inwardly: "within my memory I had just seen, leaning over my weariness, the features, strained, preoccupied, and disappointed, of my grandmother . . . not her whom, to my surprise and self-reproach, I had regretted so little, and who bore only her name, but my veritable grandmother, of whom, for the first time, I was finding in an involuntary and complete memory the living reality."

Here it is not by savours or scents or sounds that the living part is evoked, as in the case of the "little *made-*

leine" or the "phrase of Vinteuil." It is by the inward perception of a gesture, by the movement of the body, which the author (or his hero) makes "with slowness and prudence," because he is suffering, to take off his shoes. It is the movement which forces his love for his grandmother to emerge from the unconscious.

Immediately this love grows painful. At the same time the author recalls the impatient and wounding words which he may have said to his grandmother while she was still alive: "as the dead exist only within ourselves, it is ourselves that we unrelentingly strike when we remember insistently the blows which we have dealt them." And yet, "cruel though they were, I clung to these pains with all my strength, for I felt sure that they were the result of the memory of my grandmother. . . . I felt that I could recall her to my memory only through pain." And so, if it is by means of the unconscious, it is mainly by the suffering of love hidden therein that we are capable of resuscitating our dead. So much do the dead survive within us that they can still inspire us with the feelings of pain.

Further, Proust adds: "I clung not only to suffering, but to respecting the originality of my suffering." The phrase must not be taken in a romantic sense. Proust does not attach himself to it because nothing is nobler, nothing grander, than a great grief, but because there is nothing more *true*. And he writes: "Certainly I did not know whether, from this impression, painful and at the moment incomprehensible, I should one day free a morsel of truth, but I did know that if ever I was able to extract this morsel of truth, it could only be from that impression. . . . Thus, the duty imposed upon the artist obliges him to maintain within himself his living emotions, to yield himself in their respect to a kind of self-autopsy.

Our unconsciousness, in the whole reckoning, is altogether the great reality of our inner life. It is there that our dead and our childhood live on, our passions too, and our joys and sorrows. And never is it so real, so near to our comprehension, as when it is traversed by pain. Starting from this pain, the artist attains life and conveys joy.

At the same time, these dreaming and half-waking impressions serve as a starting-point, or as transitions to the different chapters of the novel. An entirely new process: in place of passing from one subject to another through a logical sequence of ideas, the author relies upon the obscure memories of the hidden self. He uses them as joints, or hinges, and it is this which gives the work its inward and original composition. In an unpublished letter Marcel Proust explained himself in this connexion: "It is a book," he wrote, "of the utmost reality, but *supported*, in a way, in order to imitate the involuntary working of the memory (which in my opinion, although Bergson does not make this distinction, is the only true one, the memory of the intelligence and of the eyes giving us back the past only in inaccurate facsimiles, which do not resemble it any more than the pictures of bad painters resemble the spring, etc. . . .) by abrupt recollections. One part of the book is a part of my life which I had forgotten and suddenly find again in eating a piece of cake which I had dipped in a cup of tea. . . . Another part of the book springs up again from those moments of awakening, when one does not know where one is, and imagines one is in another country, and two years ago. But all that is only the *scaffolding* of the book. And what it conveys is real, impassioned. . . ." These supports at the base of the novel form likewise the first seven of the "themes" which, like the *leitmotiven* of Wagner, alternate, return, and return again, in accord with an inner rhythm which is of the essence of the novel. And in the end, from these various phenomena, there will emerge "a whole theory of memory and knowledge," though not promulgated directly in logical terms.

CHAPTER IV

THE RÔLE OF DURATION AND TIME

"W E bathe not twice in the same stream," wrote Heraclitus. The world of our sentiments is an uninterrupted flow—a continuous gushing, say the modern philosophers. It is to this thought that we are led by the psychology of Proust. Our ego is modified every moment. Every sensation, every sentiment, grows old by the very fact of its duration. And here lies the second great idea of Proust's: that our conscious and unconscious life is in an unceasing process of evolution.

We all know of course that the things of this life are transitory. But this commonplace truth, coming glibly off the tongue, is one which few men really appreciate. For most of them hours and days resemble each other like the faces of people belonging to some strange race. And just as Proust, when he depicts the life of fashion, establishes personalities, his whole aim, in the life of sensibility, is to reconstitute each moment in its own individuality.

Things do not change only in themselves, but change also in relation to us. A landscape, a town, a dwelling, form an æsthetic vision and, at the same time, a surrounding atmosphere. Usually fresh surroundings are inimical to us. Little by little they are modified. The habit we form of living in a particular room slowly deprives the objects in it of their disturbing aspect. Proust (or his hero) tells us of his first arrival in the hotel at Balbec: "Every regular guest returning to his room, every girl coming down to dinner, every maid passing in the corridor, in the strangeness of their delineaments, casts upon you a look in which one reads nothing of what one would have liked." Later, when he comes back to Balbec, everything seems familiar to him. He feels himself at home. He has, in fact, advanced a stage in that operation which has "always to be recommenced, longer and more difficult than the turning back of the eyelid, and consists of investing things with the spirit which is familiar to us, in place of their own, which is hostile to us." And when he leaves Balbec at the close of a second summer, the surrounding country, the place-names of the country-side—everything has lost the mystery it had at the beginning.

Persons undergo a metamorphosis analogous to that of objects. The lovely features of unknown women, seen for an instant in the street, which awake our desire, would become, if we had time to come near them, plain or vulgar. The little band of girls, always together on the *plage* of Balbec, leave Proust spellbound, enchanted with them all at once, with their group. Then he chooses one of them: Albertine. When he finds her again in Paris, she has changed, because she is torn from the *plage* where he had always known her. And then she changes again, as he falls in love with her. Elsewhere Proust sees Swann again, grown old, and transformed by the approach of death: "I could not help being struck, moreover, by how much he had aged in relation

to myself . . . I could not bring myself to understand
how I had been able to stock him with such mystery that
his appearance in the Champs Élysées made my heart
beat faster." All the characters of the novel, the several
groups, the "sets," the *salons*, are drawn forward in a
twofold evolution: they grow old, not only in themselves, but also in relation to the central character, the
"I" of the narrative.

Works of art and ideas are similarly submitted to this
lowering of rank to which persons and things are subject. One writer has delighted Proust in his youth—Bergotte. But before long our hero is admiring him less,
because the sentences of his books have become less clear
for him. "The painter of originality, the artist of
originality, proceed in the manner of oculists. The course
of treatment by their painting or their prose is not always pleasant. When it is concluded, the practitioner
says to us: 'Now look.' And behold! the world (which
was not created one single time, but as often as an
original artist has arisen) appears to us entirely different
from the old world, but all in perfect clarity." And to
this Wildean conception Proust adds: "And I came at
last to wonder if there was any truth in that distinction
which we always draw between art, which is no further advanced than in the time of Homer, and science,
with its continuous progressions. Perhaps, on the contrary, art in this regard resembled science; each new
writer of originality seemed to me to be progressing beyond the one who had preceded him, and who told me
that in twenty years, when I shall be able to accompany
without fatigue what is new to-day, another would not

appear, before whom the one of the present moment would go to join Bergotte."

Thus, in the everlasting dispute of the ancients and the moderns, Proust stands resolutely with the moderns. He is determined to prove to us that he believes not only in evolution, but in progress, if not in the sense of Condorcet, as a continual improvement, then in the Nietzschean sense of the eternal round. Doubtless he has observed too often that the images of nature, the mystery of mankind, the unknown element of a new art, give us relative impressions, ephemeral joys, and he wishes to imagine that these perish only so that other and finer joys may succeed the first. Perhaps, indeed, death exists only to engender a new and always better life. This belief would be only a kind of corrective to the desolating philosophy of Proust, to the philosophy of instability, mobility, and general flux.

In this cycle of life, nevertheless, love holds essential place; it yields, as does the great mass of things, to this great law of evolution. In vain, amid these unceasing rapids of time, do we strive to raise up some enduring monument of love. From Swann and his passion for Odette, to the Baron de Charlus and his captivation by the musician Morel, love has its roots in one and the same phenomenon: it is a simple modification of our unconscious, an accident in its flux. Often it is born from some phrase of this sort: "This evening" (answers the woman one desires) "I shan't be free." It is prolonged by anxiety and jealousy. It sets up a nervous condition which overwhelms us, and upsets our scale of values. None of the desires of our ego in love will be that of our future ego. And when the ageing of our inner life draws our love towards its end, we remark in the ultimate analysis that it has perhaps been only a nervous condition. Thus is made clear the fleeting quality of this great agitation.

Birth and habits, the fair faces of women, friends, parents and relations, the life of drawing-rooms and fashion, philosophy and works of art, passions and jealousies—in regard to all these there constantly returns, brief or insistent, the theme of universal flux. The universe and mankind are made subject to the category of time, under its twofold form of the social hours that go by, and of our inner duration in its flight. This theme of *time* emerges over and over again in the most different scenes of the work, to remind us that we must content ourselves with relative joys and ephemeral illusions; that we can never, even for an instant, attain happiness—that is to say, immobile and absolute happiness—save only in death.

. . . .

Although their appearance has now (1925) continued for over ten years, the books which make up the whole of Marcel Proust's work are far from being all published. None the less, if *Le temps retrouvé* is still unknown to us, we know at least that it will provide us with the key of the whole work. "All that," wrote Proust, in his correspondence with Louis de Robert, "will be shown clearly in the third volume," the volume which to-day has become the ninth. He writes further: "I have in effect tried to envelop my first chapter in the impressions of the wakening state, the significance of which will not be complete until later." However, I do not consider that this last part will bring us a veritable revelation.[3] In spite of the criticisms of the ignorant or foolish, the work is so magnificently constructed that its conclusion is already enclosed within its starting-point and is only one great expansion. In the two themes of the unconscious and of evolution it is present in its entirety. One proceeds from memory to art, the other from birth to death; the first is developed in our inner duration, the second in time itself. And Proust teaches us that all that exists in time is lost, that what is in our own duration is a treasure revealed.

In this way alternate these two leading motives, with the aid of which the writer, in accordance with a superior order, expresses his creative genius. And each one of the mingled scenes of the novel has the grandeur of a chain of mountains. The reader is like a traveller: at every bend in the road he discovers a new aspect of the world, and trembles in his emotion. And then mountain chains anew, then lakes, then the spreading fields, and mountains once again. He advances further into the work, and each new volume seems to him like a new continent. When *Le temps retrouvé* appears, the reader, back at his starting-point, will have been right round the world.

---

[3] Cf. *Introduction.*

CHAPTER V

THE EVOLUTION OF THE CHARACTERS

THE characters in Marcel Proust's work are multiple in time and space. From this comes their extraordinary novelty. He used to speak of them as he might of contemporaries or of historical figures. He would quote, in one and the same phrase, and in the same tone of voice, the Comtesse Greffühle, the Duchesse de Guermantes, and Madame Récamier. He told how he was not free to make them act as he might wish and the reader receives the same impression. He is interested in their changing humours, in their quarrels; without wearying he follows them through the thousands of pages of the work: he is their impassioned friend.

The characters of Proust, unlike those of Balzac, are not the heroes of an intense activity; their characteristics do not emerge from their deeds and actions, nor, as in Stendhal, from the dissection of successive actions. Whence then do they derive their astoundingly living quality?

"My characters," explained Marcel Proust,[1] "in the second part of the book do quite the opposite of what they do in the first, and of what could be expected of them." In fact, they pass and repass before our eyes,

---

[1] Unpublished correspondence.

and each time in unexpected circumstances. With that, the light falls always on another aspect of their character. The more complex it becomes, the more does the personage take on a quality of relief. He is continually enriched; he grows more and more solid, with a new quantity of psychological notations, strengthening our impression from his first entrance; often enough when he does appear, he is not defined with complete clarity. But his outlines grow sharper and sharper with each reappearance, viewed by other people in other circles, mingled with the various groups, old and new.

It is a striking method. A dinner-party with the Duchesse de Guermantes takes up one hundred and fifty pages! An evening reception with the Princesse de Guermantes fills the half of one volume! How does the action advance in such conditions, and how do the characters evolve? How can time flow on over a period of seventy-five years? The episode of Swann's love-affair, *Un Amour de Swann*, opens thirty years before the birth of Proust, and the novel extends right to the period of the war. It is here that the marvellous art of Marcel Proust is manifest. Under the guise of a static work he presents us with a work which is in continual evolution. The truth is that the most important events are unfolding themselves between great motionless frescoes, and more often than not in the wings of the stage.

Just as in life itself, the characters disappear from the scene of the novel over long periods. We lose sight of them. They have other friends, and so have we. And suddenly we come across them again, just when we are least expecting them, and very different from what they were at the moment we left them. The evolution has been going on, not on the stage, but behind the scenes. We can measure it by the contrast between the character who has disappeared and that which we find again. He bears the same name, but he is no longer the same. Each time that he reappears before the spectators, Proust plies him with a thousand questions, contrasts his present state of consciousness with that which was his in the past, and from this extracts a course of remarkably living force.

Take Swann as an example. In the first book we see him in his most brilliant period. He is sought after by the Faubourg Saint-Germain. He is the gifted man of fashion; he is the Jew who has attained his entry to the aristocracy; he is the *blasé* favourite of women. Then he makes the acquaintance of Odette and the Verdurins. And here comes the magnificent story, perhaps Marcel Proust's masterpiece, of Swann's passion, and Swann's jealousy, until the day when, returning into the *monde* at Madame de Saint-Euverte's party, he is listening to the Vinteuil sonata and understands that his love is ended. Such is the first fresco from which the figure of Swann stands out. Here is the second: Swann is married. To whom? To this *demi-mondaine*, Odette, whom he loves no longer. The character, then, has undergone a distinct evolution. It is our part to re-create it. We must imagine Odette paying her court assiduously to this ageing man of fashion, and how he, weak and fearful of solitude, is powerless to resist the solicitations of a woman, although nevertheless he no longer loves her. Swann is married: the light shows itself again. What becomes of Swann, the social figure? He has almost entirely renounced the Faubourg Saint-Germain. He frequents, alone, without his wife, his former friends. He seems suddenly to attach great importance to republican connexions, because the ministers or advocates, whom formerly he used to despise, consent to visit him. In short, he is protecting his wife, seeking to force recognition for her in spite of all the difficulties and humiliations which he undergoes. To console himself he wants to make himself believe that the connexions which he has maintained unbroken are the only ones that have any value. Here the fresco is completed afresh—a dark fragment. And the third fresco: Swann has grown old, and ill. France is cleft in twain by the Dreyfus affair. Swann is a supporter of the Dreyfus party: Jewish nationalism has declared itself within him, to the detriment of the exclusive taste which he had in his youth for the *monde*. A few aristocrats approve his attitude, unbeknown to all the others. These are the last pleasures that Swann knows before he dies.—Finally, after another interval of obscurity, comes the last fresco, throwing an ironic light on the destiny of the character. Swann pays a visit to the Duc and the Duchesse de Guermantes, one evening when they are making ready to go to a ball. Swann informs them that he is going to die. But they have barely time to listen to the news of one who once was always their best friend. Swann is indeed left solitary. Night. And just as it was behind the scenes that Swann was married, so now it is behind the scenes that he dies.

All the characters of Proust are painted thus in large incomplete frescoes, like statues of Rodin, leaving room for some suggestion of mystery. The missing portions correspond to the evolution of the character in question, and the chiselled fragments are of sufficient strength to suggest this to us, at once in his past and in his present. The most striking changes are those undergone by the women. Thus the "lady in pink" of the café concerts whom the child Proust sees on his uncle's knee, later becomes the fashionable *cocotte,* Odette de Crécy, received at the Verdurins in a bourgeois circle. She will in time become Madame Swann, and we shall meet her in the drawing-room of Madame de Villeparisis, which the Duchesse de Guermantes leaves when Odette enters. Later still, after the death of Swann himself, Proust throws an abrupt ray of light on to the *salon* of Madame Swann: it is now one of the most elegant in Paris, frequented by Bergotte, by princes, and finally even by the Duchesse de Guermantes, whom Swann tried in vain all his life to attract to visit Odette. And thus, from one fresco to the next, a woman rises in the scale of social life, each time renewing our surprise and obliging us to re-create the movement which has been going on in the intervals.

Under this particular theme of time we can consider each of the characters of the novel successively: Dr. Cottard, for instance, an irritating blockhead busily letting off little puns, ends by becoming a celebrated and fashionable surgeon, for the wit of a commercial traveller is not incompatible with medical science, and a poor decent man can become a revered master. Elsewhere the hero of the book recognizes with stupefaction in Elstir, the painter of genius, a certain Bohemian whom he used

to meet long ago at the Verdurins'. The Verdurins themselves [2] are first of all simply a family of the lesser bourgeoisie; they grow rich; with the Baron de Charlus as
intermediary, they make their first contact with the
aristocracy. I think that before long we shall find them
again in the drawing-rooms of the Faubourg Saint-
Germain.

[2] For the benefit of the amateurs of keys—but with the general reservations I have made regarding keys to Proust's work—it may be recorded
that certain traits in Madame Verdurin must have been taken by the
author from Madame Ménard Dorian, and certain traits of Cottard from
Professor Guyon.

CHAPTER VI

LANGUAGE AND SELF-EXPRESSION

MARCEL PROUST, it may be, passed a great part of his life in listening to the conversation of his friends, the people in a drawing-room, and in ceaselessly provoking answers to his questioning "But tell me, please. . . ?" But he had a reason: with him there was no better light into the hearts of men than their language. Guided by their own peculiar phraseologies, he descended into their consciousness, as a miner follows the veins of ore through the obscurity of the galleries. And in the same way, in Proust's novel, the youthful hero listens to the discourses of his old aunt Léonie, the long complaints of Françoise at his parents' table, and tries to lose not one word of what is said by distinguished guests. If he interrupts, it is but to incite Swann or M. de Norpois to continue their remarks. Insatiable, divinely patient, hypnotized by his attentiveness, he retains by heart the diatribes of a Charlus. Just as, after the departure of Montesquiou, before an amused gallery, he gave imitations that were hallucinating in their verisimilitude, so in his book he brings to life the characters which he has created by the aid of other imitations of genius, no longer mimed, but written, authentic pastiches. The Verdurins, the Guermantes—he plays them on the stage of his novel. Unable to let himself be heard or seen by the reader, grimacing, waving his arms, changing his intonation, laughing, he makes them speak, in monologue or dialogue, and he makes his commentary, with the aid of parentheses—or incidents placed within dashes—their nervous tricks or their eccentricities.

It is, of course, the most familiar, the most everyday, of their conversations that he reproduces. And just as there is not one intrigue in his novel that shapes itself in continuous progression, just as the principal events occur off the stage, so the conversations of these characters are not designed to hasten the action, to oppose the characters, to create a situation. Most novelists take moments of crisis as those for their heroes to speak. Marcel Proust, on the contrary, considers them in their normal, habitual life. The ambassador M. de Norpois chatters with some bourgeois acquaintances to whose house he is invited on some quite unremarkable evening of his life; he exchanges courtesies in the drawing-room of his friend Madame de Villeparisis. Another novelist would have put him on trial in some exceptional time, on the eve of war, exchanging notes with other diplomats. Anatole France would at the least have placed beside him at a dinner-party a number of important guests, prelates and ministers and scholars. And yet we know the very secrets of the soul of Proust's Norpois, a profound and universal type.

How does the reader succeed in extracting his most secret states of consciousness from his most commonplace conversation? What the writer brings out into the light is not so much what is actually said by a Swann or a Saint-Loup, as the manner in which they say it; not so much the logical sense of their phrases as the construction of their periods, the nervous tricks, the words that they are continually repeating, those that they isolate, or lengthen out, or throw into prominence. It is, in fact, by the pathology of the language, interpreted in all its exactitude, that Proust reveals his characters to us.

" 'I do not say that [the Duchesse La Trémoille] is *profound*,' [Swann] pronounced the *profound* as if it had been a ridiculous word . . ." The fact was that in the set of the Duchesse de Guermantes, where Swann passes his life, the discussion of general ideas in a tone of seriousness is not tolerated, and Swann, intelligent though he is, is so fully conquered by the *monde* that he has submitted to these imperious rules and has caught the tone of these drawing-rooms. It happens, none the less, that the aspirations of his hidden nature rise to the surface of his mind in spite of himself. And then, in order to thrust them back, he detaches the word, be it unbecoming, pedantic, or heavy, in this instance the word *profound*, as if to excuse himself.

"All the same [*quand même*], to prefer Racine to Victor [Victor Hugo] is something *tremendous* [*énorme*]," exclaims Saint-Loup. And Proust adds: "The pleasure of saying '*quand même*,' and particularly '*énorme*,' was a 'consolation' to him." But while Swann pronounces these words between quotation marks, Saint-Loup throws them out in triumph. In this aristocrat they are the expression of his desire to realize his high aspirations, a work of art, a great deed. But being imprisoned within his own circle, where discussion, save of genealogies, does not exist, and leading a life devoid of significance, these words intoxicate him, give him an illusion, console him. And ten years later, a thousand pages later, Saint-Loup will be found again saying: "The *Chartreuse* [*de Parme*], that's something tremendous [*énorme*]."

Thus what interests the writer is not what his characters are thinking of each other; it is the manner in which they express what they are thinking. Proust is too much of a Bergsonian not to be aware that words never correspond to the fineness of our sensibilities. Language was created by man when he was seeking his nourishment, when he struggled against the beasts of the wild, when he was contriving instruments of war, of iron, for utilitarian ends. So language is precise and supple when it is applied to the sciences,[1] but vapid and clumsy when it is obliged to convey our states of consciousness. It is not, in fact, the talk of a Saint-Loup or a Charlus, least of all their conversations imitated and reproduced by Proust, their extremely commonplace and everyday conversations, which allow us to understand their soul. But the writer interprets all their pathology, their conduct, their nervous tricks. In fine, Proust is here carrying out a true process of psychoanalysis. He is ransacking the unconscious.

Thus, if one analyses the conversation of Madame de Gallardon as if to "discover the key of a ciphered language," one observes that there is no expression which

---

[1] To such a point that a purely mathematical language, such as Couturat dreamed of, would not constitute a stage of progress.

recurs in it so frequently as "at my cousins', the Guermantes'." By its constant repetition this expression tes-
tifies to the unsatisfied snobbery of this person, who
finds consolation in pronouncing as often as possible
one of the most aristocratic names in society and in
underlining her relationship with that name: "at my
cousins', the Guermantes'." In any case they receive her
only once a year, and that, moreover, only because she
is their cousin.

When Freud declares that *lapsus linguæ* are not
simply matters of distraction, but correspond with certain obscure feelings pushed back within us, is he not
working on the same lines as Proust? The *"profonde"*
of Swann, the *"énorme"* of Saint-Loup, the "at my
cousins', the Guermantes' "—are not these a sort of
lapsus linguæ, escaping from the lips of these people
without their taking any heed of them, and revealing
in one a dogmatic nature, in another idealism, in the
third snobbery: traits which form their true nature,
but which they are anxious to conceal in their outward
life? Whence it can readily be understood why Proust
is so interested in the most ordinary of conversations,
in which he discovers a thousand signs, errors, processes,
and mechanisms, which are the most revealing symp-
toms he could want.

Almost on every page of the book they are to be
found, over and over again: "They are young *bour-*
geois," declares the Baron de Charlus to Proust, making
certain words stand out, preceding them with several
b's, unable to resist the pleasure of showing some degree
of insolence towards the youth. This pride, in aristo-

crats, is generally suppressed from their high degree of politeness. But none the less we find it again in the Duc de Guermantes, the brother of Charlus, who, "in order perhaps to give a Jewish name a more foreign air, did not pronounce the *ch* of Bloch like a *k*, but as in the German *hoch*." Here again is poor Saniette, who had a bubbling in his mouth in speaking, a fault in enunciation which Proust attributes to a "relic of the innocence of his early days which he had never lost"—that is to say, a great measure of primitive goodness. His precious and pretentious expressions, such as "Is it not curious? [*Est-ce pas curieux que?*]" or "singularly [*singulière-ment*]" in the sense of "particularly [*particulière-ment*]," reveal in him further the boldness of the shy man. Thus the long conversations of the Verdurins, those of the dinner with Saniette, Brichot, Ski, recall to our memory certain novels of Max Jacob's in which the concierges and the street vendors exchange talk that has no end and is yet of absorbing interest. The truth being that the mental and spiritual dispositions of these characters take on bodily form, and are localized, in their lispings, their pronunciation, the composition of their vocabulary.

But Proust goes further. As in life itself, where the slightest thought of other people's could not pass unnoticed by this veritable wizard, so, attentive in listening to Albertine's conversation, he seized hold in this way of the tiniest movement of her mobile conscience. She was fifteen years old when he met her on the beach at Balbec. When he comes upon her again, she "had ceased to be a mere child." In fact, she now says, in thanks for a gift: "I am confused [*Je suis confuse*] . . ." or, speaking of a girl of somewhat vulgar stamp: "She has a foot of rouge on her face [*Elle a un pied de rouge sur la figure*]." And later on, when she is the prisoner of the young man, she expresses herself quite differently. Talking of a political event of which she disapproves, she says: "I think it frightful [*Je trouve ça formidable*]," and Proust adds: "I do not know whether it was about then that she learned, if she wanted to convey that a book was badly written, to say: 'It is interesting, but look, it must have been written by an utter jackass [*C'est intéressant, mais par example, c'est écrit comme par un cochon*].'" But he is much more anxious still when he discovers in her restricted vocabulary expressions which do not come from herself. At Balbec she used to make use of a certain number of phrases (such as *"c'est un type," "Je n'ai pas d'argent à perdre," "Je te trouve magnifique"*) which Madame Bontemps, who had brought her up, had taught her. Thus, "a mother surrenders her own jewels to her daughter with each successive stage in her growing up." But here is Albertine, since the previous summer, saying of someone that he is *"tout à fait distingué"*; of golf, *"c'est tout à fait une sélection,"* or that a certain *"laps de temps"* had passed. These are words which Madame Bontemps could not have bequeathed to her, for they are words which Madame Bontemps never employs. The truth is that Albertine, since last year, has made the acquaintance of a young man and has engaged in a lengthy flirtation with him. No doubt, then, she will be less rebellious to-day against kisses than formerly. And so when Proust hears the word *"distingué,"* he is reassured and comes nearer her; from the word *"sélection"* he infers that Albertine's flirtation must have been a very free one, and clasps her; and finally, with the expression that follows, *"laps de temps,"* he embraces her. It is a method of interpretation which might profitably be used in judicial procedure. By a confrontation of the expressions of the accused and the family of the victim, the *juge d'instruction* would be able to tell whether they were known to each other. The police at present apply only material procedures, finger-prints, bodily measurements. If it had recourse equally to psychological analysis, they would no doubt be less negligent.

Later, when Proust is to experience an agonizing passion for Albertine, every word of her conversation imported from without, every "alluvial addition originating in soils formerly unknown to her," will, in contrast with the preceding scene, cause him the most terrible suffering. Jealous and complex, as he was in life itself, he will then study with minute care the words the girl uses, and especially those of the least significance. Albertine, he will tell us, "used to say, speaking of anything at all: 'Is that true? Really? [*C'est vrai? c'est bien vrai?*]' "—a locution corresponding to the "isn't it?" which crops up continually in English conversation. In a similar sense Odette de Crécy used to say: "Is it really true, all this nonsense?" and then the formula is explained as coming from "a stupid commonplaceness of

mind of a woman." But such is not the sense of Albertine's *"C'est vrai,"* for the girl accompanies it with a
look of sincere interrogation which she manifestly would
not have if the formula were only a piece of mechanical
politeness. So then Proust envisages a second possible
solution: could Albertine be so distracted that she had
need of continual confirmation of the smallest observations of fact? (When she was told: "It's an hour since
we set off," she asked: "Is that true?") But Proust observes that her questioning interjection is accompanied
at the same time by a slightly coquettish pout. And
henceforward, abandoning the second solution, he finds
"at last the true solution of this formula. It seemed
rather as if these words, from the time when Albertine
became of a marriageable age, had been answers to:
'You know, I have never known anyone so pretty as you
are,' or 'You know, I'm very much in love with you'
—affirmations to which these interjections—'Is that
true? Really?'—answered with a modest consenting coquetry, and they were no longer of any use to Albertine with me but to answer with a question to an affirmation, such as 'You have been dozing far more than an
hour'—'Is that true?' "

It is in this way that the analysis of "certain modes of
speech of Albertine's made me suppose—I do not know
why—that she must in her short life have received a
great many compliments, a great many avowals, and
have received them with pleasure, with sensuality." That
"I do not know why," placed in his quotation between
dashes by Proust, is doubtless modesty on his part, as

he devotes a page to finding out exactly why. But I am not anxious in my turn to analyse this "I do not know why," after this unprecedented analysis where Proust, tortured by jealousy, leads us as far into the interior of a consciousness as it is possible to go.

PART THREE

THE UNIVERSE OF MARCEL PROUST

CHAPTER I

THE *SALONS*

THE first groping classification of general opinion, as irresistible as the legacies of heredity, had placed Marcel Proust in the category of "society" writers. His articles for the *Figaro,* as we have said, gave him the reputation of a mere frequenter of social functions. And the crowding names of Princess This and Duchess of That which he strings together in any of his books had still further confirmed his reputation for snobbery.

Snobbery? When Rastignac, twenty years of age, stands on the summit of the Butte and sweeps all Paris with his glance and vows inwardly to conquer this, the most elegant capital of the world, is he a *snob?* Drawing-rooms are to him the battle-field of the fiercest passions. Old Père Goriot has just died, and the same evening his daughters, to earn their gowns, have gone to dance in the drawing-room of the Baron de Nuncingen. And these people claim to be civilized? The young man quivers. He will be stronger than they, the prime minister of the king. First and foremost he is a man of ambition. Ambitious likewise is Julien Sorel, the peasant, the son of peasants, who longs to marry Mathilde de la Môle. The world of fashion appears to him as the domain of hypocrisy; he is familiar with its mechanism and he will vanquish it; but he will end under the knife of the guillotine!

What is this *monde,* this world of fashion, in the eyes of Marcel Proust? A distant country, with its frontiers barred and its passports hard to obtain. From his childhood he has heard speak of one of the inhabitants of this marvellous country, the Duchesse de Guermantes. He imagines her as beautiful as a fairy creature. One day he catches sight of her at a distance in the church at Combray, and does not understand that she is a creature of flesh and blood like the commonalty of mortals. Willingly the child, when taking a walk with his father, leads him round by "the Guermantes' way." Alongside the road flows the cool stream of the Vivonne, and on its banks he finds expanses of nenuphars, of white water-lilies and buttercups. If the path towards this forbidden country is thus beset with enchantments, what must be the castle itself wherein the duke dwells with his duchess? As the child cannot go there, he dreams of it. Up through his memory there surges the history of France which he has lately been learning. The Guermantes are descended from the great Condé, from Geneviève of Brabant, and their ancestors go right back into the days of the Merovingians. Already under Charlemagne they were renowned.

And so henceforward we find the *monde* associated in Proust's mind with the landscapes and the centuries of history. Round each aristocratic name of which he hears mention, he creates a poem. This aristocratic society is set for him in inaccessible heights, a dream which continues his own dreams, a pure and free vision which he is to cherish intact, until the day when he actually enters its drawing-rooms.

"Man does not readily resign himself to remain eternally in ignorance of the fundamental truth of things," the learned Henri Poincaré has written. And Proust says: "We are attracted by every life that offers us something unknown, by a last illusion to be destroyed." It is this sentiment which drives men to love (to know a woman so as to divest her of her mystery); to travel (to divest a town of the legend of its name); to enter the fashionable world (to remove the prestige that encircles aristocratic names). That quality in Proust to which the name of snobbery has been applied is this philosophy of desire and disenchantment, the essence of which is to invest with mystery all that is in our unconscious, and which then, brought little by little to the centre of our ego, into the light of the intelligence, is thereby stripped of savour and of life.

Desire is a sequence of inevitable deceptions which we are compelled to experience "in relation to beings, as at the theatre, in travel, or even in love." The *salons* of the Faubourg Saint-Germain are more alluring to Marcel Proust than Venice or the Berma, Gilberte or the hawthorns. Before long they will be as naught. The long contact of Proust with the world of fashion will be the story of the stripping-off of successive skins. Little by little, all that is most peculiar to himself, extreme politeness, the subtle grades of salutation, lightness of wit, everything, will become commonplace and void of any power to please. As with someone who has been loved to distraction and, after the love has passed, is no more than a mere anybody, so Proust will come to see hardly any difference between certain vulgarities of the Duc and those of the bourgeois, between the flawless speech of Oriane de Guermantes and that of Françoise.

The richer a man's imagination and sensibility, and the greater his power to restore on top of the ruins of shattered mystery a new mystery, the longer will he be in finally abandoning the objects of his desire, as the lover who renews himself will prolong his love. Can Marcel Proust be styled a snob because after the deception which he experienced at the dinner of the Duchesse, the *salon* of the Princesse de Guermantes appeared none the less in his eyes to be a place of mystery and glamour? The Prince seemed to be a man for whom "only highnesses and dukes counted, and who made a scene at every dinner-party because he did not have the place at table to which he would have been entitled under the reign of Louis XIV (a place which, thanks to his extreme erudition in matters of history and genealogy, he was the only person to know anything about)." When Proust (or his hero) received an invitation for this evening reception, it is the greatest and most unexpected event that can possibly happen to him, so much so that he doubts whether he has been invited at all. But nevertheless, after an hour of boredom, he will make haste to escape from this function in order to rejoin Albertine, who at that moment is his incarnation of mystery.

"It is only imagination and the power of belief which are competent to differentiate certain objects and cer-

tain beings from others, and to create an atmosphere."
Here is the idealistic and subjectivist philosophy which
Proust applies to every form of life. We are going to
accompany Proust into this "world," to familiarize ourselves with its peculiar characteristics and its laws; it
is nothing less than the history of the author's disillusion-
ment.

. . . .

It was once remarked by a newspaper writer that
Marcel Proust is the best of all professors of snobbery,
and that his novels are, for beginners, excellent manuals
of social strategy. It may be so—if the society of 1895
which they depict had not undergone considerable development, if, on the one hand, the Dreyfus affair had
not crystallized the kernel of the Faubourg Saint-
Germain, and if the war of 1914 had not, on the other,
left it utterly worn out.

But fortunately the life of fashion is not envisaged
in Marcel Proust's books only from the point of view
of history and documentation. What interests us is not
so much to know all the rules of correct conduct, what
was "done" and what was "not done" in the drawing-
room of those days, but rather to learn the manner in
which these rules were applied, their deeper meaning,
their human value. The Proustian study is something
more than the resurrection of an epoch. A generalized
spirit emerges from it, and to grasp this a certain effort
is necessary. Proust's method of fathoming depth brings
only impressions, but so rich are they in unexpressed
ideas that we shall be able to give exact formulation to
only a few among them.

Seen under close analysis, the poetic greatness which enveloped the *salons* of Proust's dreams is resolved into the immeasurable pride of their inhabitants. This world of the nobility rests in its entirety on a sentiment of hierarchy, a natural voice which is placed by God in the depth of our consciousness. But none the less, just as the sanguinary instincts of mankind are checked by the laws of the criminal code, so these stern instincts of pride and humility, the foundations of the noble class, are marked and softened down by the rules of polite conduct.

Just as the primitive clan obeys the law of solidarity, and the nation of the present day that of patriotism, so the Faubourg Saint-Germain is given shape and form by the law of social politeness. It is the first duty that everyone owes; it is the axiom preliminary to the ten commandments themselves. Human society says to man: "Thou shalt not kill." The society of the Faubourg Saint-Germain says to him: "Thou shalt honour the law of politeness." There are thousands of its articles to be observed, codified by custom, and accompanied, each of them, by an abundant jurisprudence. It is as natural to submit to these as it is to abstain from infringing the law. The accomplishment of these polite duties does not enhance the merit of a man of noble birth, for this is based rather on the choice and the importance of his connexions.

Some of these articles, which have been transmitted intact from the days of Louis XIV, are unalterably congealed in the structure of etiquette: as, for instance, the obligation of presenting to a royal highness, without an instant's delay, any person unknown to him or her in the drawing-room, and of not leaving the room before his or her departure. Just as God is adored in accordance with traditional rites, so must kings be honoured by their courts according to rules of a rigorous precision—and this does not always help to make certain drawing-rooms very amusing. But fortunately, setting the procedure with highnesses on one side, the rules of correct conduct admit of a certain degree of variation and suppleness. If you are a duke, they consist in making a bourgeois believe that he is none the less your equal; in fact, rather more, that you are actually his inferior. On the part of the latter, they consist in declining to believe the avalanche of amiable expressions and in protesting. This play of mutual dupes, when well carried out, is proof of a good education. Thus, when the young Proust (or his hero) is presented for the first time to the Princesse de Parme, he is welcomed by her as an old acquaintance; she invites him to the theatre with her son, and noticing that the young man is tired, she pushes forward a chair to him with her own hands. "She had not the slightest knowledge of my family or of myself, but, sprung herself from the noblest of stocks and possessing the greatest fortune in the world, she was anxious in her gratitude to the Creator to show her neighbour that, however poor or humble his extraction, she did not despise him."

Amongst the bourgeoisie, on the contrary, the great fear of everyone is of making too marked an advance to one's neighbour, which would be considered a humiliation. A member of the nobility, again, is so fully aware of his greatness that, however marked his amiability may be, he cannot stoop towards an inferior; at the most he will put a little "balm" in his heart. And so the politeness of the noble is never exaggerated. It is expressive only of his immense pride. It is no more deceitful than that of the bourgeois. But starting from a higher plane, it presupposes so great a distance between him who accords it and him who receives it that, to reach the latter, it is necessary to use more amiable phrases that will travel further. And so at that moment the two interlocutors have the illusion of being, for some instants, at the same level. Between them a moat is filled up, and although of different ranks, they are provisionally allowed to make use of normal relations.

The code of politeness as thus conceived gives us some explanation of the Marcel Proust of whom we have spoken, the man fulsome in praise, eager with his compliments and his homage, the Proust who protected himself by this excess of formality from the intrusion into his life of the people surrounding him. The very generosity of his tips was perhaps due to his idea of the distance that separated him from servants: no sum of money could ever seem to him sufficient to soften their sense of humility. It is in this highly individual sense that a service rendered would never seem to him to be adequately recompensed.

Of this comedy of politeness the bourgeois will remain in ignorance. If a certain duke happens to show him this cordiality, he will have every confidence in the duke's sincerity, and take his cordiality at its face value, and a few days later he will be astonished to find that he

has not been invited to that reception, at which the duke
after all receives only his peers. Well, it is just because
the duke knew that he could not invite this good bourgeois, just because he has a very sharp consciousness of
the hierarchy, that he displayed so much gratuitous affability towards this inferior. If the bourgeois had understood, he would have replied with a sincere manifestation of his humility. So in the end politeness is one of
the outward signs of the pride of the nobility, and one
which characterizes this class.

Another such sign is to be found in the salutation.
It is the first gesture which puts two persons into relation with each other, two persons often of different
classes, and must give an exact measurement of the distance that separates them. The salutation which is of
truly capital import, and is so complex, implying like
politeness a certain responsibility, is that of the superior to the inferior. In this class of comedy it is notably the women who have a magnificent degree of skill.
Madame de Courvoisier (and here Proust had in his
mind the Comtesse d'Haussonville) "approached the
head and bust towards you at an angle of forty-five degrees more or less, the lower part of the body remaining
immobile. But scarcely had she thus inclined the upper
part of her person towards you, when she drew it back-
wards from the vertical with an abrupt withdrawal of
approximately equal distance. The reversal that followed
neutralized what had seemed to be conceded to you.
. . . The advances made in a first movement were no
more than a momentary feint."

Men, on the other hand, proceed in an inverse way,

and begin by neutralizing "the amiability which they proceed for a moment to concede. At first one of the Guermantes does not seem decided to give you so much as 'Good day.' " But when in the end "he had judged you worthy of meeting himself, his hand, stretched out towards you at the end of an arm extended to its full length, had the appearance of presenting you the foil for some singular combat, and the hand indeed was itself at that instant so far distant from the Guermantes that when he then inclined his head, it was hard to make out whether it was yourself or his own hand that he was greeting." The salutation becomes a kind of duel. This first attainment of contact between two strangers, under its civilized externals, is a real drama, until each of the pair has taken the true place befitting his rank.

Each group, each set, has its own salutation: those of "lofty stiffness" or of "rapid negligence." Each separate person has his own, such as Saint-Loup, whose customary handshake detaches itself "as if in spite of himself at the moment of his hearing your name . . . without any participation by his glance, without the reinforcement of a greeting."

And there are the salutations of those who are receiving guests and, being obliged to repeat their actions, strive not to weary themselves out. The Duchesse de Guermantes expresses her greeting by making "only her eyes gleam with a flame as of wit"; at parties she "kindles them for the whole evening." Or there is Charlus, "leaning an elbow on the rail of the balustrade," replying to the guests who come to greet him "by naming people by their names," and calling out very loudly.

Or there is that very brusque salutation of the duke who is enraged by being presented to a musician whom he does not want to know, and runs the risk of "butting him alarmingly in the stomach."

It frequently happens, of course, that the impossible pride of the nobility breaks down the feeble barriers provided by politeness or salutation. Many among them, Proust tells us, are so badly educated, and the civilization of the *monde* is so scanty! Their grossness of language, bearing, and conduct, reveals the silent hostility which was hidden in the relations of the aristocracy with the bourgeoisie; it is then an open warfare of classes. Every insolence of the noble is a small revolution. It chases the intruder or the importunate, driven by the same spirit of revolt as the people, who go down into the streets and erect barricades. The state of peace, represented by the rôle of politeness, is abolished. So precarious, alas, is the state of peace! Instinct is always bearing it away, and wickedness is left in unbridled triumph.

It may be M. de Charlus recounting horrors concerning Madame de Saint-Euverte, who cannot but hear him, and ending triumphantly with an infamous couplet. Or it may be Madame de Guermantes, exclaiming in front of Legrandin: "His sister, Madame de Cambremer, is just as much of a toady as he is, and just as tiresome." When these insolences break out between two men, it is war; that is to say, the duel. Marcel Proust, extremely sensitive to what he imagined must be an insult, had recourse to arms on one occasion and frequently was on the point of resorting to them. But for the most

part, if the man of fashion had to reply to every grossness, he would be pacing the drawing-rooms with his
sword in his hand, and playing with it unceasingly. History has known such epochs. And to-day, on the outer
boulevards, the Parisian apache has so quick a sense of
honour that, for sometimes only a simple gibe, he whips
out his knife.

It is this continual fear of humiliation which has
given so much suffering to certain natures, at once
proud and susceptible, in their incursions into the world
of rank and fashion. Jean-Jacques Rousseau was one
such: he was extremely touchy, he had no turn for rep-
artee, he could not take the rough with the smooth.

As a matter of fact, the world has various methods
of accommodating itself with honour. Madame de
Saint-Euverte makes pretence of not having heard the
diatribes of Charlus, and greets him "as if she were
kneeling before her master," and without any transition
sets out to invite him to her next evening party. Others
will be anxious at any price to consider an insult as an
innocent and pleasant piece of fun and thus to disarm
their adversary. The "historian of the Fronde," being
"blackguarded" by the Duc, does not even comprehend
it, blushes, and trembles in every limb. Proust teaches
us that the cowardice of the fashionable is almost without bounds.

For the fact is that this mean-spiritedness is often
necessary to them, to be received as to receive. Be mean,
or be vile, it matters little so long as you have social connexions. Such is the supreme moral law which emerges
here from the Proustian picture. The law of good breed-

ing is a social law; the noble who violates it is not degrading himself any more than is the citizen who defrauds the treasury authorities. Be a barbarian or a hog, no one will think any the worse of you. But for each drawing-room door you have forced, your value will have taken on an increase. You are nothing in yourself. In the consideration of the fashionable, Newton or Balzac do not exist. You begin to have existence in proportion as you are admitted to participate in the functions of the various *salons*. And if not one of them is closed to you at any hour of the day, then you are the complete man. Look, all the joy and all the drama of life centre in and around those slips of pasteboard on which the lady of this house or that who is preparing for a reception inscribes the list of the guests, lists of proscription in the eyes of the rejected more frightful than those of the most tyrannical of governments. And for a Madame de Saint-Euverte, no doubt, exile or capital punishment is less terrible than their exclusion from the elegant drawing-rooms.

In his *Aphorisms on Wisdom in Life* Schopenhauer speaks of the stupidity of men who are preoccupied to their dying day with public opinion. "Lecomte, who was guillotined in Paris for an attempted regicide, was beset during his trial by one especial regret, that he was not able to appear in appropriate clothing before the Chamber of Peers, and even at the moment of execution his great chagrin was that he had not been permitted to shave himself beforehand. To have death staring you in the face, and yet to be concerned solely with the effect that one will produce on the crowd of gaping idlers assembled, and the opinion one will leave behind—is not this a unique example of folly?"

Here similarly the goal of life rests upon exchange of visits. Bourgeois morality does not intervene upon the judgment of the *salons*. A man is free in his private life. The Duc de Guermantes invites his mistress, Madame d'Arpajon, to dinner at his house. And Madame d'Arpajon has no better friend than the wife of her lover, in whom she confides, and under whose roof she groans every time the Duc "has not come to see her; that is to say, almost every day." And the Duchesse de Guermantes in her turn recounts to her friends, without any reservations, the woes of her husband's mistress. Virtuous women do not here share any of that repugnance for those of free behaviour which the most intelligent women of the bourgeois class display. No doubt a life of completely scandalous kind is capable of ruining a woman's reputation. But in general "there was a pretence of ignoring the fact that the person of the mistress of a house was handled by anyone who wanted to, so long as the *salon* remained inviolate." What makes a woman lose caste is an absence of severity, not in the choice of her amorous relationships, but in the choice of her fashionable relationships; that is, in the composition of her receptions.

What, then, are the final qualities needful if one is to receive and be received? First and foremost, one must have a name—one of those names into which Proust puts so much poetry and history, so much geography, so many dreams. But the merit of a title of nobility can be sustained only when its bearer keeps it in its due place, not by accomplishing deeds as glorious as those of his ancestors, but by eliminating from his receptions all those whom he must needs consider as his vassals.

Marcel Proust frequently insists on this idea, that one rates the worth of a *salon* "according to the persons whom the mistress of the house excludes, rather than to those whom she receives." In this way there is made clear the negative character of the qualifications for an exalted position in the *monde:* a title, but a title surrounded by the void.

.　.　.　.　.　.　.　.

Here then is the *salon* of the Prince and the Princesse de Guermantes, the ceremonial of which was no doubt suggested to Proust by that of the Princesse Mathilde. It is a meeting-place of royal or imperial highnesses. But a few families of less splendid connexions are admitted within its enclosures, on account of their immense wealth, or because of a bond of kinship uniting them to their host and hostess. An almost perfect grandeur reigns in the midst of a magnificent ennui. Almost at the same altitude we have the *salon* of the Duchesse de Guermantes, already less circumscribed. In fact, one can meet there, in the proportion of one in a hundred, an artist, or a politician, or a favoured amateur, but without their wives, for their personal merit alone. This boldness on the part of the master and mistress of the house is severely criticized by their peers, but excused by others, who are charmed by the surprise given them by the intrusion of these strangers. Much lower down comes the *salon* of Madame de Villeparisis. In her youth Madame de Villeparisis has flung her best connexions to the winds, and nowadays, so far as persons of elegance are concerned, she receives only the members of her family, who are obliged to pay her a visit once during the year. And then the Faubourg Saint-Germain, which, seen from outside and from afar, has the appearance of a motionless lake, is really in a perpetual agitation, traversed by a current rising up from its bottom, an agitation as violent as the eddies of a river at its mouth when the tide drives it back towards its source. One identical desire, that of gaining entry to the *salon* ranked above their own, is the obsession of all these persons of nobility. Nowhere more than here does the sense of rivalry hold the field, here among these people who still seem to the bourgeois to have touched the most exalted heights.

From this seething swarm of passions emerges a life of great intensity, with fine gradations of movement. And here once more we can grasp the genius of Marcel Proust's art. His descriptions of an afternoon party, a dinner, a reception, are endowed with an imposing and static amplitude which must surely give a reader the impression of heaviness. But in and about all these studies of polite usage, salutations, grossness, malice and scorn, amongst these fashionable personages, there passes so strong a breath of authentic snobbery that all these beings take on an abrupt animation, just as a machine, of which we may have first examined the separate and heavy components, will suddenly, thanks to the balanced forces of its mass, move under the pressure of the steam into perfect action. Just as some men devote themselves to art or to business, so here they apply all their creative faculties to the completion of their social relations. A *salon* is never a finished work; it must always be made more truly select, and embellished. And thus a certain measure of the ideal enters into these existences with their vain goals. The Princess de Parme, a royal highness, strives to attract to her house the friends of the Duchesse de Guermantes, intellectuals or artists, but they decline to go to these evenings of portentous solemnity. When an old lady makes her way into the *salon* of Madame de Villeparisis, she immediately "casts a piercing glance all round the company in order to pick out any fragment there might be in this *salon* which could be made use of for her own; and if such there were, she would have to discover it for herself, for Madame de Villeparisis, she had no doubt, would be spiteful enough to hide it from her." This "fragment" turns out to be composed of these two or three cousins of the great aristocracy, who have only come to Madame de Villeparisis's on a visit of obligation. In this way certain ladies were trying to build up their *salons* with those of others, and rivalries came into being, estrangements, scenes of jealousy.

Applying here as everywhere his methods of fathoming depths, Marcel Proust has discovered in all *salons* a kind of subdivision, the *coterie*, which is for him the true unit of fashionable society. Below it one can descend no farther. The coterie is a small group of persons amongst whom, as a result of long association with each other, there has arisen "one uniform method of judging small affairs." Again, at the same time as he explores the *salons* which form the divisions of the aris-

tocratic world in accordance with the wonted rules of
tradition, the writer penetrates into the *clans* or sets.
And in the interior of each of these small groupings,
which are bounded, not by the walls of a room, but by
the frontiers of a certain cast of mind, he engages in a
magnificent work of analysis. A striking resemblance is
worthy of notice, as it makes the sureness of his procedure understood: he will fathom the Guermantes coterie and the Courvoisier coterie in the same way as he
does his separate characters. Just as favourite words,
nervous tricks, slips of the tongue, have enabled him
to penetrate to the unconscious self of Swann or of
Albertine, so, thanks also to these, he enters into the
social consciousness of the coterie. In this way, for instance, "Swann and the Princesse de Laumes [1] had . . .
close analogies in their methods of expression, and even
in pronunciation. . . . They were the same phrases,
the same inflexions, the tone of the Guermantes coterie." Elsewhere, speaking of Madame de Cambremer,
the Princesse de Laumes says: ". . . I do not think that
she is a *contemporary* of mine." And Proust adds: "This
expression was one common to the Gallardons and the
Guermantes." But the true characteristic of the social
consciousness of the coteries is, in conformity with the
Bergsonian theory of laughter, their witticisms. It is
from these words of wit that Proust, just as he de-
duces the nature of an individual person from his language, extracts the character of the Guermantes coterie, starting from the physical aspect of the chief
personages who compose it ("a manner of bearing,

---

[1] Who later becomes the Duchesse de Guermantes.

walking, saluting") and working back to their general ideas: the love which they affect for intelligence, and their contempt for the titles of nobility.

But these ideas which they are pleased to affirm are often only the expression of an hypocrisy, unconscious though it may be. While still an unmarried girl, Oriane had shown herself somewhat untrammelled in bearing and manner, making allusions to Tolstoy, and manifesting sympathy with this man whom the aristocracy regarded as a great revolutionary. But none the less she married the Duc de Guermantes, who belonged to one of the noblest families, and one of great wealth as well. If Saint-Loup, on the other hand, wanted to act in conformity with his theories, to work, to marry his mistress, it was said that this was dangerous behaviour. Yet, though the Guermantes set claims to worship nothing but intelligence, it still does not go so far as to invite at random the artists or intellectuals of repute; it contents itself with making a severe selection, admitting those from among them who are well-born enough to figure in a *salon*, but, on the other hand, it excludes from its connexions the Courvoisiers, for example, for, in spite of their noble title, they are such stupid creatures that they are not far from imagining that to be intelligent is probably much the same as "having murdered one's father and mother."

But above all, starting from the witty word to fathom the depths of the Guermantes coterie, Marcel Proust comes once more to the spirit. The fact is that intelligence, as the Guermantes conceive it, consists in speaking of serious subjects, not seriously, but with "charm," "simplicity," and "tact." Intelligence, at the most, can exercise its critical spirit on persons and on things, and try to express it as precisely as possible with words of wit. It seems as if the study Proust is making of the Guermantes coterie extends beyond the individual case, and can be applied in general to the *monde*, as opposed to the bourgeoisie. In the set of Madame Verdurin, one Brichot, a professor at the Collège de France, and one Cottard, professor of the Faculty of Medicine, carry on a dogmatic discussion of the great question of the day. But in the *monde* this pedantry is considered as showing insufferable lack of good breeding and reserve.

And no doubt this spirit is full of grace, and the sayings of Oriane, which in her circle are called "very intelligent," are sometimes extremely witty. They even take on an extraordinary importance, as the Duc de Guermantes spends his time in stimulating them in his wife or in making her repeat them in the new *salon* which she frequents. And these phrases and witticisms are subsequently hawked round from mouth to mouth. " 'I don't know,' declared Oriane, 'whether M. Esterhazy is worth much more than [Dreyfus], but he has a quite different style in the mode of turning phrases, a different colour. It cannot be very pleasant for the partisans of M. Dreyfus. What a pity they cannot change their innocent victim! . . .' 'You have heard Oriane's remark?' asked the Duc greedily." And in the Guermantes coterie the members present immediately change countenance, assume for the moment an expression of tragic stupefaction, while a heavy silence descends. At last, with an effort, one of them finds his voice just enough to remark: "Admirable!" in colour-less stones. Oriane's remark is admirable! From that moment it circulates from set to set, from the present *salon* to the *salon* immediately below it on the scale. "It was still being eaten cold the next day at luncheon among intimates invited for that, and during the week it turned up again under a variety of sauces." It is like-wise from this same spirit that there proceeds the taste of Oriane, and of the fashionable world in general, for "imitations," caricatures of men under the form of *tableaux vivants*, the instability of Oriane's judgments, her paradoxes, the perpetual contradiction of her opinions, of her humour, her sudden infatuation for a man or an art; in a word, a delightfully superficial aspect of intelligence.

There can be no doubt that Marcel Proust was intoxicated by it. We have mentioned the gift he had of talking in the style of "Count Robert." In the Guermantes coterie he has left all the fascination, the joy of giving pleasure, the pleasures he tasted in the years of his fashionable youth. In his childhood he had magnified the names of noble families with a kind of poetry, and this poetry was not yet to fade away immediately into thin air. At first he was only amused by the early discoveries beneath the veil, the pride, the brutality, the lust of advancement, the spirit of hierarchy that inspired the suzerain chiefs of the Faubourg Saint-Germain.

He left these evenings in a state of excitation not un-like that produced by wine or liqueurs. Life, with all its plans and all its loves, seemed to him to be made easier. For the *monde* by its external agitation infused him with a sense of movement which animated him in his turn, and gave him a fallacious exaltation. The profusion of words which Madame de Guermantes bestowed on him, attributable to idleness, makes him believe in some degree of affection on her part. But he soon realizes the extent of his illusion. True exaltation is a joy, "that which liberates the life of creators," that which springs from experiencing the hospitality of our unconscious, so rich, so truly rich, in memories and impressions, and allowing us to draw near to reality itself. And suddenly he feels himself divorced from his true nature by the world of fashion. His inward life was unable to wake, during these hours of social activity, and "I was an inhabitant," he said, "of my epidermis, my well-trimmed hair, my shirt-front; that is to say, I could feel nothing of what this life of pleasure held for me."

The poetry of names had vanished. And he understood that all the fashionable crowd were terribly insignificant, and that those who were gifted with my intelligence renounced its use almost completely, except for a certain wit, one of its most seductive forms perhaps, but how narrowly, how poorly circumscribed! The professional workers, physicians, painters, artists, have one and all had to make real renunciation of themselves from the day they entered this life of the coterie. And Proust, revolted by the idea of sacrificing his most precious attribute, his art, abandoned the people of fashion. He may see them again, he may continue to be passionately interested in them, but none the less he is henceforth separated from them.

From the *salons* he is separated by all the space of
time stretching between *Les Plaisirs et les jours* and his
main work. And with what eyes he sees them now!
Doubtless he had remarked the inconceivable pride of
the nobility as deriving from the sense of their hierarchy. But, in the first place, are they not very often
ignorant of their own rank? A Madame de Cambremer,
of course, like so many ladies of bourgeois stock introduced into the body of the aristocracy, imagines that
her parents-in-law, small provincial landowners, are
"the most brilliant people in France." But the Duc himself, and very often his equals, are only poorly acquainted with their genealogy, often though they may
speak of it.

Apart from questions of rank, sometimes the only
ones they know, and the subject of many conversations,
what limits are there to the usual ignorance of the fashionable *monde!* Proust had not much frequented such
coteries as that of the Courvoisiers (in the background
in his book), which is closed against every innovation,
every fineness of feeling, every flash of imagination,
and does not even comprehend the play of wit. It is
true that in them all Proust observes just such an absence of culture. When Oriane makes a play upon words
about *Taquin* and *Tarquin the Proud* (meaning Charlus), the Duc feels obliged to explain to the company
that Tarquin was a king of ancient times who—and so
forth. But on other occasions the Duc himself is still
more ignorant. What touches Proust more closely, however, is "to reflect on what an absolute void of true

taste the artistic judgment of the world of fashion is based, a judgment so arbitrary that the veriest trifle can make it reach the most pitiful absurdities, on the path to which it encounters no genuinely felt impression which will check it." No doubt it was the fashion about 1895 to perform *saynètes* or sonatas at the afternoon parties given by the Mesdames de Villeparisis! But the only works of any worth were given, by chance perhaps, like the unpublished quartet of Vinteuil, in the bourgeois set of the Verdurins. It is ridiculous, on the part of the journalists and fashionable chroniclers, to criticize the occasional alliance of art and fashion, the fleeting utility which a literary or artistic snobbery may possess; and no less ridiculous to deem the world of fashion capable of grasping the rôle of utility which it is occasionally brought to play without being aware of it. It will suffice to hear this same Madame de Villeparisis talking of Balzac or of Victor Hugo—both of whom she knew in her youth—calling them by their Christian names, but finding not one word to say of them except, of the one, that he was lacking in tact, and of the other, that he had a red handkerchief. And if she discusses the ideas of Hugo, she will still go on considering him, even nowadays, as a revolutionary. The majority of these women have never advanced beyond romanticism. And Madame de Guermantes, who has the finest masterpieces of Elstir in her drawing-room— the finest Monets, that is to say—will remark in her appreciation of them: "Finely observed—amusing—Parisian—and then one passes on!"

Face to face with such ignorance, what a poor sort

of pride is this pride of name! And what excuse can there be for the attitude of all these persons of nobility, for their impertinence, often enough for their incapacity for self-respect even among equals, for that kind of veiled malice which shocks Marcel Proust's great goodness of heart, his goodness that reaches even to generosity, humility, and mysticism?

Even in the presence of death their frequent egoism remains invulnerable, and the care of their immediate pleasure yields to no force of circumstance. No doubt they respect etiquette with the utmost punctilio, and their name appears "in the fashionable intelligence of the *Gaulois,* on account of the prodigious number of funerals at which they would have found it culpable not to have their names inscribed"; but in one of the Guermantes, "touching in his kindness and revolting in his hardness, the slave of the most minute obligations and absolved from the most sacred understandings," one finds the scruples of conscience transported "from the realm of affection and reality to questions of pure form." From the particular insensibility of a Duc de Guermantes Marcel Proust has extracted the greatest prodigies of his moral effects, and scenes of comedy which, in their cruelty and their violence, attain the deepest levels of Shakespearean irony. Thus, the Duc de Guermantes, knowing that his cousin, gravely ill, will not survive the night, but anxious at any cost not to miss a ball to which he is invited with his wife, manages to obtain news of his state before dinner, and from that moment, when his cousin was still alive, is anxious that no one should speak to him of the illness, that no one should manage to alarm him, or prevent him from going out: to such an extent that in the end he is found declaring with his own lips that his cousin, now in his agony, is decidedly getting on much better, very much better.

This scene, as frequently happens in Proust, is taken up again later, as he moves, in accordance with his unceasing search, still further towards the basis of things, if it be possible, enlarging the scope of its comic sense with regard to the death of Swann shortly before he disappears. Elsewhere as well, amongst the Verdurins, Proust shows us this monstrous indifference, which seems to set the world of fashion in his mind finally, not at the top, but at the bottom rung of the social ladder, on the same level as valets and domestics.

.   .   .   .

Moreover, both of these are equally human to him. The first impression that strikes Swann in the *monde* (and here Swann merges with the figure of the author himself) is the number of servants he comes across at Madame de Saint-Euverte's party. For a long time before he enters into the *monde* itself, he is traversing another *monde*, no less extensive and powerful, a counterpart of the other. For there are the footmen who welcome the arriving guests in the street, like gardeners "drawn up at the appoaches to their flower-beds," and there is "the scattered pack, magnificent and idle-handed, of the tall flunkeys" in the cloak-room, who show the members of the nobility "contempt" for their persons and "every consideration" for their hats. Then, all along the magnificent staircase, "on one side and the

other, at different heights . . ." are a door-keeper, a
major-domo, a house-steward, each in his "dazzling livery." Here again is the enormous *suisse* who strikes "the
tiles with his staff at the passage of each of the guests";
here the valets, "sitting like notaries," who put down the
name of every arrival; and here at last the "chain-hung
steward" who opens the doors of the drawing-rooms as
if "handing over the keys of a city."

Throughout the progress of this interminable journey, more extended than that which he is to make in the
monde itself, Proust can already foresee all the vanity
of the latter. Moreover, as soon as the doors are once
passed, he finds "in opposition to the spectacle of the
servants . . . the sense of masculine ugliness," and at
the same time that foolish affectation the symbol of
which is discovered by the author in all those monocles,
then so fashionable, of M. de Bréauté, of the Marquis de
Forestelle, of M. de Saint-Candé. It is by the fullness of
his painting of the world of the "below-stairs" that
Proust, more perhaps than any moralist, after holding
up all the glittering lures of the *monde* before our eyes,
lets us see its hollowness. Everywhere, beside or in the
midst of the description of a reception, of a sparkling
and sumptuous dinner, the author sets a parallel description of the kitchen, like a caricature side by side with a
portrait, or Sancho Panza alongside Don Quixote, but
without ever diminishing the value of the first. In this
way, indeed, it often happens that the imitation is superior to the original. Here are these cooks and ladies'
maids and head butlers who, in speaking of their master,
say "*we*," or in addressing the servants of another house,

and referring to its master, say *"you"*; they are imbued through and through with the same passions as are those whom they serve—pride, baseness, insolence, the feeling of hierarchy; and they are envisaged by Proust from a human point of view, and set on the same level as the Duc de Guermantes or the Cour-voisiers.

There is nobody, perhaps, who has entered so deeply into the inmost mind of the servant. Françoise, along with Charlus, is probably the most successfully created character of the whole book. Until the present, servants have never been independently studied with this splen-didly complete disinterestedness from any object-lesson or thesis. They have always been used either as mechan-ical aids in the development and *dénouement* of a piece (the confidants of the theatre), or for a contrast of ef-fect (as Iago with Othello), or through their agency to attack the established code of society (as in *Le Mariage de Figaro* or Mirbeau's *Le Journal d'une femme de chambre*), or as symbols of devotion or poverty of life (as in *Un Cœur simple*). But Françoise lives by herself. Proust has pierced right into her soul, "almost animal in its quality of watch-dog," devoted to her mistress, surly towards strangers, proud of her master's wealth, but sorely upset because they have not a motor-car to make some display, and finding in them "the share of contentment which was indispensable to her life"—and at the same time, thanks to that state of "symbiosis" that makes her live in the intimacy of her masters, she knows them so thoroughly that, love them though she does, her bearing towards them is hostile, contrary, peevish, not hiding her hatred of Albertine, the stranger, and expressing her contempt by silence.

And there once more, just as the writer explores the consciousness of a coterie or a character through their words, so he studies Françoise through her highly characteristic conversation, and is able to report that her language, if fathomed aright, will reveal the same fundamental characteristics as the speech of the Duc or the Duchesse, apparently so highly refined.

The psychology of the servants is closely akin to that of the members of the nobility. There is a deficiency of culture in one class as much as in the other. No doubt, while the ignorance of the Duc is principally due to the absence of culture, that of Françoise can be attributed mainly to disregard of grammar. Her errors of speech depend above all, like the fables which Plato believed in, on a false conception of the world and on preconceived ideas. Thus, properly interperted, the long chattering with the *maître d'hôtel,* during that taboo hour that follows on the meals, when the masters have not the right to disturb their servants, instructs us in the limited and absurd philosophy of Françoise: "All that could very well change," grumbled the *maître d'hôtel,* "the workers must make war on Canada, and the minister said to monsieur the other day that for that he has received two hundred thousand francs payment!" And Françoise answered him with no astonishment, but meeting him with her somewhat narrow fatalism: "So long as the world's what it is, look you, there will be masters to send you trotting, and servants to do their bidding."

In another direction Françoise made use of a whole category of expressions of the utmost purity, which came to her intact from the little corner of France where she had her origins. She would say *"faire réponse"* like Madame de Sévigné, or "Antoine with his Antoinesse," creating the feminine form with an unconscious recollection of *chanoine* and *chanoinesse*. Or again, "she used the verb *plaindre* in the same sense as La Bruyère does," in the sense of *to be sparing*. And Proust: "From Françoise I had learnt, from the age of five, that one does not speak of the *Tarn* but the *Tar,* not of *Béarn,* but of *Béar,* and the result was that at twenty, when I went into society, I did not have to learn that one must not say, as Madame Bontemps did: 'Madame de Béarn.' " These expressions of the country-side he finds again, likewise drowned in surrounding floods of errors, in the mouth of the Duchesse de Guermantes, herself with a touch of the peasant woman in her, and proud of being so too, and, like Françoise, having her roots in a region essentially French, where the classic tongue has been preserved intact. . . . And thus, in the great lady as in the servant woman, we find the same conversation of the past.

Let us note further that this tradition only barely survives. One day Proust hears Françoise exclaim: *"Je vais me cavaler presto!"* And it turns out that the old servant has brought in her daughter to help her, who, considering herself "up to date," has picked up the Parisian argot. And so, in the same way that we saw the speech of Albertine modified by her flirtations with different young men, so "the influence of her daughter was beginning to altar the vocabulary of Françoise a little. Thus do all the modes of speech lose their purity through the assumption of new terms."

We see, then, running through the different social classes, certain aspects of human nature, ignorance and stupidity, tradition, fatalism, and vanity, linking up persons who are far removed from each other. The Faubourg Saint-Germain is no longer that barred and distant country of the writer's childhood's dreams. It is a world that is in its essence relative, little different, in spite of appearances, from the world of the bourgeoisie, and even less from that of the common people. When M. de Norpois, the ambassador, converses with the Prince of Faffenheim, this dialogue of diplomats seems to offer Proust a great many analogies with a conversation of a couple of apaches. And in the end, when the hero, in the Champs Élysées, goes into the famous *chalet de nécessité*, its old woman guardian talks to him of her clientele, of the uncleanly people whom she is obliged to exclude, of her faithful regular customers, of the selection that she makes among those whom she receives—all in the same tone as the Marquise de Villeparisis. Into a name we can place all the renown of history, and the expanses of land behind the name, but words make all men appear as on one and the same plane.

CHAPTER II

SODOM AND GOMORRAH: THE INDIVIDUAL AND SOCIETY

A MONGST the coteries that make up the world of the bourgeoisie and the nobility, there is one of which Marcel Proust has sounded and studied the depth, in the same way, for instance, as he has the coterie of the Guermantes: it is that formed to-day by the descendants of the dispersed populations of Sodom and Gomorrah.

"I am obeying," wrote the author to Louis de Robert, "a general truth, which forbids me to think of friends who are sympathetic any more than of those who are antipathetic: the favour of sadists [1] when my book has appeared will afflict me as a man; it could not modify the conditions under which I make trial of the truth, conditions which are in no way chosen by my caprice." How could one find a nobler expression of the sentiment which inspired and obliged him to depict these two accursed cities? Just as his characters impose themselves on him, just as he did not think himself free to make them act according to his own fancy, so he saw the society which he was bringing back to life as necessarily composed of a certain number of groups, and, unless he was to act the traitor to his own conscience, to touch

---

[1] And, in general, of all amateurs of pornography.

up and falsify the vision created in him by external reality, he felt constrained to make them all take part in his novel. The courage of the artist thus carrying out his duty was not inferior to any other heroism. He knew, as we have seen in our examination of his life, that he was running the risk of losing "applause, decorations, honours, the entrée to fashionable houses." [2] If he exposed only so much as his project in conversation to a friend, the latter would in alarm have hurried to shut the door, as if he had to listen to the story of some crime. [3] Marcel Proust is probably the first of the great French men of letters to penetrate the tragic gates of the flaming Sodom.

Every time, doubtless, that a writer of stature, at no matter what epoch of history, has cast his glance round the general structure of the society of his time, he has been struck by the red glow cast upon the sky from the fires that consumed that city. Saint-Simon, in his *Memoirs* of the court of Louis XIV, frankly faces the question on several occasions, in connexion with Monsieur, the brother of the King, or with the Elector Palatine, but drops it at once. In his *Comédie humaine,* less in *La Belle aux yeux d'or* than in *Les Illusions perdues,* and principally in his *Grandeur et misère des courtisanes,* Balzac stages this terrible passion with Lucien de Rubempré in the *monde* and with Vautrin in the prison. But the reactionary morality of Louis-Philippe forces the writer, respectful of the established

[2] André Gide.
[3] Cf. *"Quelques instantanés de Proust." Nouvelle Revue Française,* January 1st, 1923.

powers, to treat of his subject in covert phrases, prudently submitting it to his own preventive censorship. Émile Zola, in tracing the history of the Rougon-Macquarts, was attracted by "the great social and psychological interest" of this problem. "I have sought in vain," he wrote to his friend Dr. Laupts, "for a form in which to present it to the public, and this has made me in the end abandon the project.—At the time, I was passing through the most trying hours of my literary battle, and the critics were every day treating me as a criminal capable of every vice and every form of debauch: I should have been duly condemned. And what an outcry if I had allowed myself to say that there is no subject more serious. . . ."[4]

Marcel Proust braved the clamour. And thanks to his genius, the critics have not protested: they content themselves with organizing round this part of his work a sort of passive resistance or non-co-operation. A certain journalist, the first to discover the worth of the writer, declared: "It is horrible! A whole book on this subject! I cannot speak of it."[5]

Nevertheless, this conspiracy of silence gives token

---

[4] I ought to mention here M. Francis Carco's novel *Jesus la Caille*, the only novel of any worth, so far as I am aware, before Marcel Proust, to paint the picture of Sodom. A fragmentary picture, however, the author having travelled only through those quarters in Sodom which correspond to the Montmartre of Paris. This little book, which ought to meet with much success, has a great measure of touching sincerity and unapproachable freshness, proving that from such a subject it is possible to draw the purest tones.

[5] In the article following the appearance of *Sodome et Gomorrhe* the critic did not conceal his satisfaction at being relieved from a great apprehension: "Fortunately," he remarked, "the whole book does not deal with this subject. . . ."

of the most flagrant literary incomprehension. How is it that criticism has not yet learned that whenever a writer discloses a new subject of study, conventional morality must necessarily take fright; that whenever he enters an unexplored domain, he is regarded as one committing a sacrilege? But all the same it is a necessary quality of art to encroach continually on those parts of life which are not yet subject to it, and even to create new modes of life. Before the younger Dumas studied the modern courtesan, or Flaubert the adulterous wife, these were certainly to be found in real life, but they did not *exist* in the way that they did when art had once revealed them and made them lasting. But the taste of the crowd is characterized by its horror of all art giving it the illusion of life being presented in its most profound reality—that is to say, a horror of the very aim and object of art. And faced with a Marcel Proust, widening the frontiers of literary explorations, bringing into the pages of his book a passion which hitherto has rebelled against submission to artistic form, is criticism, far from keeping silence, not in duty bound to draw the attention of the public to this effort?

And there is more. If a critic has resigned himself to writing articles "suitable for young persons," he can in case of necessity skip one or two scabrous episodes in a book and justify his omission. But this free-and-easy procedure cannot be applied to the work of Marcel Proust. The writer has not just conjured up these scriptural cities in one or two chapters. No, in accordance with his customary mode of composition, he takes up the subject again and again throughout the whole length of his work, raising it sometimes to a tone of lyrical and romantic invocation, as in the opening pages of *Sodome et Gomorrhe*, or reducing it to the tone of the drawing-room comedy, of the *saynète*, as Proust said. All the participants in the action of the novel seem to be grouped round the principal character (after the narrator, or "I," that is), round the Baron de Charlus, the hero of Sodom. As for the other inverts, the author having met them in the most widely different circles, in the drawing-rooms of the Faubourg Saint-Germain no less than in its kitchens, in the families of the bourgeoisie or those of the Jews, he is led to mention them in different parts of his book. From the very beginning, in *Du côté de chez Swann*, he repeatedly alludes to the subject, though almost imperceptibly to the reader.[6] And continually he will take it up again, in frescoes, for fresh observation, and, like his other main themes, the present one is indissolubly joined up with the substance of his work.

This arbitrary silence on the part of the critics is all the more absurd because it is in Sodom and Gomorrah that Marcel Proust has made his most important explorations. "Emotion is further augmented," wrote Proust on the subject of Baudelaire, "when one learns that these 'condemned' pieces were not here merely on the same footing as the others, but that, in Baudelaire's eyes, they were to such an extent the central key-pieces that he was anxious at first to call the whole volume,

---

[6] "Charlus regretted his wife very deeply," declares Madame de Guermantes, in all innocence, "but like a cousin, like a grandmother, like a sister. True, they were two saints, which makes the mourning rather special." *Du côté de chez Swann*.

not *Fleurs du mal*, but *Les Lesbiennes*." In the same
way Proust thought of entitling his work *Sodome et
Gomorrhe*, instead of *A la recherche du temps perdu*.
How was he able to interest himself so particularly in
this subject, and to wish to give its name as title to
the whole novel? This question, which Proust put with
regard to Baudelaire, we are asking now with regard
to Proust.

. . . .

"That [which the sexual inverts] call their love (and
to which, out of a social sense, playing on the word,
they have annexed all that poetry, painting, music,
chivalry, and asceticism have been able to add to love)
flows, not from an ideal of beauty which they have
chosen, but from an incurable *malady*." This quotation
contains practically the whole of Marcel Proust's
thoughts upon this vexatious problem.

For Marcel Proust inversion is a pathological fact
which from this point of view concerns principally, and
even solely, physicians and psychiatrists: a pathological,
physiological, and neurological fact, which in no way
affects the general psychology of the individual. The invert's passion is the same as that of the normal man, in
the sense that it dashes itself, like every other amorous
passion, against the rocks of anxiety and jealousy, that
it is submitted to the tormenting force of crystallization,
that it is familiar with eternal vows that acknowledge
no to-morrow, with the yielding up of self to the point
of sacrifice, the bewilderment and ephemerality of all
the movements of the conscience. But the invert, more
luckless than mankind in general, and set under a curse

by society, is obliged to defend himself against it, to conceal his dearest, his deepest, his most moving aspirations, and to struggle in hypocrisy, far more than other men, to achieve his happiness. Marcel Proust, in his perpetual searching of the pleasures of life, encountered a certain group of hapless individuals. What brought him to measure the impression they left on him was that he felt in them, under a form at once exacerbated and highly intensified, the desire to find whole-hearted joy: that he felt their fettered impulses, that he felt, chief of all, their love. He saw in them the age-old struggle of the individual against society. Apart from the obstacles which a man finds within himself, when he wants to affirm himself, to seek his own happiness—such as his incapacity to come out of himself, to hold and fix an emotion of happiness—we find society adding all kinds of hindrances. And these overwhelm the invert more especially. Proust thus comes to regard him as the symbolic victim of society. This conception of sexual inversion is at all points in direct opposition to that of the writers who have made allusion to the topic.

Many poets, no doubt, heedless of reality and letting their voices sing within themselves, have been unable to resign themselves to the belief that a passion which gave birth to sentiments of tenderness as pure and disinterested as those of Romeo or of des Grieux found its origins in an involuntary malady of the brain. These poets, imagining that they were studying inversion, have actually only been speaking of neighbouring and kindred passions, which are capable of being confounded with it and being substituted for it in their minds and in literature. Some, concealing their subject under the cloak of symbols, evoke only a heavy and troubled atmosphere. They make allusion to debauches, which they wrap about with the perilous veil of beauty. And they are haunted, these writers, by vice, a sumptuous vice, a magnificent nightmare, the fruit of the tree of good and evil, which serves to enrich the monotony of life. Immorality in their eyes is one of the essential motives of art. Others, again, seek to idealize it through æsthetics and through ethics. They celebrate friendship, the affection of the master-protector for his disciple, the strength of the masculine body in the gymnasium or beneath the portico, the marvellous characteristics of the adolescent, who is at once the ultimate beauty and the ultimate good.

They draw analogies with antiquity. But in those times all forms of love which had not the continuance of the race as their object were placed on one and the same level, stripped of the mystical, moral, and practical complications which Christianity and our business-like civilization have incorporated with love. For love then was a simple and natural gesture, and in that different state of opinion the idealization of Sodom could be understood. But "for nineteen hundred years now . . . all the customary homosexuality of the youths of Plato and the shepherds of Virgil has vanished. There survives only an involuntary homosexuality, that which is concealed from others and travestied even by its representatives." To celebrate inversion as a passion chosen by man of his own free will, from a taste for beauty, friendship, or the masculine intelligence, is an absurdity. Only a few men of genius, great enough and frank-minded enough to live above their own times, in a younger and fresher world, can rise to a superhuman and sublime friendship. The others confound their "mania" with friendship, which, says Proust, "has not the slightest resemblance to it."

Thus it is clear that this passion could not be the expression either of an ideal of beauty, or of an ideal of satanic debauchery: that would imply that it was an act of volition. It is a malady with social consequences. The writer does not naïvely try to raise this passion above its proper level. He observed his characters. He sees nervous "involuntaries" set in the midst of a society which carries a scourge for them. And he adds: "For the invert, vice begins, not when he engages in relations (for too many reasons can command them), but when he takes his pleasure with women." And Proust tells us that "some of them, if one surprises them still in bed in the morning, display an admirable woman's head, so much is the expression general and so much does it symbolize the whole sex." Here the writer, penetrating into one of the most troubling mysteries of nature, sets out several questions, though not answering them; they are questions which are doubtless familiar, but their terms are so perfectly thrown into the light by him that, under his pen, they take on an aspect of tragedy which shakes the firm stance of reason. He is astonished at the way in which, among the men-women, the sexual instinct leads by such certain paths towards a sex opposed to their own —that is to say, towards other men—and triumphs over the aberrations which might drag reason and the social constraints headlong away. "One has but to look at this curly head of hair on the white pillow to understand that if, in the evening, this youth slips from between his parents' fingers, in spite of them, in spite of himself, it will not be to go and find women. . . ."

Proust is thus brought to comparing this passion with certain forms of madness. During a whole conversation the madman in our presence may easily appear to be quite normal, and it is just at the moment of parting that, all of a sudden, he will reveal his madness to us. Similarly, the inverts are just like other men—until the moment when the veil suddenly falls from their fatal love. At the Prince de Guermantes' reception, the author takes a cross-section of the drawing-room: in the remotest corner of the room Charlus, in the middle of a group of his friends, is freely exchanging with them, in their esoteric language, remarks about the manservants and footmen of the hotels or clubs that they frequent. —Another problem: whence comes it that an insignificant physiological flaw, like an invisible bump on the skull, takes outward manifestation in gestures, in laughter, so effeminate that they seem nothing short of the signs of a madness? How is it that this beginning of hermaphroditism, limited to the development of the haunches and the whiteness of the skin, is often, among the persons affected by it, the mark of a pronounced taste for the arts? A taste, it is true, supported on the false literary idealism that we have explained, but one capable in spite of everything of producing astonishing works.

Certain moral or philosophic theories, no doubt, attempt explanations of this mystery of physiology. In the *Symposium* Plato speaks of "androgynes." Schopenhauer thinks that inversion is a provision of nature in order to sterilize unions in which the old man or the extreme youth, if they were to procreate, would no longer be in the full enjoyment of their faculties.

Marcel Proust adopts none of these general theories. Just as when he declares that he knows nothing which can make him believe in the immortality of the soul, and alludes nevertheless to the possibility of an anterior life, so, in remaining in a state of expectancy, inversion, he thinks, may perhaps be attached to "another and higher law . . . to epochs of experimentation, this initial hermaphroditism," an ultimate reversion which would to-day hold in check the excessive forces of fecundity on our over-peopled earth. However, he does not develop this hypothesis. It does not belong to litera-ture, but to the psychiatrists, and these in any case are content to classify and label the maladies.

. . . .

What is of interest to Proust as a writer is that this abnormal passion is none the less of the same psycholog-ical nature as normal love, and that the invert's processes of mind, in so far as he is not pursued by society, are those of all men. Here again Marcel Proust is the first to maintain this parallelism.

Thus, he says, the inverted adolescent finds his own passion in the reading of "Madame de Lafayette, Racine, Baudelaire, Walter Scott." With the heroes of these romances or poems he proceeds to effect an unconscious substitution of sex. He visualizes a man when his text tells him of a woman, he replaces *she* by *he*, the fact being indeed that "the sentiment is the same," and only "the object differs." So, reciprocally, some writers have been able without difficulty, without falsifying psychological truth, to present a woman in their pages whilst inwardly having in mind all the time a man. This transposition passes unnoticed by the public, as in the *Vierge folle* of Rimbaud, while the probability of the *social* situations is maintained.

Certain male inverts, no doubt, possess a feminine psychology, marked by vanity, versatility, weakness, egoism; and certain women inverts are endowed with a man's sensibility. The inverted couple reproduce the normal couple, having the same aspirations, the same jealousies. But the malady of the invert remains strangely localized in a part of his brain, without any influence on his general consciousness, modified only in so far as society makes the weight of its constraint felt upon the individual.

The true object, then, of Marcel Proust's study in his journey through the Cities of the Plain, will not be the idealization of this passion; nor will it be a philosophic explanation of its mystery, nor the amorous psychology of these beings, a psychology that simply enters into his general study of love; but it will analyze the soul of the man marked down by society, in latent revolt against it, the individual against society, nature opposed to morality.

· · · · · · · ·

The case where the social injustice appears to him as most striking is that of what Marcel Proust calls the "solitary." His evocation of this will become classic. His voice assumes suddenly a gravity and eloquence that reminds one of the tragic appeal of a Pascal overwhelmed by the misery of the lot of mankind. Behold, he exclaims, the depth of the abyss into which society can fling an individual, the martyr of his passion! And the author, whose tone grows calm, shows in a couple of pages, like Maupassant, the whole life of the solitary—his youth, his marriage, his relapses, his surrender, and finally his solitude. For he is afraid of the severity of mankind's judgments. He has withdrawn to the country, far from the world, with what he believes to be his monstrous vice, as it were a leper. Perhaps he will sometimes encounter some tatterdemalion who will make pretence of being interested in him, "but for a material advantage only, like those people who, at the Collège de France, in the room where the professor of Sanskrit lectures without any auditors, go and follow the course, but only for the sake of keeping warm." How is it that the solitary does not succumb beneath the burden of this destiny of perpetual seclusion? Is not his life like the desert that is traversed by lovers, but without any oasis? Proust (or his hero), being in love with Albertine, finds this same accent of tragedy, the most beautiful in his book, when he observes that, living with that girl, he is nevertheless so much alone that he can find a morsel of pleasure only "in watching her lying asleep."

The other inverts have the daring to engage in a struggle against the collective body. But they will be the eternally accursed, like the Jews, to whom Proust compares them, because, the one like the other, they

are the victims of a social prejudice, and stand accused
of having betrayed a god or violated the sacred laws of
nature. Disseminated over all the regions of the globe,
nowhere in their own home, everywhere repulsed, everywhere hated, they are the victims of an error of justice
that cannot be undone. The life of the invert is the history of his dissimulations, of his hypocrisy, like that of
a remorseless criminal who should renew his crime every
day in quietude and dread. Like Raskolnikov haunted by
the magistrate who plays the game of cat and mouse
with him, he remains to his dying day in fear of the
scandal which may deliver him over to the mercies of
society.

With a truly Shakespearean power Proust has chosen
as the type of the marked man, the most haughty of
great gentlemen, a man whose head is almost turned
with pride, who is yet forced in humility to conceal his
desires. Whence the extraordinary repressions of this
passion in the Baron de Charlus, which explain his ups
and downs, his outbursts of anger, his incompatibili-
ties, his tyrannical and at the same time surly temper.
His secret passion is the key to this magnificent character.

"What does thou desire?" asks Nietzsche of the Stranger. "What would'st thou have to comfort thee?"—
"To comfort me, O curious one, what word is that? But
give me, I beg you——" —"What? Go on!"—"One
more mask! Another mask!"

The whole life of Charlus is something that is played
with a mask. At no moment can he bare his face to the
sun. Sometimes, for the space of a second, he makes the

gesture of raising it so as to let himself be recognizable
to his kind—but immediately, trembling lest he may
have been discovered by others, he resumes "a mask—
another mask." In a drawing-room he is always close by
the side of the most elegant woman, persistently, says
Proust, covering himself with her robe, with its train
hiding his feet and the bottoms of his trousers. In the
presence of young men he displays "an air of absolute
indifference," when he is not even "hostile and provoca-
tive." No one is so difficult as he in the choice of his
acquaintance. The number of people to whom he has
refused to have himself introduced is fantastic. To explain his attitude towards so many persons who are not
of his class, he has fashioned for himself a legend of kind-
heartedness. Of the persons of humble origin whom he
does admit to his affection, it is said that he protects
them.

And in spite of all the exhaustive pains he brings to his
precautions, he is never sure that his terrible secret is
well guarded. Do certain people have "some doubts as
to his morals?" As soon as he meets anyone, he has his
suspicions: does he *know*, or does he not? In the end it
is no longer he who is the enigma, but those who sur-
round him form an enigma for him. A terrible reversal
of circumstances: in the eyes of this man with his mask
it is henceforward the whole world that wears a mask,
and it tortures him. It is he who hides himself, and he
who no longer recognizes anyone, who can no longer
distinguish his friends from his enemies. His passion,
fatal and implacable as the incestuous love of Œdipus,

holds him back at every step before the cruel sphinx
asking of him: "Are you recognized, or are you not,
under your disguise? Vile mummer, under your fard
and your powder, are you identified?" And so the drama
is played for him as much in his own conscience as in
that of each of those about him. Here is this noble lady,
offering him the plate of cakes with a smile, but does
he not see, there, in her look that is glowing with
affability, gleams of hatred and contempt? Has she any
proofs? Must he plead guilty? Should he make search
for extenuating circumstances in playful conversation?
Or feign innocence? In spite of himself every individual
is a judge, and he is passing before their tribunal. He is
brought back to those prehistoric times when man lived
in a state of perpetual fear and defence. To his ear the
most innocent words in a conversation take on the aspect of directly wounding allusions. He is obliged to
watch over his honour, which as often as not is not even
impugned, and his susceptibility, for which he finds a
justification in his pride of birth, makes him pass from
the tragic to the ridiculous, from excessive politeness to
an incomprehensible rudeness. And this man, the de-
scendant of the most noble families of history, will
never dare to be the first to offer his hand—from fear
that it will not be taken.

The man who pays his court to a woman or a girl
adds to the pleasure of triumphing by his intelligence
or wit that of vanity in being envied by a drawing-
room or a circle of acquaintances. But a Charlus pays
his court as one prepares for a crime. In some magnifi-

cent and celebrated pages,[7] where the Baron meets the young Proust (or his hero) in the street without recognizing him, the writer, penetrating into the unconsciousness of the surprised child who does not understand the tricks of this occasional seducer, and fathoming his surprise, unveils the most extraordinary refinements of hypocrisy that a man can invent to free himself from society. Here, to begin with, are two openings through which the passion of Charlus slips: the eyes, which throw "a supreme glance, at once bold and prudent, rapid and profound. . . ." Continually Proust returns to the eyes. They were "like the single crack, the single loop-hole which he had not stopped up," or they made one think "of some incognito, of the disguise of a powerful man who is in some danger," or again ". . . like an emissary of police on a secret mission," or again "like the eyes of certain frightened animals or those of street hawkers . . . exhibiting their illicit wares," or again "like those of a street vendor in dread of the arrival of 'the cops,' " or again like "the glance of a tailor who betrays his profession by his way of fastening them immediately on one's clothes." The other gap in the mask is the mouth; that is to say, the voice, which seems to shelter "a brood of young girls," and the singing of which seems like "the alternating duet of a young man

---

[7] These were the first pages of Proust to appear in the *Nouvelle Revue Française* in 1913, and they greatly contributed, as we have said, to the spreading of a knowledge of Proust's name among literary people and the young. Why did no one ever speak of them? And when the book in which they appear was published (and it was the one crowned by the Académie Goncourt), no one, even in the *N.R.F.*, drew attention to this passage, though it is one of the most moving.

and a woman," and likewise the laugh, "the sharp, fresh laughter of a schoolgirl or a coquette." Lastly, and also gaps in the mask, are those effeminate gestures, which, as we have said, are like those that indicate the madman —as for example this, admirably observed: "At this moment, noticing that the embroidered handkerchief which he had in his pocket was showing its coloured edgings, he pushed them hurriedly back, with the startled look of a woman of excessive modesty, but not innocent, affecting concealment of some glimpse which through excess of scruple she considers indecent."

Let us notice how frequently the words *crook* or *police* recur as terms of comparison from Proust's pen. Not only does Charlus act in spite of himself like a criminal, but with his own kind his bearing is such that he might belong to a band of malefactors. None too sure of their feeling of solidarity, he is afraid of being denounced by them, and with them even more than with strangers he is forced to fit his mask on more closely,[8] suspecting them of greater perspicacity, and to justify the presence of even a brother beside him, or of a cousin younger than himself. Each of these guilty ones, as in the parable of the mote in the neighbour's eye and the beam in one's own, imagines that he is less deeply compromised than the other. The better to defend himself, he is ready to denounce everybody. He does not even find the security and repose of a ticket-of-leave man in the midst of his own people.

---

[8] For instance, M. de Charlus is walking with Proust and has given him his arm. But on meeting M. d'Argencourt he hastens to withdraw it, to stand apart from the youth, and to offer innumerable explanations.

But it is just this kind of hostile perspicacity which allows these outlaws to make reciprocal discovery of each other, and, on occasion, to raise their masks and allow free play to their passion. Proust shows the importance of this game of reconnoitring, which is the principal object of the conversation they exchange amongst themselves. When they are discussing a case, each one brings his brief, and pleads it; and the inculpated person, who is naturally not at hand, very rarely emerges acquitted from this accumulation of gossip, for if the adolescent "believes himself . . . alone in the universe, he later comes to imagine, with another exaggeration, that the unique exception is the normal man."

. . . .

Here once again Marcel Proust brings out the importance of language. Just as the nervous tricks of his characters, or the interminable conversations of his fashionable personages, throw light upon their deepest character, so the futilities and jests so peculiar to the class of inverts whom he brings on to the stage are the expression of their status as hunted beings. They speak, in fact, a special language of their own, in order to conceal themselves the better in society. "Slang," wrote Victor Hugo, "is neither more nor less than a dressing-room in which language, having some evil deed to prepare, assumes a disguise. It covers itself with mask-words and tatterdemalion metaphors." And it is indeed a sort of cant language which inverts have created among themselves for the purposes of a clandestine action. And the writer, in reproducing the grossness and crudity of their terms, is not trying to produce even a *resemblance,* but, in accordance with his favourite procedure (we are now familiar with it), to penetrate thereby into their consciousness.

If their slang gives them better facilities to mask themselves, it sometimes serves also to pierce this same mask. For in the course of conversation with normal people they will introduce one of these special words not meant to pass out of their freemasonry. And Proust explains to us: "The people who can be charged with certain things are persistent in their anxiety to show that they have no timidity in speaking of these." When Charlus utters the word *truqueur,* Proust (or his young hero) pricks up an attentive ear, much surprised. Thus, in spite of the skilful disguise that Charlus continually wears, one single word, voluntarily uttered, but going just beyond the mark where a pleasantry is no longer innocent, is enough for Proust to afford proof of the criminal passion of the person he is talking to. As we have said, the interpretation of speech on the lines of the Proustian method could often be useful to a judge conducting a preliminary inquiry to obtain truthful admissions from an accused person.

"The most dangerous of all the accessory acts," writes Proust, "is that of the fault itself in the soul of the offender. The continual familiarity which he has with it prevents him from knowing how generally ignorant people are of it. . . ." Thus, in order to contradict certain rumours which he believes to have obtained currency, Charlus makes the following profession of faith: "I have had a great many ups and down in my life, I

have known all kinds of people, thieves as well as kings,
and I must say I have a certain preference for the
thieves; I have pursued beauty in all its forms. . . ."
Let us note that it is not only to give an air of probability to his attitude that Charlus flings out these rash
words, thinking them to be apt, but that he suddenly
feels the need to speak of this passion which he hides
with such pains, to set free his conscience, too long
weighed down by the terrible discipline that he imposes
upon it. He is compelled by the same feeling that forces
the murderer to return to the scene of his crime. Nothing makes more plain the constraining power of the
mask he wears than this brutal reaction of the individual who, in a moment of forgetfulness or abandonment,
in his need for liberty, will break with all his past,
through a scandal.

.   .   .   .

It is in this way that the writer, in his evocation of
Sodom and Gomorrah, brings before our eyes in a continuous and alternating opposition the apparent life and
the inner life of their inhabitants, society and the
individual. Out of this harsh struggle, pursued through
the whole length of the work, the author seems to extract a double significance, social and individual.

Hypocrisy in moral matters generally acts in such a
way as to prevent the grasping of the true and profound
motive of events. But beneath the painful disguise which
the group of inverts, despite itself, assumes, their actions, which remain sometimes inscribed in history, do
not meet with their explanation, so secret is it, and so
much concealed under a solidified crust of custom and

prejudice. In his picture of contemporary society Marcel Proust chooses to bring into emphasis the part played by inversion, a part as important as it is unsuspected.

Charlus has given, at the Verdurins' house, a magnificent party. The unpublished quartet of Vinteuil is played for the first time, and it is a revelation of one of the greatest masterpieces of music. The press, next day, will take possession of the event and discuss it, an event which one already feels to be imperishable; it will give forth a moral eulogy of Mlle de Vinteuil, the daughter of the composer, who has passed her nights in deciphering the almost illegible score of the work, and of Morel, the musician who performed it, and of Charlus, who, by his authority and connexions, has made it known.

But none the less, Proust reminds us that "if . . . the Under-Secretary of State for Fine Arts, a man of truly artistic temper, of good family and a snob, a few duchesses and three ambassadors with their wives were at Madame Verdurin's that evening, the close and immediate motive of this attendance lay in the relationship existing between M. de Charlus and Morel, a relationship that made the Baron desire to give the greatest possible brilliance to the artistic triumphs of his youthful idol and to obtain for him the cross of the Legion of Honour, while the remoter cause which had made this gathering possible was the fact that a girl who maintained a relationship with Mlle de Vinteuil parallel with that of Charlie [Morel] and the Baron had brought to light a whole series of works of genius; and such a revelation had these been that a subscription was very soon going to be opened, under the patronage of the Minister of Public Instruction, with a view to the erection of a statue to Vinteuil."

Public celebrity and the immortal masterpiece itself are thus seen branching forth from an interplay of passions which are held to be horrible vices. But it is one of the mysteries of life, according to Proust, that this alliance of madness and art, that the most dazzling facts in a society, should have their origins in the humblest facts of the individual. History, to be fully understood, must necessarily have light thrown upon it, not just in its small corners, but in its deepest foundations; that is to say—we have said it only too often—it must have its depths fathomed. In the same way Proust has effected a juxtaposition of the world of the nobility and the bourgeoisie with that of the kitchen and the servants' hall.

·   ·   ·   ·   ·   ·   ·   ·

In spite of the constraint of society we can observe the inverts succeeding sometimes in producing a work, in realizing themselves as social beings; will they succeed likewise in attaining their own happiness?

With the man of his choice the invert will be able in the end to let his mask fall. As he thinks he is no longer observed, the features of his face unbend. The true face of Charlus reminds us of a woman's. His instincts will be able to blossom out. But until such time as he has been able to find the man he is looking for, are not the difficulties such that his happiness has something exceptional, something rare and beautiful and sacred about it? And it is this marvellous victory of the individual, who succeeds in finding his happiness in spite of all the obstacles of society, which the writer admired, and which was probably one of the motives for the importance he assigned to this subject.

The great moral idea dominating all the work of Proust is this, that "the search for pleasure and the expectation of pleasure are, if not the end, at least one of the ends, of nature, the pursuit in which man is ardent to the point of madness." Well, the man who loves men would surely despair of ever finding a being who could love him if there did not exist a certain other category of men who desire him, and if the little workings of chance, in spite of the small opportunity the one and the others have of meeting, did not favour their "conjunction." And it is here that Proust has traced, as a simple comparison, the history of certain plants, which reproduce their kind only if the bumble-bee, going there in search of his honey, should all unwittingly carry on his feet from the flower of the male kind to the flower of the female kind, some of the fecundating pollen. How many thwarting accidents are possible before this success! When it is achieved, it can only be the result of a kind of miracle!

Inversion, no doubt, is a dreadful passion, and Proust seems to have taken a malicious pleasure, from the first pages in which he brings us into the bounds of the accursed cities, in presenting Charlus and Jupien in the most crude and repulsive light, in giving their pleasure an air of bestiality. But in another direction the writer gets from the spectacle of this connexion a lesson of value. For no one could bring home to us better than the invert the almost total impossibility of all desires, the vanity represented by the search of no matter what happiness, and yet the beauty and grandeur that are born of these vain pursuits.

"Mutual love," wrote Proust, "apart from those great and sometimes insurmountable difficulties which it encounters among the ordinary mass of men, adds to these abnormal beings difficulties of so special a kind that what is always for everybody something of great rarity becomes for them practically an impossibility . . . and that their happiness, even more than that of the normal lover, has in it something extraordinary, something selective, something that is profoundly necessary." So henceforth we can understand the conception held by the writer of love in general. After having sought in the *monde* to find pleasure, the great instinct to which man has to submit blindly and hopelessly, he expects, in spite of everything, some joy from love. "Here, on this earth, every being" must give to someone "his music, his flame, and his perfume." But love—is that possible? Charlus and Jupien, Charlus and Morel, Proust and Gilberte, Proust and Albertine—no doubt they succeeded, some easily, others painfully, in encountering each other. But will they really come to know love?

CHAPTER III

DESIRE AND LOVE

IN the interval separating my childhood from the present day," wrote Marcel Proust in a dedication, "there lies a whole life of pleasures and sufferings."

What despair is in those words! What a desolate horizon opens up behind that simple phrase! The writer was drawing near to death, and looking behind him, he saw again the forty years he had lived, like those passed by Moses in the desert. Sand, everywhere sand. No corn, no water, no cattle, no wine. Under the dome of azure, the infinite expanse. Not even the hope of an after life. Man had not yet a soul. But God existed. A good and just God. Every day God made manifest His presence. From the sky He made manna to fall, and from the rock water to gush forth. And Moses lived with Him. But in the universe of Marcel Proust God does not appear. Only *desire* exists, and desire is an eternal mirage. Man is abandoned to himself. His life is "a life of pleasures and sufferings." But none the less he turns his steps towards the Promised Land, rising up there in the distance, but advancing at the same pace as he who would fain draw near to it, and keeping between itself and man a distance that is always the same, that seems impossible for him to traverse.

And in spite of everything man cannot confine himself to "living his own life"; that is to say, if the expression has any meaning, to leading a purely animal
existence. In order to escape a mortal melancholy he
must force himself to escape out of himself. And there
is still only *desire* to incite him to come forth from his
ego. Escaping from duration and from time, which are
his laws, he must strive to unite himself with nature,
with the beauty of works of art, and, in love, with
woman. It is those few exceptional, almost absolute,
moments which for Marcel Proust are perhaps worth
the pain of living.

.   .   .   .

A communion with forces exterior and superior to
ourselves is at the basis of happiness. It is this communion which gives birth to desire, with its multiplicity
of branches, the deepest nature of which, under almost
infinite variety of forms, remains identical. We love the
hawthorns, the churches, the statues, the spires of our
native town. In each of those things we can "believe
as in a being that has no equivalent." Under a form
much more banal, was it not Lamartine who exclaimed:
"Inanimate objects, have you then a soul?"

Desire begins to take on its veritable existence from
the moment it ceases to be a vague and aimless aspiration, and fixes in a precise way on some object, whatsoever that may be. A name is enough to hold it, the
name which recurs so often in the work of Proust, the
name of a town or of a person. Under the name of Florence Proust's imagination places a corolla "miraculously
perfumed"; under the name of Parma, something "com-

pact, smooth, mauve, and sweet." Likewise in the name
of the Duc de Guermantes he has enclosed centuries of
heroic history. As soon as desire takes on an individual
form it hooks itself on to a reality, and our indecisive
dreaming finds food for itself, to enlarge and prolong
it. When Proust (or his hero) goes out, on foot or in
the carriage, with Madame de Villeparisis, or else is
travelling by train, and catches sight of the fresh cheeks
of some country girl, the effusion of his sentiment is
borne immediately towards one of those beings whom
he has hardly caught sight of, and whom he will be able
all the better to embellish as he submits the "reappearance" of the girl within him to the "peculiar laws" of
his spirit.

And from that moment, love can come to birth. If
some chance brings us to come upon this fugitive
creature again, we shall confront it with the image we
have fashioned of it for ourselves. If the girl should refuse to see us again as often as we might like, if our
desire continues to be thwarted, we shall live all the
more with her image, we shall explore it and make it
more solid with all the riches of our own consciousness.
Love is a subjective phenomenon, "a kind of creation
. . . of a supplementary person, distinct from that
which bears the same name in the world, and most of
whose elements are drawn from ourselves."

This idea we find over and over again, like a haunting refrain, beneath all the loves of this novel. No doubt
it is in the passion of Swann for Odette de Crécy that
it is given the clearest expression. The other love-stories
seem afterwards to be no more than corollaries drawn

and developed from this first postulate. And yet what
diversity there is in these accounts! The love of the child
for Gilberte, the little girl who plays the coquette in the
Champs Élysées; the love of the schoolboy for the
Duchesse de Guermantes, who passes in her carriage unheeding; the young man's desire one evening to possess
Madame Stermaria, who does not come to the rendez-
vous; and finally the great passion for Albertine, whose
unfinished story stops short with the last volume that
has so far appeared, and allows a glimpse of terrible
dramas to come. And how many other intrigues revolve
round the hero! Robert de Saint-Loup is associated with
Rachel, once a woman in an infamous house. The Baron
de Charlus, infatuated with Morel, submits like the
others to the hard law of passion. In the fashionable
world the ambassador M. de Norpois remains faithful
to old Madame de Villeparisis. The Princesse de Guermantes makes vain advances to M. de Charlus. But here
sentiments are weakened, because the desire to receive
or to be received is already a passion. On the other hand,
what ardour there is in the loves of these fashionable
personages for servants or prostitutes! Suddenly for
several months on end Swann will assiduously frequent
a certain aristocratic drawing-room because he has desired the cook of the house.

These loves, whether they be superficial or obsessing,
light, tender or brutal, brief or irremediable, are all
derived from the same phenomenon: they are all a
simple modification of the unconscious, an accident in
its flux. Whatever it may be, love substitutes another
self for the habitual self for some time, and this other

self soon disappears without our having been responsible for its death any more than for its birth.

. . . .

In order to understand the originality underlying this conception, we must think of the romantic idea of love, which only yesterday Henry Bataille was still setting forth. In one of his last plays he makes one of his characters say: "Two beings who love each other belong to each other by right." (By natural right, no doubt?) These two beings have chosen each other probably after long deliberations. Or else they were predestined for each other. According to them, their love is already a reality exterior to themselves, solid and immutable. They can lose it only by their fault, as one loses a fortune, or a place in society. Over this love, which they come to include among their material goods, they have a kind of proprietary right, which guarantees them of its stable possession. Alas! this calm certainty, this reasonable and rational possession, is indeed the ideal to which all love instinctively aspires. But the error of romanticism is to consider these illusory aspirations as reality. The reality is different, and more deceptive. The truth is that love is only an individual creation, due to the chance of some malcontent caprice, and prolonged so long as the desire is unsatisfied or thinks itself so.

Over and over again Proust is at pains to tell us that if a certain conjunction of circumstance had been different, it would not have been Odette that Swann would have loved, but some other woman. She who to-day seems indispensable for our love might very easily have been another, without whom we should have been no less certain that we could not live. There is no necessary relation between her and us. So little does the choice of the mistress loved depend on our intelligence that often, "when she has gone, we could not say how she has been dressed, and we realize that we have not even looked at her." And this is the explanation of why she hardly ever corresponds to our moral and even physical ideal. Later, when he no longer loves Odette, Swann will be able to exclaim: "To think that I ruined years of my life, that I wanted to die . . . for a woman who wasn't even pleasing to me, who wasn't my sort!" She was not even of his own circle in society: she was a *demi-mondaine;* but none the less he married her. Most of the persons who are violently loved in the books of Marcel Proust are unworthy of being so. The mind has small share in this desolating passion: "I have been shaken in my loves," he writes; "I have lived them, I have felt them, but never have I been able to see them or think them."

It is no doubt this contingent conception that has made certain readers, and even certain critics,[1] think that Proust (or his hero) and the characters of his work have never themselves known a veritable love. And certainly, if one were to claim that a Swann or a Saint-Loup never at any moment knows an absolute love, as divine love ought to be, that would be perfectly true. No passion, unfortunately, is perfect. Often in adolescence, at that age when the relative does not afford satisfaction, two friends will argue after this fashion:

---

[1] Cf. André Germain's study, *De Proust à Dada.*

"You are a donkey," says the first, "*and in the first place you don't know me in the slightest;* I've already suffered a lot."—"I too," answers the other, "*and you don't know any more about me. . . .*" These naïve conversations make us smile, for we know (and no one has shown it better than Proust) in studying his characters that the "I" is something incommunicable. If the sympathy of two young people linked by friendship does not allow mutual comprehension even to their intelligence, it is not through the contact of their two bodies in love that their two sensibilities will find the possibility of communion: ideas penetrate each other more easily than sentiments. Moreover, it is only at fifteen years old that these illusions are tolerable. But the man will often cherish throughout the whole of his life the dream he has made as a child. At fifteen, according to popular tradition, the adolescent believes in the unique, the infinite love. He seeks it outside of himself, like the adventurer who sets out to discover gold-mines. What seems to him to be difficult is not to find a woman, but to find a great passion. Like the believer who waits trembling for grace, he grows impatient at not being touched by a love descending from the empyrean. He imagines that it is he who is responsible, through his ignorance, for not experiencing an all-powerful sentiment. He would like to be taught the way to seize it. He imagines that there are beings who never know what love is, and that there are others who are the privileged, the elect. Sometimes he thinks that the lack of culture and education amongst the masses of the people, for instance, does not allow them to know this terrestrial beatitude. "I shall never love anyone but you," or "I love you for all my life"—these are the vows which put this belief into words.

So far removed is it from love that there is often an opposition between the idea of love and love itself. The idea expressing needs of tenderness in the search of an absolute is dissociated from the needs of sensuous pleasure. For many men still, there is no fusion between their sentiment of love, which they set on the ideal plane, and their sensual desires, even when these are of great violence. It would seem to them that this alliance of their sentiment with vulgar appetites would be cheapening or a profanation. Such men, moreover, will frequently become Platonic in their ideas, ending in sexual aberrations.

The whole intellectual work of Marcel Proust, and that doubtless of the true artist in general, consists in a penetration of the crust of ready-made judgments. Man does not like to be made to enter into profound reality. What is more, the discoveries of Proust were of necessity bound to administer a shock to opinion; but nowhere perhaps will he meet with so much resistance as in stripping love, to which men cling most closely, of that magnificent tissue of illusions with which they have enwrapped it. In the Middle Ages the scholars who made a discovery that shocked the ordinary common sense of their time were at once accused of atheism. We need not then be astonished that Proust should be met with the reproach, the false, revolting, and evidently absurd reproach, that he denies love and belongs to that class of hapless creatures who have never experienced it.

Ironical paradox! The splendid pages which Proust has devoted to love show too well to what point of intensity his sorrow could rise. And yet he continues to believe that love is "the only portion of happiness in what is, no doubt, the only life that we have." To love he sacrifices all other pleasures; and for the sake of a woman, even if he be in the company of Bergotte or the most elegant of aristocrats, he will leave them, headlong, and at the risk of discourtesy. Only, he does not think that love exists in itself. Love is no more than our own desire in its differently modified forms within us. We cannot hope for it as a boon from heaven. It is our personal creation. That deep disquietude of our adolescent days is precisely that which will be the spring wherein we dip in order to bring it to life. The great passion is already within us, and what is difficult to find is a woman. The poet says: "Whom shall I love? Life is short and draws dream after dream behind it." And we await the woman whose image may possibly coincide with that of our brain; that is to say, whose beauty can give satisfaction to our senses. The need of giving "one's inner music, one's flame," to another is felt, as we know, by every being on this earth, valets and servants as much as great noblemen. What differentiates one love from another is simply the strength of the desire and the quality of our imagination, with both of which we give sustenance to our inner creation. Whence physical pleasure is indissolubly bound up in our desire. The working of our mind has taken the form of a passion only when our body has hoped to achieve union with another body. And when our bodily pleasure is satisfied, the image of our love will gradually fade away and we shall see before us only a human being, like any other. Nothing, it is evident, can be further removed from the popular conception of passion than this Proustian conception. Yet it approximates more closely than any other to the psychological reality. Love, in its birth, its development, its death, has in this work so great a measure of beauty that it deserves our consideration of its mechanism in the different stages of its evolution.

   .   .   .   .

How is it born? After a period of elaboration it is a thwarted desire fixed in a crystallization. "The charms of a person are a less frequent cause of love than a phrase of this kind: 'No, I shan't be free this evening.' " The unexpected absence of a woman whom we were not yet in love with is enough to awaken in us "an anxious need," a need that henceforward is an exclusive one. And with the prolongation of this anguish will come the prolongation of our love. It is the essential nourishment of our love, and here, without any doubt, lies the most important original contribution of the author, in having continually drawn attention to the immense part played by this in the life of passion.

For several weeks the young Proust (or his hero) has been encountering on the beach at Balbec the famous group of young girls, *les jeunes filles en fleurs*—"the budding grove." He has learned that the name of one of them is Albertine, and he has no other thought but to be introduced to her. It happens that the painter

Elstir, with whom he takes his walk, is on terms of close intimacy with the little band, and here they are, coming forward to meet each other. At that moment the young man, certain at last that his desire is on the point of being realized, steps a few paces aside from Elstir, feigning indifference. But suddenly he feels the indifference become real. "The pleasure of knowing these girls seemed to me smaller than that of talking with Saint-Loup, or dining with my grandmother, or making expeditions in the neighbourhood. . . ." The fact is that this pleasure had henceforth become "inevitable." It was no longer an unsatisfied desire, and that is as much as to say that it was no longer anything. But as soon as the hero sees Elstir leave the girls without having called him to be introduced, the same desire of his is reborn, and with increased force. "I realized that the variance in the importance which a pleasure or a pain may have in our eyes . . . can depend on the displacement of invisible beliefs. . . . Variance of a belief, the annulment likewise of love; which, pre-existing and mobile, halts at the image of a woman simply because this woman will be all but impossible of attainment. From that point . . . a whole sequence of agonies develops, and is sufficient to fix our love on to the woman who is its object, though she may be hardly known to us." This little scene of comedy throws an admirable light on the Proustian psychology. Of Albertine the hero knows only one or two profiles against the sea, assuredly less beautiful than "those of the women of Veronese." If these profiles successively assume for him an unequalled degree of value, then become of no interest, and then are restored, not only to their first place, but even to a more exalted position, the reason is that into his consciousness there has entered an element of anxiety; it has vanished, and then it has returned—all under the influence of insignificant incidents.

This coming and going of anxiety will form the whole history of his love for Albertine. In him she will continually be creating new images of the girl, and inasmuch as he exhausts one, another will come to birth from it. When he is able to make her come to his house at his will, he will want to embrace her. And when he has possessed her, he will want to keep her for himself, to isolate her, to make her a prisoner. Having deprived her of all her physical mystery, jealousy, that supreme anxiety, will keep his love alive. In the little Balbec train Albertine innocently tells him the whole story of her childhood, and at the same time lets him know of her relations with Mlle de Vinteuil.[2] This, for the hero, is a terrible revelation: a thousand presentiments which he had not understood are now suddenly made clear as day. He was on the point of breaking with Albertine, but this brusque revelation of a secret has provoked such an inrush of suffering in his heart that he proposes there and then to marry her. He takes her to Paris and shuts her up in his house. Grief has made his love burn up again. The budding girl is dead. It is the friend of Mlle de Vinteuil whom he keeps so strictly beside him. And then—"I should have been able to tell

[2] Marcel Proust used sometimes to say that, in the whole body of his work, this was the passage he himself preferred to any.

anyone who asked me the meaning of this retired life, for I had isolated myself to the point of no longer going even to the theatre, that it originated in the anxiety of one day [the evening of the revelation] and the need to secure for myself on all the days that might follow it the certainty that the woman whose grievous childhood I had then learned of should not have the chance, even if she had so wished, of exposing herself to the same temptations." And the author adds this fine thought: "Under every bodily charm of any depth there lies the permanence of a danger."

Proust's jealousy was almost necessarily bound to take on an amplitude which has never yet, I think, been matched in any work, in any language. In the account of Swann's love-affair (*Un Amour de Swann*), the author makes a preliminary sketch of his subject. He resumes it and develops it through the two volumes of *La Prisonnière*, with such an arsenal of complications and tortures that the painting reminds one of those subterranean parts of mediæval keeps where, side by side, separated by stone doors that two men at least must push against to move, are dungeons on the walls of which hang all the instruments of torture that ever sprang from the imaginations of the executioners of the Inquisition. We are familiar with the extraordinary natural complexity of Proust's mind, with the multiplicity of hidden motives which he attributes to the most commonplace gesture, and which he associates, compares, and connects with others recalled by his unparalleled memory. Here then is this spirit interesting itself, not in a stranger, but in the person who in his present life represents the whole object of his existence. He is here applying his analytic process to the acts on which his happiness immediately depends.

To know at any price what Albertine was thinking, whom she was seeing, whom she loved, he was naturally forced to dissemble continually. The girl, in order to recover her lost freedom, continually unrolled before the hero a tissue of lies, and the man, on his side, in order to penetrate this curtain, wrapped himself similarly in other lies. Thus love ends by transforming the relations of two beings into a succession of mutual deceptions, taking their origin as much in the lover as the loved. Social relations, no doubt, always imply a certain measure of hypocrisy. But Proust insists with vigour on this idea that love brings it immediately to its maximum. The greater part of the lies which Proust imposes on the girl, and, conversely, the girl upon Proust, would be of no use if love did not make the two young people live together. Here the lie is still further complicated, not only by the perspicacity of the hero, pushed indeed to such a degree of intensity that it sometimes appears to border on mania, on disease, but still more by the peculiar character of the tastes of Albertine. We have already seen how the victims of inversion, male or female, wear in society a natural mask, with which they strive completely to conceal their true features. And in this way, in the case of Albertine, there is added to the ruses and coquetry instinctive in a woman the habit of a long dissimulation imposed by this passion that cannot be avowed. And from his side, the discoveries which Proust makes in the girl's life assume for him a more tragic character. Not only does he learn that she deceives him, but that she does so with beings who afford her a sensual pleasure which he, for his part, will never be able to give her.

The hero likewise pushes falsehood to an extreme point. He does not rest content with simple feints. When his suffering grows so strong that it might become evident, he plays what is really a complete comedy. His supreme care is that he shall not show to the girl that he actually loves her, being certain then that the small desire she has kept for him would utterly vanish. "As at Balbec, on the night following her revelation of her friendship with the Vinteuils, I had immediately to invent a possible reason for my chagrin." Every time that Albertine unwittingly betrays herself, by beginning a phrase which she does not finish, or by talking in her sleep, or by throwing out meaningless expressions like her *"C'est vrai? c'est bien vrai?"* (but expressions which are revelations of her coquetry towards the hero), the latter feels his heart change its beat; anxiety, like a running noose, catches him tight; and to conceal his torment he invents some pretext, or accuses himself of some imaginary wrongdoing. "I call love here a reciprocal torture," Proust finally declares.

Often these falsehoods culminate in bursts of anger. The need of possession in the one is in conflict with the desire for liberty in the other. There come "these brief but inevitable moments when one detests the person whom one loves."

"Bloch told me," declares Proust (although it was

not the truth), "that you had known his cousin Esther very well." (She was an invert.)—"I should not even recognize her," says Albertine with a vague air.—"I've seen her photograph," adds the young man.—On nights of discussion Albertine will leave the hero's room, to go back to her own, without embracing him. And then he experiences the same anguish as on those evenings when his mother "scarcely said good-night to him, or even did not come up to his room." And in this way there reappears here the profound identity of all desires and of all the disappointments they bring with them. Proust considers Albertine "as a mistress, as a sister, as a daughter, and as a mother with a daily good-night as well. . . ."

But to her he does not dare, as long ago to his mother, to say: "I'm sad," so that she will come and kiss him. When the girl has left his room, he wanders about the corridor in front of her door, hoping that she will come back, returns into his own room to see whether she may not have left a bag behind, and at last goes to bed and weeps the whole night through. But when, on the other hand, she has come to sleep beside him and embraces him, "incomparable as were those two kisses of peace the one to the other," she left in him "a store of calm almost as gentle as when my mother set her lips upon my brow in the evening at Combray." Very much of the same nature is the anguish of Swann in love, "the anguish there is in feeling that the being whom one loves is at some place of enjoyment where one is not present, where one cannot join her."

I apologize for these long quotations. They bring us

back to our starting-point: to desire, and to love, which is nothing else but a creation of the individual. In the long span we have traversed we observe the uselessness of our effort. Doubtless those who are so naïve as to accuse the author of depicting, in place of love, only a demented jealousy, believe in Love with a capital L, pre-existent to the individual, real, outside the individual himself, and are those who have really never understood the most fundamental laws of this agonizing passion. However, if it be indeed love which the author brings forward before our gaze, he shows at the same time its inanity. We are very soon forced to conclude that reciprocal love is so great a miracle that it is better to live without this hope, for it is one which would only add to our inevitable sufferings a series of fresh deceptions which we can well dispense with. Thus, although this passion may be, among all the bonds of tenderness, the one which leads most naturally to the grateful relaxation of the reposed and satisfied senses, to these mutual confidences, to that spontaneous trust which is one of the great consolations of life, it is surely preferable, if the man wishes to keep his mistress, that he should not avow his love to her, or not at least the whole force of his love.

And in spite of all it is only desire that will "make us find interest in the existence and character of a person." For the sake of a desire, "that of going to see in some mansion a picture by Elstir, or a Gothic tapestry," we are ready to make light of danger, to brave all obstacles. And nevertheless we know that a short time afterwards we shall pass with indifference in front of the same picture, the same tapestry. Similarly, in the being whom we most desire in a carnal sense, we can recognize, says Proust, as the primary motive an idea of perfection for which we would sacrifice our life. But before long the idea is forgotten and we no longer understand the effort we were anxious to make.

In fact, in the ultimate analysis love is perhaps no more than a nervous condition which overwhelms our ego and overturns our table of values. But it is submitted also to the modifications of the perpetual flow of time about us. A little while afterwards our table of values is arranged in a new order, approximating to the old, although different. Those things which were of the greatest indifference to us become suddenly precious, because this woman loves them. And for her "we shall barter all the future against a power in itself insignificant." And then again the desires of our self in the future are no longer the same as those of our self in love. Often, when we are suffering too keenly, we desire to reach the day when we shall love this woman no more, when we shall be able to avenge ourselves on her. But when the day arrives, our vengeance means very little to us; she interested us only because we were under the sway of passion. And thus the fleeting quality of this great agitation is made evident again. The evolution of our inner life draws our love towards its end, which is delayed only by our anxiety, our pain.

Birth and duration and death, jealousy and upheaval —all the great drama of a love is played in the interior of our self. We can never come forth from our personality. And certain of never attaining happiness, we must content ourselves with relative joys and with our illusions. Never has a writer given us a more beautiful lesson than when Proust recounts how he found his greatest pleasure with Albertine one evening, watching her as she lay asleep, and stretching out beside her. "When Albertine was asleep, she seemed to have found her innocence once more . . . her sleep was the sleep of a child . . . my jealousy calmed down. . . ." Here the phrases of the writer soften and grow shorter, as if he wished that they too should take on suddenly the innocence of the girl. Thus the most beautiful and the purest moments of his love are savoured by him with a being in unconsciousness and immobility, passive and incapable of making him suffer longer, stretched out in sleep as if in death itself.

———

CHAPTER IV

ART AND THE SENSE OF THE DIVINE

THE reader who traverses the Proustian universe, overpeopled with characters, is overwhelmed by the impression of a continuous desolation. In the author's company we pass through the drawing-rooms, through Sodom, Gomorrah, Venus.—One after another we are confronted with the vanity of love, the vanity of social activity, the anguish of desire, and, on the margins of madness, the passions which haunt the degraded as much as the superior, which throw their lives out of balance and overshadow all their pleasures. And in every class of society each single individual is the slave of the same illusions and set on the edge of the same abyss. Death brings no hope. The search for self-centred pleasure is the great and general law. But pleasure does not exist, and its pursuit is as vain as the zeal of the occultists to find the esoteric traditions, the philosopher's stone, the formula of happiness. Is the writer to end, then, like Buddha or Schopenhauer, in a definite pessimism? The word *nothingness* recurs over and over again in the books of Marcel Proust, like a warning signal that ought to safe-guard us. Does the Proustian philosophy lead us to nirvana, where suffering is annihilated in non-being, or rather to the Sheol of Ecclesiastes, the mysterious and undefined common grave of the after life? Or, if man is thus reduced to this single present existence, can he hope, like all the atheists from Lucretius to the scientists, that to the evolutionary process of the universe there corresponds a "Progress of Humanity"?

The ideal of Marcel Proust is not that. But hope is not extinguished in the world he has created, rich in spite of everything by reason of its marvellous diversity. Above the roof, as in the verse of Verlaine, the sky is so blue, so calm.—Are there not, in his work, dominating from on high the seething mass of men, certain persons of lofty build, who seem to be the *raison d'être* of the others? In his private life the musician Vinteuil is merely a shy creature pushed to the background; Elstir, known among the Verdurins as "M. Tiche," is a painter made ridiculous by the little group of followers; Bergotte, the writer, and Berma, the famous actress, are commonplace persons when seen at close quarters. But from time to time in the course of Proust's work each of these characters rises transformed by his own work: the artist detaches himself from the man, and suddenly assumes the proportions of magnificence. While still retaining his poor individual character, he becomes the incarnate representative of painting, of music, of poetry. Architecture itself, the expression of a collective existence, is portrayed in the church at Balbec, so living a thing that it appears, like Elstir, like Vinteuil, to stand as the symbol of a whole art while still keeping its own visible features. Thus these exceptional beings rise up in succession, as if complementary to each other. Considered together, they form the total image of artistic activity, on an almost divine plane and on the heights where dwell the Muses, and, like the Muses, assuming the outward human form.

They are greater still. It is they who provide Marcel Proust's work with its true and final explanation. They are like those *epigonoi,* of taller stature than the mean, who stretch forth their hands across the centuries of history and over above humanity, to guide and console it. In the moments when their gleaming genius thrusts their everyday selves into the shadow, at the moment when they are creating, they appear to Marcel Proust to be the very essence, and the reason even, of life. In the void, the "nothingness," of his universe, art is the basis of morality, as well as being the immediate postulate of metaphysics.

. . . .

No doubt the merit of a novel is not made by its philosophic ideas. But when a novel has the vastness of *A la recherche du temps perdu,* it is they alone that allow us to penetrate it. They are the true keys to the work, those keys which the public has sought for every character among our contemporaries, and sought so vainly. It is true that to-day *Le temps retrouvé* is still unpublished, but I think that the detailed study of each aspect of the work, so far as it has already appeared, allows us to fill up this lacuna without difficulty. *Le temps retrouvé* will probably not be so much an intellectual surprise as a splendid artistic confirmation.

Human consciousness, to take the Bergsonian image no doubt dear to Proust, is covered with a thick crust into which our habits, the feelings customary to us, have solidified. It is there, in this outer covering of consciousness, that we find the machinery mounted, the ready-made sentiments, requisite for our everyday work and conversations. But beneath this superficial layer there lies in us the richer part, the essential part of our self, which scarcely ever intervenes in our daily activities. For the truth is that we are perpetually playing one single part, like those actors or actresses who are La Dame aux camélias, or L'Aiglon, to their dying day. We cry out, we laugh, we even shed real tears, but all without our deeper personality's having to come upon the stage. Our reflexes, our memory-habit, make us perform the necessary gestures and utter mechanically the necessary words. Two or three times, at the most, in our existence, in those circumstances which Maeterlinck has called "the everyday tragedy," but are for the great majority of men only very exceptional (the death of one dear to us, a parting on the threshold of a door, a lost love), the innermost part of our consciousness rushes suddenly up, flows forth, and for a moment we commune in a new sentiment with another being. In that instant is expressed the true individual who is within us. For the first time he has his free-will. But immediately he is caught up again by everyday existence; once more he no longer acts save in accordance with the habits and reactions which heredity and education and society have deposited on the surface of his true self. Impotently he is submitted to an implacable determinism.

The artist, on the other hand, is free. It is from the

heart of his individual consciousness that he draws the sources of his art. "Vinteuil . . . with all the strength of his creative effort, attained his own essence at those depths where, whatever the question that faced him, it was with the same accent, his own particular accent, that his essence responded." And Bergson writes: "Between nature and ourselves, or rather between us and our own consciousness, a veil is interposed, a veil that is opaque for the generality of men, but thin, almost transparent, for the artist and the poet." And he adds, giving a definition of art which is almost that of Proust: "Art has no other object than to set aside the symbols of practical utility, the generalities that are conventionally and socially accepted, everything in fact which masks reality from us, in order to set us face to face with reality itself." Thus, according to the writer, the reality of the external world lies in the inner life of things and of ourselves, and this reality, if art did not give it expression, would remain for ever unknown to us. It is upon art that the Proustian universe is founded.

And art multiplies and perpetuates the world. In the consciousness of every artist the world is reflected in a manner at once particular and unique. "Every artist seems thus to be the citizen of an unknown country, forgotten by himself, different from that from whence will come, sailing towards the earth, some other great artist." And the nearer an artist draws to this native land of his, the loftier will be the beauty of his work. At the same time, just as, settling down into a country, the inhabitants shadow forth the type of the race and grow more and more closely alike, so the artist likewise discovers the true spot of which his soul is a native, affirms his personality and gives his whole work a greater unity—a unity not formal but proceeding from within, almost inexpressible, which would be like a tonality. It is to this country, lost so deep in the consciousness, that Proust himself tries to return, to find the essence of his impressions, and to reproduce them, a labour which is at the very basis of his books, and one which we have described as his method of exploration by the fathoming of depth.

Drawn forth from everything most secret within him, the work of art will not reproduce the world according to the conventional images of the public. To attain this reality it will distort the appearances of reality, it will destroy its envelope in order to express its content with a marvellous exactitude. Proust cites the case of the portraits of Elstir, which women never find close enough in resemblance, the truth being that, for the type which a woman has provided for herself, the artist substitutes the type of woman as she exists in his innermost country. Each one of his portraits has a partial resemblance to the model who sat for it, and has also a partial resemblance to other portraits by the same painter. And this is the explanation of why the public has so much difficulty in acclimatizing itself to every new form of art: an effort is demanded of it, and the greater number of people are incapable of such an effort.

It is an effort which corresponds to that made by the artist himself. This reality, which he must reach by piercing the solidified rind of his ego, by shunning determinism by every means within his power, never presents itself to him in bare and naked form. But this effort will bring him his reward, for it leads in the end to joy, a joy that is the expression of the *reality* of the world, to the only *absolute* joy that can be given us on this earth. The ethics of Proust are in harmony with his metaphysics.

Our joy, in fact, results only from the communion of ourselves with a part of the external world, a communion which really associates our profoundest being with the essence of things or of other beings. The true Proustian joy is a kind of beatitude. Neither the *salons,* nor travel, nor love (or love only very rarely), can bring us that mystical fusion of our life with the life about us, because neither one nor the other is strong enough to allow us to escape from our self and to shatter its outer crust. But art, and art alone, brings this miracle to pass. It gives us the happiness which alcohol or opium procure for us artificially—but at the cost of what punishments!—and frees us from the weight of our flesh, makes us enter, radiant and light of body, into an unexpected world, a world of white angels and disincarnate spirits, so unburdened by the heavy cares of life so distant from it, that we think of the world of sleep and of death. For mankind absolute happiness can be conceived only through the absence of life: it is a state of liberation of such a kind that, while being aware that we continue to exist, we nevertheless experience already the blessings of eternal rest. "This appeal towards a superterrestrial joy," which is that of Proust when he hears the little phrase he knew so well in Vinteuil's sonata recurring in his quartet, is indeed a joy of this kind, and also like that satisfaction which sometimes, but only for the space of an instant, follows the pleasure of the senses in love, a pleasure during which the whole world seems to have dissolved in order to allow two intertwining bodies to lie outstretched and afloat in space.

This absolute of the artist's joy reminds Proust of "those impressions which at distant intervals I found in my life, like landmarks, lures for the construction of a veritable life: the impression felt . . . before a row of trees near Balbec," an impression which we have analysed in the early pages of this study as an example of the method of Proustian investigation. It not only represents for the writer the proper path along which to produce the work of art, but is the sole source of joy. What the writer will find beyond the image, in a communion between the external world and himself, is so widely different from the habitual course of his life that he feels that happiness lies hid in that direction, and he is all eagerness to devote himself to the quest. Thus, beyond ordinary language, beyond purely logical ideas, art allows the individual to give expression to his original impulse. The combined efforts of his intelligence and his intuition allow him to touch reality in joy.

A legend takes shape with rapidity: Marcel Proust —novelist of memory and of the life of fashion. Nevertheless, it is forgotten that he is first and foremost an artist, that no one loved art, the supreme goal of life, more passionately and more disinterestedly than this so-called "snob."

His articles on Baudelaire and Flaubert, his prefaces to the translations of Ruskin, bear witness, as does the whole of his existence, to his passion for the labour which is the artist's lot. The works created by the artist, Proust brings back to life in his own books; and the astonishing intensity with which he has done this has not perhaps been adequately noticed. Most novelists, when they have to speak of some work of art in their books, will cite some definite historic masterpiece—the Sistine Chapel, or the Cathedral of Rouen. But such works are not given a name in Marcel Proust's pages. Following his usual procedure, he borrows from Debussy, from Wagner, from Saint-Saëns, different phrases of their music, and makes a literary re-composition of the sonata and the Vinteuil quartet, a sonata and a quartet which emanate entirely from his own imagination—and a sonata greater perhaps than any real sonata, for it allows the reader to enshrine within it the corpus of his own most cherished musical memories. He is not here performing the functions of an art critic. He does not expound the beauties of the Wagnerian *Nibelungen* cycle, or the charm of a painting by Vermeer. He does not talk like most professional critics of the *colour* of this music, or of the *singing* tone of that colour, resting content with these transpositions of the values of an art from one direction to another. In his pages he re-creates a work, the sonata, the quartet, the church at Balbec, and, investing it with an abstract and general character, he penetrates it and sinks into it so deeply that it becomes animate and enduring, making us dream of the morality and philosophy which, by virtue of art, lies there within it.

．　　　．　　　．　　　．　　　．　　　．　　　．　　　．

We are brought finally to the conclusion that from Proust's books there emerges the same lesson as from his life. This writer, whom love and pleasures played false, who might easily seem to be a man given over to despair, suddenly recovers his strength as admirer and idealist. This man who gave up so many of his years to the life of fashion, is in reality nothing less than the type of the pure artist.

In our epoch, when the writer or the painter falls into the accepted mode of commercializing his production, the instance should be noted of this man of fashion, rich and an invalid, who offered to art the gift of his whole self. Our cold and sport-loving generation stands stupefied before the overwhelming and architectural mass of his work. And in all truth it hardly seems as if this writer had "lost" his "Time," but as if he had retired into his tower of ivory (say, rather, of cork), to have, in the long run, "recovered" it. And without any doubt the essential part of this work is the exalted worship it offers to the great artists. For them Marcel Proust has that enthusiastic love which a girl has for an actor or an author. One day, particularly courageous, she decides to ask him for his photograph, in a letter that is full of burning passion, hyperbolic and sincere. The photograph is ardently kissed, for this is a love of the fetish kind. If the writer continues to reply, his admirer soon makes confession; she receives encouragement. One day she forwards a poem of hers which she had forgotten, she says, in a drawer, and which the great man, please, will try to place with some provincial review. To offer him her thanks, she calls on him; and both are undeceived. But nevertheless their relations are resumed by correspondence after a while: the one has the need to protect, the other to admire.

This passion for artists was felt by Proust in his childhood, and towards the end of his life, when he was surrounded by hardly anyone save writers. It is in their company that he had found the greatest joys of friendship. The hero of his book tells us of his great desire, as a youth, to know the painter Elstir, and how he addressed to him one of those letters brimming over with love, which gave him the chance of entering his studio. Again, when the young man reads Bergotte, he informs us of that same desire he had, not only to know him, but to know his opinion on all the things that interested him. He attributed a quasi-divine value to the writer whom he thus adored. He imagined that all his judgments must partake of that sacred nature and would bring him unexpected revelations. Like Flaubert, he took the bit between his teeth, but with this difference, that Flaubert vowed his worship first and foremost to the past. Proust, while turning back to the classics, loved to discover new forms of art. He was too strongly imbued with the spirit of evolution and of life for his taste to remain fixed, or for it not to seek out the art that creates itself, that is born, that comes, the art like his own. At the present day another pure lover of art prefers the life of the study to the life of activity. M. Valéry Larbaud extols the pleasure of "reading, that unpunished vice." But among a few pure artists Marcel Proust is the most astonishing: it was after he had made study of men, of duels, of love, of the vices, that he withdrew like a monk into his chamber, and began his adoration of art as of his God.

It is possible, no doubt, to conceive of a different ideal. Faust knew the intoxication of wine, of women, of beauty. But none the less he continues his search. And at last one evening a fleet that is his own, the symbol of his activity, sails back with sails unfurled into the harbour that he has created. It is then that he exclaims: "*O Time, suspend thy flight!*" The feeling of battle, of politics, of business, are all absent from the work of Proust. For him art is the supreme form of action. Proust has taught us to probe into the depths of every fact, and we know that it was illness which thus oriented his life, which thus determined the vocation of this man. But it has in no way detracted from it. The movement of thought is worth as much as the movement which displaces matter. Without emerging from his room, a man, with the activity of his brain, can become the equal of any leader of peoples, no matter who. Action has two great complementary tendencies. For Proust, as for Goethe, an interested pleasure leads to a void. Only forgetfulness of self can let us know a moment of happiness. Faust finds that moment in life, Proust finds it in art. And it is then that he calls out to *le temps retrouvé,* to time recovered: "*O Time, suspend thy flight!*"

EXTRACTS FROM UNPUBLISHED LETTERS OF MARCEL
PROUST [1]

ABOUT 1905, Fernand Gregh sent his latest collection of poems to Marcel Proust. After many expressions of eulogy Proust makes a reservation on the
subject of a use of the word *comme*. One can appreciate
here the importance attached by the author to exact expression—

". . . The *comme* which seems to me not exactly open to criti-
cism, but perhaps a little useless, is not the *comme* meaning *just
as:*
  Comme un marin qu'aveugle, etc.
  Comme un village, etc.
  Comme un nageur, etc.
  Comme s'ils m'attendaient, etc.
  Comme le tain d'un miroir, etc. Etc., etc., etc.
"That is indispensable. No, I mean the *comme* used to mean
so to speak:
  D'un pas délibéré, comme désespéré.
  C'étaient comme pendus au fond, etc."

Elsewhere Proust speaks at length to his friend of
the book he has just received. His unique critical spirit,
as always, is here seen investigating the depths:

---

[1] These letters have connexion with different points of our biography,
and may be regarded as in a way complementary to it.—L. P.-Q.

"I said to myself that it was perhaps Flaubert's page—'*Sur ses yeux, sur sa bouche, sur ses pieds,*' etc.—which had given you in a purely accidental way the idea of the beautiful development (otherwise absolutely different): '*Leurs fronts, leurs yeux, leur col . . .*' etc. Moreover, you know that Sainte-Beuve and Balzac (Balzac twice) made the development of Flaubert the same, which is, for the matter of that, from Bossuet. While yours *has no kind of connexion.* I tell you that, simply as if I said to you: 'Perhaps it is the heat that makes you prefer to remain working to-day' (accidental things). . . .

". . . No doubt it would be lacking in gratitude for all the perfection which your work has attained, to advise a 'curious' form to you when you have the simplicity of the masters. But you know as I do that the fusion of moral emotions with natural sensations, which is the only great poetry, tends always to give too much abstraction to the style, and as you are on the true path to the true source of great poetry, you run no risk of losing yourself or taking a wrong turning, even if you take your delight and diversion and condescend sometimes to underline occasionally with a singular stroke a perfect form. . . ."

And here again is Proust bringing out his character of professional writer:

". . . Have you by any chance (my apologies for speaking of this work, you know moreover that it no longer exists) the *Renaissance latine* within your reach? If you have not, I should like to send you a number in which I wrote an article, because you know the almost unique confidence I have in your taste, and I should like you to tell me, without any kindness, which would be rather unkind really, exactly where I stand, whether there is any progress or the reverse on *Les Plaisirs et les jours* and *La Bible d'Amiens,* and, on the other hand, its relations with other things of mine, and how that stands in itself. I should like a note, as at school. And if it were not abusing your kindness, some corrections in the margin. Naturally there is no hurry about any of this. It could be any time. . . ."

In 1913, at the time when René Blum took *Du côté de chez Swann* to Grasset, this is what Proust himself wrote of his book:

"I have taken as a general title *A la recherche du temps perdu.* The first volume (but it would be better not to say the first volume, for I pretend that it is all in itself a little whole, like *L'Orme du mail* in the *Histoire contemporaine,* or *Les Déracinés* in the novel of *L'Énergie nationale*) is called *Du côté de chez Swann.* The second and third are announced on the cover as going to be called, the second, *Le côté de Guermantes,* and the third, *Le temps retrouvé.* But perhaps the second will be called *A l'ombre des jeunes filles en fleurs,* or perhaps *Les Intermittences du cœur,* or perhaps *L'Adoration perpétuelle,* or perhaps *Les Colombes poignardées,* but it is useless to tell all this. It is a book of extreme reality, but supported in some degree, to imitate involuntary memory —(which in my opinion, although Bergson does not make this distinction, is the only true memory, the voluntary memory, the memory of the intelligence and the eyes restoring to us from the past only inexact facsimiles, which no more reproduce it than the pictures of bad painters have any resemblance to the spring, etc. . . . So that we do not believe life real because we do not really recall it, but if we happen to catch some smell of long ago, we are suddenly intoxicated; and similarly, if we think that we no longer love the dead, it is because we do not really recall them, but if suddenly we see some old glove again, we melt into tears)— by sudden reminiscence: one part of the book is a part of my life which I had forgotten, suddenly recovered, in eating a morsel of cake which I had soaked in tea, which delighted me before I had recognized and identified it as having been something I used long ago to take every morning: immediately my life of those days comes back to life, and, as I say in the book, like the Japanese toy in which tiny morsels of paper, when soaked in a bowl of water, become people, flowers, etc. . . . all the people and gardens of this period of my life have emerged from out of one cup of tea.

Another part of the book is reborn from the moments of awakening, when one does not know where one is, and imagines oneself to be two years before in a different country. But all that is only the framework of the book. . . .

". . . I do not know if I told you that this book was a novel. At least it is from the novel that it diverges least. There is a narrator who says 'I'; there are a great many characters; they are 'prepared' in this first volume; that is to say, they will do in the second exactly the contrary of what one expected from the first. From the point of view of the publisher, unfortunately, this first volume is much less narrative than the second. And as regards composition, this is so complex that it becomes apparent only very late in the day, when all the themes have begun to combine. You see that none of this is particularly inviting. But subject to what we have said, it seems to me that in any case M. Grasset can lose nothing, and from a literary point of view I do not think that it will do his reputatioin any harm. . . .

". . . I should be very happy if my book pleased you. I should also be very happy, as I have written to you already, if you should ask a service of me. Is it not possible? And finally I should be happy if you are keeping well. Somebody or other, I cannot remember who (and yet I see nobody), told me that he had it from . . . (I think from you) that you have sent me a questionnaire, for me to say what are the ten novels I like best. I have never received this, otherwise I should have acknowledged it to you. But all the same I am quite glad not to have received it, for if the question is of living authors, there are very few whose books I care for, and very few whom I care for in person, and as these are generally not the same, I should be hurting the feelings of the second in announcing the first."

With regard to the proposed dictionary of the characters in the work of Marcel Proust, here are the guiding lines given by the author to François Fosca, who will undertake the task of compiling it when the novel has been issued in its entirety:

". . . I should introduce, if I were you (and I would willingly do it in concert with you)—I thought I had written all this to you, but I have been so ill, perhaps I am confused—an original element; that is, for instance, in holding in check the financial, social indications, etc., which take up so great a place in Balzac. But I repeat, you will do that according to your own ideas. Pay no heed to these indications if it pleases you to do differently. What I had in mind was the following: in a Balzacian dictionary you will find indications inevitable of this kind: '*Duchesse de Maufrigneuse, later Princesse de Cadignan, had inscribed 20,000 livres income in the* "grand livre," *on the advice of de Marsay, then her lover. In 1827, thanks to the liberalities of Madame, the fortune of the Princesse was raised to 37,000 francs income,*' etc. . . . Well, even while maintaining ourselves on a purely social ground, I should prefer that this class of facts, too Balzacian, should be eliminated, and replaced for instance by this kind of thing: '*Oriane de Guermantes, Princesse de Laumes, later Duchesse de Guermantes, refuses to go to the Iénas' at the time when she is Princesse de Laumes* (see Du côté de chez Swann), *then becomes their intimate friend and even wishes to induce the Princesse de Parme to go to their house* (*see* Le côté de Guermantes).'

"If you come to Paris after Bourbon-Lancy, in spite of all the difficulties which arise for me in receiving anyone, you would give me great pleasure if you called during the day at my address, 44, Rue Hamelin, to warn my servant that you will be coming the same evening at 11 o'clock. Her husband, who is a chauffeur, will be able to go and meet you and bring you back. We shall talk more of Degas than of the dictionary. At any rate, I hope that the latter is not indispensable to the maintenance of our reciprocal intellectual sympathy and that if some day you renounce your idea of compiling this dictionary, we shall not be left any less friendlily disposed. . . ."

NOTES

PAGE 24. For a long time Marcel Proust was an enthusiastic student of metaphysics. He loved to discuss the great metaphysical systems with his friends. But before long, after becoming a regular frequenter of the *salon* of Madame Arman de Caillavet, Anatole France, by his scepticism, was to cure him of this passion, but none the less it remained always with him, more or less, to the end of his life.

PAGE 56. When Marcel Proust read a few pages of his book to some friends, before it had appeared, he was repeatedly seized with a nervous laughter which forced him indefinitely to give up his reading.

PAGE 57. About 1901 Marcel Proust's family left the Boulevard Malesherbes and took up their residence at 45, Rue de Courcelles. It was this apartment which he left, after the death of his mother, to go and live on the Boulevard Haussmann.

PAGE 59. The asthma, towards the end of his life, had resulted in a development of his chest. This remark, made by some of Proust's friends, might have a different explanation: historic truth obliges me to add that Proust almost always wore starched shirt-fronts, and it was perhaps his shirt-front bulging out.

PAGE 67. Not only had Proust an extraordinary gift of divination, but further, it was impossible to conceal anything from him. "A thought would be just emerging to the surface of your consciousness," writes Paul Morand, "and, at the very instant, Proust showed by a slight shock that he had received communication of it simultaneously with yourself." When Louis de Robert wanted to spare him the pain which would be given him by the brutal letter of refusal from Ollendorf, Proust remarked at once that his friend was hiding something from him. When he happened to be taken in by someone and paid no heed, the fact was that he had seen it all, understood it all, and just preferred not to protest. "You think him your dupe: if he *feigns* to be, which is the greater dupe, he, or you?" said La Bruyère.

PAGE 85. His extreme sensibility might make one believe in his susceptibility. One of his best friends, who saw him right to the end of his life, had drawn his attention in *Les Plaisirs et les jours* to a somewhat lengthy sentence. Proust made no reply. But much later, when *Du côté de chez Swann* was on the point of appearing, Proust said to the same friend: "I do not think you will care for my style, for the sentences this time are must longer than those in *Les Plaisirs et les jours*. . . ." He was replying twenty years after to a small literary criticism which he had never let slip from his memory.

PAGE 91. Proust's peculiar taste for reconstructing deep-hidden and secret motives for people's actions found constant occasion for exercise during the war. The censorship was in full swing. Proust amused himself by searching for the words left as blanks, by finding the sense of the suppressed passage. He made a study of working out an expanded interpretation of the official *communiqué* with a sagacity, a power of penetration, a gift of divination, which enabled him to catch sight of the truth long before the professional commentators did. From 1915 onwards he was sincerely convinced that Germany would be completely vanquished. He compared her to a woman stricken with cancer, who knows it, but still goes to the ball.

PAGE 100. I should add that, a short time after the award of the Prix Goncourt, Marcel Proust was given the decoration of the Legion of Honour (in the same list as the Comtesse de Noailles, whom he had often encountered in his youth in the *monde*). This event, quite unexpected by him, as was all his fame, gave him profound satisfaction.

PAGE 105. He was so familiar a figure at the Ritz that he used to tell how once he had been embarrassed, at a dinner given there by the Princesse X., by seeming to be the host, for it was to him, out of habit, that the maître d'hôtel offered the dishes before serving them. The confusion amused him greatly.

PAGE 106. I have remarked on page 77 that the habit of writing in bed may possibly have influenced Proust in the manner of his writing, and especially of correcting his text. Furthermore, he worked in an attitude as inconvenient as possible: a twopenny bottle of ink, always half empty, a bad pen, a thin wooden penholder. He held his sheet of paper in the air, without supporting it on a table or even a blotting-pad or a book, which explains his writing, which is almost devoid of any light or heavy lines. It was in this painful posture that he wrote almost the whole of his work, and his innumerable letters too. When one finds, in the latter, phrases such as "My dear friend—Writing is truly an agony to me . . ." he was in no way exaggerating. But he refused to be relieved, to have a shade fixed on the lamp that dazzled him, to have the table beside his bed cleared, although it was so overladen with note-books and volumes that he could put nothing more on it.

His manuscripts are extremely confused, and the writing, of course, is scarcely legible. The typist, in copying, frequently left blanks for words which she did not understand, or, worse, made errors. And so it can be understood that, not having room on his bed to keep two note-books opened out in front of him, it was difficult for Proust to search in his original manuscript for the exact text, and he preferred to put himself back into the state of mind in which he had written the passage in question, and so rewrite it. He was thus brought to complete his search, to add some fresh development, to amplify without ceasing. The attentive study of the manuscripts will prove, moreover, that some of the most beautiful passages in the book are just those which were added later by the author on top of the text.

PAGE 110. In the last days before his death, speech became for Proust an impossible fatigue. He preferred to write. Nothing could be more affecting than those backs of envelopes on which the author of *Swann*, with unchanged handwriting, asked Céleste to bring a table nearer, to give him some tea, or to soften the light.

INTRODUCTION (1928)

A great oeuvre like Marcel Proust's will never be fully plumbed by the critics. If I have decided to enter it once more by another avenue — the avenue of comedy — I have done so because this unknown route leads, as will be seen, to entirely novel insights. I fancied that I might discover, in the course of this voyage, some new and different aspects, but that in the main I would find soon again the features of a familiar terrain. How wrong I was! What astonishing riches there are in Proust's novels! They afforded me access to regions where I savored the freshness of surprise and of things never seen before. These books, so frequently re-read, suddenly proved to be the equivalent of pristine texts. Proust the psychologist of unconscious life revealed himself as an amazing author of comedy, and his Charlus, by his very enormity, made me think of a Don Quixote even more caricatural than the original.

However, the world of books is wide, and since I do not want to be the enthusiastic regionalist of one single county, I was at last going to leave the Proustian domain for new ventures. As a matter of fact, I intended to produce a monograph on André Gide, and, in addition, I had started writing a novel. The separation from Proust brought on the pains of nostalgia; I regretted the magnificent landscape, just as after an intoxication one regrets the loss of exaltation. And I moved away from Proust with that somewhat sad joy of not having known him in his unsounded depths and of abandoning him, not with an empty mind, but still fully laden with untapped treasures.

Then appeared *Le Temps retrouvé*. This time, the monument was finished, the vision of the whole complete. The panorama had unfolded circularly. And at this vast sight, I was gripped by an intense joy. Thus I was led to specify the exact place of this oeuvre in contemporary production, to imagine how it would endure, to isolate new ideas from within its framework, and to bring out its own special mystery.

The two short studies which follow guide me from a Proust, writer in the comic mode, to an almost mystical Proust.[1] Gathering my discoveries, I can measure — without a doubt, definitively — the full extent of this work, at once confessions and memoirs. It would seem to me that opinion already ranks it side by side with the most important books. In any event, I would place it there. And henceforth, I have left it behind me. I am free to go back to my own, only provisionally interrupted, work in progress. Once again, I am surrounded by the unknown.

With every work of art that marks a place in my existence, I have lived the history of my connections with Proust's books. At first, I always felt an inner shock or that slow curiosity which characterizes the beginnings of a love affair. Subsequently, I had sublime moments of elation. In the end, I knew the heartrending disappointment, that state of emptiness where the exhausted book still yields discoveries but no longer intoxicates. Passion has become affection. It is then that the most fervent reader believes that he has "read all the books..."

---

[1] Both of these short studies are appended to the present volume.

INTRODUCTION (1936)

Years ago, I began this study in order to express my gratitude to the author, and, in an attempt somehow to elucidate my personal relationship to his books. Originally, I did not approach them as a literary critic, but, rather, I was led to literary criticism through my study of Proust's work.

Later, having achieved a certain distance in time, I wanted to judge the totality of this vast confessional novel. It was then that the successive reprintings of the present monograph allowed me to complete it by adding a new essay: "Comedy and Mystery in Proust." Here, I analyzed the author's psychology in ways similar to psychological studies on Stendhal or on Balzac, considering that henceforth Proust would occupy a place side by side with the greatest novelists in French literature.

Now, ten years have elapsed. I am struck by the public's attitude, even among the cultured: a seeming lack of interest in a writer who once commanded a passionate response. Every infatuation is of course followed by a fatal reaction. I asked myself whether the present retreat from Proust does not correspond, in our society, to a general retreat from art itself, whose importance seems to diminish daily, especially since the Depression. A temporary flight, no doubt. In order to elucidate this question, I re-read *A la recherche du temps perdu* and was moved to confront memories of old with impressions of my re-reading. The present re-edition of this monograph is thus augmented by two chapters: "A New Reading: Ten Years Later" and "Proust and Today's Youth."

Finally, I have added "Remarks on the Last Months of Proust's Life," previously published in magazines, and which Paul Souday had at the time enjoined me to include in this volume.[1]

As it stands, this book presents some repetitions and perhaps even apparent contradictions. I decided, however, not to retouch any of its parts. If it lacks unity, it nonetheless proves that an oeuvre like Proust's has not ceased to remain alive, to endure, since my renewed contacts with it have allowed me to look at it from ever-changing angles, to find in it answers to burning problems of the day, to relate it to the prevailing circumstances of the moment. And, surely, future generations will discover in it pristine aspects which correspond to their own preoccupations...

Meanwhile, I do not want to exaggerate the diversity of the judgments expressed in this monograph. They doubtless rest upon a conception of life which has evolved, and which, in particular, today attributes as much worth and interest to society as to the individual. Owing to this fact, certain perspectives have shifted. However – as I foresaw it in my first Introduction – my fundamental viewpoint on Proust's work, considered in itself, has hardly changed. That is why, henceforth, I consider this volume fully rounded, definitive.

---

[1] The first editions carried, as an appendix, a text which is no longer included: a summary bibliography which, further developed and completed by other documents, became the object of a separate work: *Comment travaillait Marcel Proust* (Editions des Cahiers Libres). On the other hand, the passages from Proust's letters, which appear in the present volume, are excerpts from a correspondence which has appeared, complete, in a separate work, accompanied by commentaries under the title: *Lettres de Proust à Léon Blum, Bernard Grasset et Louis Brun* (Editions du Sagittaire).

PART FOUR

COMEDY AND MYSTERY IN PROUST

1. OBSERVING COMEDY[1]

It is odd that in the numerous essays devoted to Proust, no critic has noticed the comic element, so important to his work. A comical book is almost always thought to be joyful, short, and with an illustrated cover. It is easily forgotten that Don Quixote, Pantagruel, or Gil Blas are thick and densely printed volumes. I myself did not perceive right away the intensity of the Proustian mode of comedy. For in order to understand it one must persevere in a state of insensitivity. Compassion and sympathy inhibit laughter. A gentleman slips and falls in the street. If we orient our attention toward his weakness and his age, we are moved and think perhaps of helping him back on his feet. If, on the contrary, we see but the epileptic contortions of this body at the instant of its fall, we cannot keep from laughing.

Now the principal characters of *Du côté de chez Swann* — and of the subsequent books — were first of all pain-filled friends whose sorrows I instinctively shared: I partook of the child-narrator's nervous crises; I felt the anxiety of his puppy love for Gilberte. At such moments, I could not be receptive to anything comic.

---

[1] I state here, once and for all, that I have often drawn my inspiration from Bergson (above all from *Le Rire*) in the course of writing these pages. Since Proust was imbued with Bergson's philosophy (cf. above all, *Le Temps retrouvé*, tome II), it is only natural that Bergsonian explanations of comedy, and even of art in general, can precisely be applied to *A la recherche du temps perdu*. Thus, in the 20th century, the greatest novelist and the greatest philosopher meet.

But on re-reading *A la recherche du temps perdu*, and skipping pages in order to escape the intense emotion which animates the entire work, I have little by little glimpsed a new author, a Proust using the most diverse forms of laughter: plays on words, parodies, burlesque imitations, quid pro quo, false recognition scenes, gross jokes, quips. At last, I had the impression of perceiving, if I may say so, the wrong and the right sides of this work, where the mixture of comedy and tragedy recalls Shakespearean drama.

But only incompletely. In Shakespeare, burlesque actions and bloody ones, the buffoon's antics and the hero's meditations neatly alternate and are never found together in one and the same scene. Comedy is very clearly detached, very apparent even in the blackest histories. The spectator will burst out laughing while he still has tears in his eyes. In Proust, one would often hesitate between these two extremes, since the two genres are so closely intertwined.

At first sight it would seem unbelievable that a writer could have this dual attitude. In fact, I know of no analytical novel which would be at the same time a comic novel, except perhaps Dostoevski's.

The great French analytical novels, like *La Princesse de Clèves* or *Adolphe*, remain from beginning to end grave "confessions." The same holds true for all parts of Proust's work where he himself appears on stage, where he speaks of his anguish, of his memories, of his loves. On such occasions, he descends into the innermost depths of his own consciousness. He proceeds through introspection.

On the contrary, in all those segments where, abandoning analysis for comedy, he depicts the fashionable drawing rooms, the aristocratic "clans" of the Faubourg Saint-

Germain and the vainglorious bourgeois, his observations skirt depth, recording only the external aspect of people. This entire other part of his work in a way constitutes "memoirs" of the times (of the period from 1870 to 1917).

What is surprising is that Proust, having advanced his psychology to such an extent, would nonetheless have the gift to see the surface of things; that, engrossed in the analysis of his intense emotions, he might still have taken a simultaneous interest in the gestures of others: after having spent some moments of real ecstasy over a rose-bush in bloom or after savoring an afternoon of intoxication stretched out on the sand alongside Albertine, he could talk for hours with a friend about the wardrobe or the comings and goings of the Duchesse de Guermantes, or about the remarks of some totally insignificant prince.

There are doubtless a number of figures whom Proust considers only from the outside: they are puppets who gesticulate in the *salons*. But where the principal characters are concerned, his observations proceed successively from the outside to the inside, sometimes in depth, sometimes focussing on comical prototypes. When Swann enters the scene, first at Combray in young Proust's family, it is his amusing silhouette which is depicted. But then Swann falls in love with a courtesan. Henceforth, the character is seen from the inside. The silhouette becomes an individual. At the outset, it had been little more than a caricature lying flat on a sheet of paper. Now suddenly in relief, the cut-out has turned into a living statue.

It is this procedure which endows Proust's characters with that prodigious intensity of life. Certain readers in the end even speak of them as though they were real people who had actually lived, and whom they might have known. In his novel, Proust succeeded in presenting us with a stupifying alliance of superficial chatter and of winged poetry, tragically psychological sections and grotesque drawing-room segments.

Descartes asserted that there is no superior intelligence without, to some extent at least, a sense of comedy. His often very witty letters contrast with the rigid vigour of his reasoning. And has not that tormented mind, Pascal, in his *Provinciales*, given what Chateaubriand calls "the model for the perfect jest"? In the same manner, Proust incessantly combines the most astonishing psychological analysis with the most diverse comic observation.

2. DIFFERENT FORMS OF COMEDY IN PROUST
Comedy of Characters

Gestures and Manias

The essence of all comedy consists in the split between mechanism and life. It is continuously found in Proust.

It appears first of all in the manner in which the characters are presented on the novel's stage. In page after page, Proust describes with astonishing precision their health, their handshakes, their gaits, their manias, their ways of expressing themselves. In fact, we laugh every time when the body gives the impression of being too rigid a vestment for the soul. The more a man may suggest the idea of a thing or an animal, the funnier he will seem to us. Proust gives us a typical example of this procedure when he speaks of the page-boy at the hotel in Balbec: "The page-boy, exposed to the sun during the day, had been brought back indoors in order not to be exposed to the evening's harshness, and, swaddled in woolens...in the midst of the crystal hall, he made one think of a *hot-house plant* protected against the cold."

Proust constantly compares his characters with animals, with birds. More often than not, this comparison is suggested rather than overtly stated. Or again, the author does not directly allude to any particular animal, contenting himself with evoking in us impressions of automatism. Proust writes: in response to my greeting, "by a brusque *release*...putting between me and himself the greatest possible distance, [Saint-Loup] stretched out his arm to its fullest extent..."

If here the writer's comic power resides in the forcefulness with which he suggests mechanical impressions to us, the artistic effect will only be fully attained if these portraits let us catch a glimpse of the model's mental faculties. Thus M. de Cambremer's nose allows conclusions as to his intelligence: "By a transposition of the senses, M. de Cambremer looked at you with his nose...Aquiline, polished, shiny, brand new." Through this nose, which is assimilated to some excessively cleaned *copper object*, we understand that the psyche of this unfortunate nobleman is frozen in his body, in a part of his face "where his stupidity is most effortlessly displayed."

The face ages and a characteristic trait, which had seemed to be fixed in it until death, becomes modified in the course of time and changes altogether with the metamorphoses of the inner self. Mme Verdurin, when she laughs at an inanity by one of the "faithful" of her "Wednesday" gatherings, no longer takes care to widen her mouth, but, after emitting "a short shriek" she throws her head back and hides her face in her hands, looking as though she were making a great effort to keep herself from laughing, in order not to dislocate her jaw. And this mimicry leads Proust to an animal comparison: "She totally closed her bird's eyes which a leukoma began to veil...Clinging to her perch *like a bird* whose seed has been soaked in hot wine, Mme Verdurin was sobbing with kindliness." With advancing age and her worldly success, her tics become more pronounced. Listening to music, she had formerly felt obliged to have a "tired air of admiration": now this trait has become part of her face.

As to the elderly Marquise de Cambremer, she is compared by Proust to a bishop on his episcopal rounds. Any similarity between persons who have nothing in common, but in whom one discovers unexpected affinities, is droll. "Two similar faces, neither of which, taken individually, would provoke a laugh, produce laughter by their resemblance," says Pascal. It is in fact the frozen aspect which creates resemblance, and which contrasts with the individuality of those involved. Proust shows us the good lady bent under the "mass of luxury objects"...with which she is bedecked. She was wearing "a jet-black mantlet, like a *dalmatic*." On her chest, "a baronet's coronet was suspended in the manner of a *pectoral cross*." "in her hand, [she] held, together with her parasol's *crozier*, several embroidered purses..." Such were "the ornaments...of her *worldly priesthood*." The comparison, all the more striking since the word "bishop" is not even pronounced, evolves with magnificent solemnity.

One of Proust's favorite themes is furnished by the peculiarities and bizarre aspects of language. In sentences as well as in gestures there occur mechanical repetitions which become a source of laughter. Set forms and linguistic mannerisms serve Proust in the completion of his portraits.

Mme de Cambremer's daughter-in-law constantly repeats: "My cousins de *Ch'nouville*" instead of "Chenouville." And this pronunciation which she finds very elegant causes her a perpetual enchantment. Née Legrandin, she has married the Marquis de Cambremer only in the hope of being accepted in the fashionable circles of the Faubourg St. Germain. And since she has heard that the Duchesse de Guermantes, whom she does not know, says "Madame *d*'Chenonceau" instead of "Madame de Chenonceau," she awkwardly imitates her, eliding the wrong mute "e".

It is by this type of procedure that Proust brings out the characteristics of almost all his heroes. These linguistic mannerisms, which helped introduce them, will follow them

269

as leitmotivs throughout the novel. A single note at any moment even in the midst of drama will suffice to evoke completely the character and his comic peculiarities. And since we expect these repetitions owing to the characters' faithfulness to their manias, we have the illusion of pulling, ourselves, the strings of the marionettes.

When in certain major scenes Proust brings them all together, he achieves astonishingly sure effects, as in a burlesque symphony. Thanks to the analysis of the syntax, particular to each individual case, the preparation has been so complete that it suggests a sort of "Babel" of foreign tongues and that each word, each gesture seems familiar to us. The stage set is in place. The play begins: it is a dinner at the Duchesse de Guermantes', a reception at her cousin's, or a musical soirée at the Verdurins'. Mechanically wound up, the characters start moving without hesitation: Mme Verdurin plunges her face into her hands, pretending to laugh politely; M. de Cambremer with his enormous, imbecilic nose repeats that he does not understand what he is being told; Mme de Cambremer bubbles over with princely names whose mute syllables she swallows; foreigners make the same mistakes over and over again; Saniette gulps down consonants while speaking; Ski emits little shrieks like a spoiled child; Cottard puns; Swann articulates his words distinctly as is "the Guermantes' way."

Everyone seems to be absorbed in himself. The conversation is not general. A question does not truly evoke a response, but rather produces in the interlocutor a sort of release, whose mechanism unreels for a shorter or longer while. Then it is the next one's turn, a sort of wound-up spring which uncoils. All these people gathered together do not appear to speak to each other; at certain moments they make the impression of madmen enshrined in their obsessions. This produces a painful, almost horrible effect. And yet, we cannot avoid laughter, so true to life are the caricatures of these maniacs. The contrast between their distraction, bordering on insanity, and the suppleness which would be exacted by an attentive conversation leads us back to the very source of comedy.

At the rate at which this immense fresco, veritable circular panorama, develops, the manias become more evident, while the facial features are engraved in more incisive lines. Saint-Loup, likened to a fencer, becomes agitated, entering and exiting at top speed. In *Le Temps retrouvé*, the Baron — obese, bloated, fallen — has definitively taken on the air of a women incapable of controlling her appetites. Thus, characters whom we knew when they still were relatively well balanced, evolve in the direction of their manias and vices which, in the beginning of the novel, were sometimes barely indicated. The caricatures become gigantic. The events themselves rush down a steep slope, follow each other in ever faster succession toward the end of the novel in the midst of concentrated developments of a highly sensational nature: marriages, reversals of social status, unexpected revelations, everything concurs to confirm the impression of precipitous development in people and in things.

Proust has been reproached for having thus moved away from verisimilitude. This is possible. But what grandeur this exaggeration of movement lends to the dénouement without detriment to reality! In the final scene of *Le Temps retrouvé*, where all the novel's characters — aged, so utterly changed — are gathered again at the Prince de Guermantes', there remains almost no life, no motion in them. Little by little, the mechanism of habits, mannerisms, ready-made phrases, has invaded their entire being. Nature, like "Pompey's catastrophe, like the nymphs' metamorphosis, has immobilized them in their accustomed movement," the first form of death. Comic to a supreme degree, but in that macabre mode of comedy which would often be suggested by cadavers, if we were not almost always seized by pity or horror in their presence. Here, symbol replaces reality.

* * * * * *

At the other pole, the pole of life, opposing these obsessed creatures who are so close to the tomb, Proust has — lest we forget — brought onto the stage the radiance of the young women "in a budding grove." Adolescence does not lend itself to comedy. This is so since adolescence is precisely that unique moment where life appears in its perfect mobility, when the profile is not yet entirely frozen in features which allow "no more surprises"; when it is impossible to perceive in constantly renewed gestures one who is already dead, who can be imitated and laughed at.

One of the most beautiful pages in Proust's work shows us Marcel proclaiming his enthusiasm for Albertine's naked body. Before the outstreched young woman, he forgets the transformations she will undergo, and for the first time he celebrates life in one of its human forms. Proust writes: "...Adolescence precedes total solidification, and that is why one feels so refreshed in the presence of young women...a freshness which evokes that perpetual regeneration of nature's primordial elements that one contemplates when facing the sea."

272

Character Types and Traits of Character

If Proust were but an amusing author, he would only succeed in the creation of purely imagined characters, of generalities: gamblers, Tartuffes, scatterbrains, bores or affected persons. The defect would absorb the personality: the character would be identical with the quality which gives him his name. One says: *L'Avare* (The Miser), *L'Etourdi* (The Scatterbrain), *Le Tartuffe.* Apart from the defect, everything else would remain in shadow.

None of these traditional and classical types is to be found in Proust's work. Even in secondary figures, who only fortuitously appear, like Forcheville, Mme de Sainte-Euverte, Ski, Saniette, it can of course happen that an isolated, distracted and crystallized emotion dominates the field of their consciousness; however, they never are just this particular emotion incarnate. Always, at a given moment, Proust establishes a communion between such an emotion and the remainder of the Self; he feels the need for endowing them with a soul, a bit of his own soul. Forthwith the unique type is effaced: a true human being takes its place. A little farther on, the comical type may reappear. Similarly, according to different moments of our lives, we enter our intimate depths, our profound Selves, or, on the contrary, we externalize ourselves in Society with its inane chit-chat.

Consequently, if I wish to narrow down (as I will attempt to do below) the comical types that Proust liked most to depict, it must not be forgotten that these types do not really exist as such in his work. They are always completed, substantiated, substained by a complex and profound consciousness. Hence, they are not precisely types of character, but *character traits* which Proust has

273

described and blended in the gravest of psychological analysis.

* * * * * *

One dominant trait haunts without exception all the *personae dramatis* of this imposing and new human comedy, Proust's work: vanity. Bleating and agitated, they follow like a flock of sheep the indifferent and invisible shepherd who guides them to snobbery, the small landed gentry as well as authentic dukes, bourgeois who pretend to disdain the aristocratic *salons*, as well as applause-hungry artists, the recluse, the idle, men-about-town, the great courtesans, domestics who, under their colorful livery, swell with pride in their master's name, even the most depraved beings, the rejects of a society to which they still cling, such as "the Marquise," concessionnaire of the street lavatory, who chooses her clients and does not accommodate just any comer.

Typical sentences, what one might call "famous words," or again little farcical scenes, depict Cottard's character. "One Wednesday, their old cook having cut the vein in her arm, Cottard, already attired in his dinner jacket ready to go to the Verdurins', had shrugged his shoulders when his wife timidly asked whether he could not bandage the wounded woman: 'But I can't, Léontine,' he had whined, 'don't you see that I am wearing my white vest?!' In order not to upset her husband, she had hastened to send for the professor, head of the clinic."

On other occasions, Proust attains the tonality of grand comedy. He likes to oppose man's selfish emotions, when facing death, to his vanity. One recalls the touching scene where the Duchesse de Guermantes, when getting into her carriage to go to a dinner, learns from her best friend, Swann, that he has not long to live. Although she is very late, she hesitates for a moment between her worldly obligations and her humane duty. It is the former, however, that wins out, and without taking time to be moved, the Duchesse leaves Swann for the party where she is expected. A saddened Swann stays a few moments immobile on the stoop. But the Duchesse returns. Has she felt remorse for thus leaving her friend? No. But the Duke, noticing her black shoes, has told her ill-humoredly that she could not wear them with a red gown, and that she must put on more suitable footgear.

Scenes of this nature are extremely numerous in Proust's work and as diverse as his vainglorious types themselves. And in the endless chatter of his characters, in the faithfully reported petty gossip which may appear idle and fastidious to a superficial reader, Proust nonetheless rivals, thanks to his concern for general truth, the great memorialists of the 17th century: one thinks of La Bruyère as well as of Saint-Simon.

However, the most extraordinary figure that Proust has drawn of a vainglorious person is that of Baron de Charlus. His nobiliary self-esteem goes so far that he judges aristocrats of the oldest lineage unworthy of being invited together with him, and that his demands for exclusions from evening parties which he attends estrange the host from his best friends. Carried away by his megalomania, he renders himself in the end unbearable in his own milieu.

But if Charlus stands out in high relief from the novel's framework, already taking his place among the great figures of literary invention, it is because Proust has added to his personality many another ridiculous trait: while presenting him as proud to the point of madness, he turns him into an almost epileptically irascible personage, into a sodomite and, finally, into a bashful lover. The powerful

275

realism and the comedy of this magnificent individual derive less from his particular faults, taken one by one, than from their unexpected encounter in one and the same person.

* * * * * *

As one progresses in *A la recherche du temps perdu*, Charlus makes us aware of a new comic character trait: sexual inversion. Very close to tartuffery, this morbid instinct is seen by Proust as another type of obsession, isolating the individual from his fellow humans and marking him with all sorts of absurdities. In certain of his aspects, Charlus resembles a vast puppet. We gain this impression from his jerky speech, his cutting gestures, the entire defence mechanism he has built up to conceal his tastes.

Bergson suggests that all unbalanced individuals of the same species, i.e., all violently comic characters, "are inclined by a secret attraction to seek out each other's company." Such is the case of homosexuals. Although they fear to be even more compromised by their own kind, and though they sometimes avoid each other, they instinctively flock together and form a true sort of secret society. Thus Proust acquaints us like a biologist with the principal varieties of the sodomite species. But his always complex characters, while homosexual, exhibit other amusing features. Saint-Loup is a liar, Nissim Bernard a crude bluffer, the younger Courvoisier a bewildered simpleton...

Thus Proust has traced an infinity of comical character traits, without forgetting professional deformations: Brichot's professorial gravity, Dr. Cottard's callousness. Proust's contempt for physicians reminds me inevitably of Molière's.[1]

---

[1] Cf. a very curious study by Dr. Mauriac that was published (Ed. Grasset) regarding Marcel Proust's relationships with physicians.

In the end, the principal characters, Swann, Charlus, Saint-Loup, all addicts of their loves, do not make us laugh any more, but they move us. They are no longer general types. They have regained their individuality.

Comedy of Style

On the whole, this aspect of comedy which is created by words — no longer through their literal meaning — cannot be translated from one language into another. It is linked to the very essence of a particular language. It appears always there where supple and living thought is not rendered faithfully, and with its precise nuances, within the mold of the sentence. If the latter were ideally modelled on the incessant progress of the mind, nothing in a given style would seem funny to us. But it constantly happens that words produce double-entendre, that slips of the tongue falsify the sense of a discourse, that metaphors are taken literally, in other words, that certain terms, pronounced, spontaneously disguise the thought of the speaker, just as the maniac's gestures disguise his psyche.

There is first of all the vulgar *pun.* When Mme de Cambremer comes to pay Proust a visit at the Palace Hotel in Balbec, the page-boy calls her Mme *Camembert.* He deforms her name, of course, but, in doing so, he has found a mnemotechnical device for retaining it; it functions so well that, when he is corrected, he repeats and prefers his mistake, because of "a need for logic and clarity that it satisfies." The play on words here exceeds being a mere joke.

Often it becomes the involuntary idiosyncrasy of a character. Thus, semantic "near misses" occur in the spoonerisms of the manager of this same Palace Hotel at Balbec. He gets embroiled in two neighboring euphonies, and commits laughable malapropisms, without realizing it. Speaking of the "hotel's page-boys," he declares that these children are "busybodies" (*faiseurs d'embarras*) meaning to say that they blocked (*embarrassaient*) the passage.

* * * * * *

Parody is very close to punning. It always produces the amusing effect caused by a similarity. It repeats in a different tone (burlesque or, on the contrary, grandiloquent) an idea which was originally expressed in a natural tone. A poem is written in the lyrical style which is appropriate to the subject treated. To cause laughter, it would suffice to take up this topic again in a style either more solemn or more familiar, but in any event in such a manner that one recognizes fully a transposed copy of the original poem.

It is a device which Proust has used very frequently, and in all sorts of manners. He writes, for example, about the rigid faithfulness which Mme Verdurin exacted from the aficionados of her Wednesdays: she told them, "like the Roman empress, that she was the only general whom her legion had to obey, like Christ..., that he who loved his father and mother as much as herself and was not ready to leave them to follow her was not worthy of her, that instead of wasting his strength in bed or letting himself be hoodwinked by a whore, one would do better staying with her, her, the only salvation and the only sensual delight." Triple parody: of Caesar's military style, of Christ's evangelical style, and, finally, of the impression often given by Baudelaire's poetry. Thus Proust achieves the tone of the heroico-comic poem, which consists in systematically treating minimal matters as though they were grandiose. But, as always with him, comedy serves to put forward a psychological truth. In this instance, Proust attempts to show by the very exaggeration which lies at the bottom of this parody, to what an extent Mme Verdurin overrates the importance of these social events; that she had totally lost all sense of relative values.

Often Proust proceeds by transposing onto a page written in familiar style, solemn verse borrowed from classical tragedy, without so much as changing the original text. This time, the effect of his comedy goes farther: he wants to prove, for example, that the High Priest Joad's way of teaching the queen distrust does not greatly differ from the way in which a humble chambermaid speaks to her mistress. When Françoise says, "Flatterers know how to arrive and heap up money; but, patience! some fine day the Heavenly Father will punish them accordingly," she expresses a wisdom which could come from the lips of an old politician.

These transpositional games, so frequent in Proust's sentences, even in his Nature imagery, even in the description of a bunch of asparagus — are never used better than when he applies his style to the study of homosexuals. In the presence of the young men of an embassy, "M. de Vaugoubert [took on the astonished air] of Elise in Racine's *Esther*: *"Heavens! what a numerous swarm of innocent beauties / Crowds in on my eyes from every side / What amiable modesty is on their faces depicted!"* Thus, thanks to his parodies, Proust gives us to understand that love provokes in everyone the same reactions, the same lecherous glances. What varies are the frames, the setting (today a drawing room, formerly a palace), the social circumstances (here one hides from Society, there one brags before others). But passion always evolves within a consciousness in accordance with a well-defined rhythm:

crystallization, jealousy, anxiety are in every single case the profound elements which constitute it.

Finally, it is Proust's penetrating philosophy that we encounter again. Shifting so frequently from a tragic style to a burlesque one, from one level to the other, Proust felt above all that Society may well create separations and classes, attaching great value to them, in this schematic and abstract division; life, however, real life, appears always as a unique and spontaneous undercurrent. In spite of rigid settings which appear contradictory, all true movements of the heart, no matter how diverse, flow toward the feeling of anguish which endures as long as the individual's life lasts, and which is only extinguished in that eternal rest, so sincerely awaited and desired by Proust toward the end of his existence. It is perhaps the thought of the inanity of all things and of nothingness which is at the basis of all Proustian comedy.

* * * * * *

From semantic "near misses" and from parody it is but one step to metaphor.

Metaphor is almost always made of plays on words, words taken in their figurative sense. But ordinarily it is not comical, since it is intentional on the part of the author and expresses his thought — without any possible doubt — very precisely.

On the contrary, in Proust's style, frequently the difference separating puns from poetic images is effaced. The reader comes to hesitate between the amusing and the poetic effects, to discover, in the end, that they are both intimately linked. This is so, since the comparison, without losing its artistic beauty, remains a sort of burlesque transposition.

These metaphors which, more or less developed, can be found almost on every page, at first sight certainly do not appear imbued with an entirely original spirit. They exist, for instance, in the German Romantic humorist, Jean Paul Richter: "The sky began to change from black to red, like a boiling lobster."

Many contemporary writers use similar means. Here we recognize a modern trend which perhaps originates with Lautréamont. The black humor of his style goes beyond simple parody. His comparisons carry us from the level of reality to the ideal plane, from the level of logic to that of absurdity. He was beautiful, he writes, "like the meeting of a sewing machine and an umbrella on a dissection table." The surrealists, for their part, have pushed metaphor into the domain of dream. Metaphors create in their poems strange fusions or doublings of imagery. They give the impression of that abracadabra logic which is that of our dreams. If these poetic images can provoke laughter, it is because dream is an essentially comic phenomenon: the distracted mind ceases to model its ideas on tangible things, and sees before it the things it conjures up.

Proust's metaphors are certainly closer to surrealist imagery than to Giraudoux's fanciful images, the source of innumerable imitations. The latter are invented above all in order to surprise the reader: they exploit unexpected, pleasant and superficial details, held in common by two objects as dissimilar as possible.

As a matter of fact, Proust's images remain above all entirely Proustian: unconsciously, no doubt, he suggests in all his transpositions the profound identity of beings and emotions. Listening to the horn of an automobile and that of a Wagnerian orchestra, he rediscovers those musical emotions which fill him with identical vibrations.

But even more than evoking the unity and vanity of all things, Proust's metaphors produce new visions. His imagination splits even the closest association of images — of an object or a spectacle — breaks those bonds which habit maintains between them and recreates them, by using another formula, bringing into being new associations. His goal is to introduce us to a half-fantastic universe. And comedy is naturally added to it: "The artistic genre," he himself writes, "acts in the fashion of those extremely high temperatures which have the power of *dissociating* combinations of atoms and of *grouping* them in accordance with an absolutely contrary order, responding to a different type."

He compares to a Cotillion leader the Princesse de Guermantes, who receives him at the entrance to her drawing-room, and who, in order to greet him, executes a very graceful movement, "by the vortex of which," writes Proust, "I felt carried away." And he adds, "I almost expected her then to hand me...a cane with an ivory handle, or a wrist-watch." Listening to music in an elegant restaurant, each motif, as intimate as a woman, "suggested the secret of a sensual delight, ogled me, came toward me with a capricious or vulgar gait, accosted me, caressed me..." At this period, music occupies a minimal place in his makeup. The most vivid images are drawn from his artistic consciousness. This explains the magical and constant transformation of musical motifs, and how they can assume the form of adorable faces of women.

Once again, we leave the domain of true comedy. What remains of the style is but a quivering of colors. Metaphor, though unexpected, is molded on thought. We penetrate the very heart of life. It appears to us in its full wonder and cruelty.

I think that, with the distance in time, it is above all Proust's gift of poetic re-creation which will stand out as his dominant quality. Today, he is most of all admired for his powers of analysis. But as much as the latter, his style reveals an enchanting and quasi-unbelievable ambiance, slightly comical, also in the sublime vistas it opens on dream...

Comedy of Plot

Comedy of plot resembles that of style. Just as laughter springs from every malapropism, from each semantic misunderstanding, it appears every time that events permit any kind of confusion, are reversed, equivocal. It may be surprising that in Proust's novels, despite the seeming absence of action, there exist so many amusing combinations of facts, so many droll "situations". It is because the action evolves slowly, in vast meanderings, that nonetheless, it gives birth to a number of tributaries. Between the amply spaced lines of his plan, Proust has constantly inserted new stories. They are now simple anecdotes, then again vaudeville sketches, or scenes of grand comedy. Thus a thousand independent little sub-plots guide the reader from the most facile slapstick comedy to the most refined forms of the comic mode.

Each storiette serves as a sort of particular example of general remarks made on a character or a fashionable *salon*. We are given something amounting to proof by way of action. As to comedy, Proust seems to come upon it in his path, by chance, adding it on piecemeal to these short scenes.

Here, for instance is one, destined to illustrate Legrandin's snobbery. M. Proust would like Mme Proust and their son, who will spend their vacation in Balbec, to be put in touch with Mme de Cambremer, Legrandin's sister.

The latter, however, fearfully shrinks away at the very thought of having to introduce these mere bourgeois to an aristocrat. Yet, as a matter of courtesy, he does not want to refuse openly. M. Proust insists: "Do you have friends in those circles...?" "I have friends in all places where there are wounded but unconquered troops of trees which have grown together..." and Legrandin, in order to avoid a direct answer, launches into a nonsensical description of nature. "That is not what I meant to say...I was asking whether you know anyone there [in Balbec]?" "There as everywhere else, I know everyone and no one..." Thus two wills enter into conflict. One has the impression of watching a jumping jack spring out of his box, enter it again when one closes its cover, and come out of it once more, when one opens it.

It is a common device in Molière's comedies. Famous lines like "without a dowry," "And Tartuffe?" "But what the devil was he doing there?" which at regular intervals interrupt a character's discourse, imply in equal parts an emotion ready to explode and the adversary's will to attempt to contain it. In Proust, this type of scene is less synthetized than in Molière. It represents, nonetheless, the simplest form of situation comedy.

* * * * * *

With *chassés croisés*, elaborately choreographed changes in events, we reach a higher level of comedy. In the normal course of life, one can never go back. Facts follow an irreversible course. If the situation is brusquely reversed, it becomes funny. Thus Mme de Cambremer has been trying for a long time to make the acquaintance of Charlus, who to her mind represents the climax of elegance. She is invited for dinner at the Verdurins. "Furious about compromising herself [by going to that bourgeois event],...she arrives,

284

haughty and morose..." Suddenly she notices among the guests the last person she expected to meet this evening, the Baron de Charlus. Abruptly displeased for having shown her bad humor, she changes her facial expression at once. Like a thief who is robbed, a trickster duped, she is tricked by her own stratagem: disdainful, she is punished by her disdain. It is a typical vaudeville scene.

Proust seems as delighted as a child when he encounters these minute artifices, combined by chance. To the author's joy, unexpected meetings, coincidences, occupy an important place in his books. In the intangible and living continuity of human affairs, they reveal to him the intrusion of a mechanism that allows us to penetrate to the very core of life. "...Existence is hardly worthy of interest except on days where the dust of reality is mixed with magic sand, where some vulgar incident turns into a fabulous novelistic spring." It is then that we enter "an inaccessible world," where we find individuals whom we believe we can never see, except in dreams.

This is what happens to Proust on the day he takes a walk at Balbec in the company of Elstir. At the end of the avenue, he notices the small party of "budding" young ladies whom he has so longed to meet. All humans believe in chance, but they imagine that luck favors certain men, harms others. How mistaken can one be! Lucky circumstances intervene in equal parts in everyone's existence. It only happens that we do not know how to take advantage of chance, so we let the unique opportunity slip by. What we then call our bad luck is not due to external events, but to our own fault. We prefer, however, to attribute our faults to a fatality, and, rather than accusing ourselves, we complain about destiny.

This is the story told by Proust. He is so sure, now, that Elstir will introduce him to these coveted young ladies, that he stays somewhat behind, lingering at an antique dealer's shop window, and, ready to feign surprise, he awaits being called. Certain of seeing his good fortune materialize, he feels his luck already being compressed, diminished; it appears insignificant to him. Suddenly, he decides to turn around, and he sees "Elstir standing several steps father away with the young ladies, saying good-bye to them." "All was lost." As soon as the satisfaction of his desire is relegated again to the unknown, it is reborn, stronger than ever. Thus, not only does it not depend on us whether we benefit from a situation, but, in addition, we ourselves to a great extent create this situation. According to our feelings of anxiety or security, love varies, desire rises or falls.

While extracting these general remarks from this story, Proust has used it for its comic effect. We recognize, as shown above, a sequence of inverted facts. Feigning not to attach any importance to being introduced, he falls into his own trap. It is a game often replayed by Proust.

Quid pro quo, too, is one of his favorite devices. He extends it from words to events. He presents a situation in such a way that the spectators attribute an imaginary but verisimilar meaning to a given event, while the reading public or the other characters of the novel see it in its real light.

Thus, the Princesse de Luxembourg, heavily made up and followed by a black page, crosses the hall of the Palace Hotel in Balbec. In a corner of the hotel, a group consisting of the wives of the notary, the President of the Bar Association and the Presiding Judge assume that she is a courtesan. The reader, however, and Proust know her true identity. On this fundamental idea develops the *quid pro quo*: the wife of the judge fancies that the name "Princesse de

Luxembourg" is a pseudonym. As a matter of fact, she commits the same mistake with regard to the Marquise de Villeparisis, this time for the opposite reason, since the Marquise is modestly dressed. "Wasn't I right to be on my guard!" exclaims the magistrate's spouse.

"Moreover, one must not believe," writes Proust, "that this was a momentary misunderstanding like those which are produced by the second act of a vaudeville show, only to be dissipated in the last act." Proust himself explains that the short vaudeville sketch which he has staged has a profound and general import. He adds, "Mme de Luxembourg, niece of the King of England and of the Emperor of Austria, and Mme de Villeparisis always seemed (to the notary's wife and the judge's) to be two strumpets of the species that, in spas, it is hard to keep out of one's way. Three quarters of the men of the Faubourg Saint-Germain, in the eyes of a goodly portion of the bourgeoisie, are seen as penniless scoundrels...who, consequently, are undesirable, not received anywhere by anyone." The short scene shows to what an extent "the two worlds [of bourgeois and aristocratic societies] hold a chimerical...view of one another." The group's opinion on the individual, and the individual's opinion on the group are almost always erroneous. Society rests not only on hypocrisy but also on non-recognition.

Moreover, if the friends around us and, above all, the woman we love, change according to our moods, our desire or our indifference, they are modified, too, by our social milieu from which we perceive them: depending on whether we are on the same level as they, whether we look at them from near or far. Artists, who, upon closer acquaintance, almost always disappoint their admirers, are a striking case in point. This perspectivism serves Proust in another way. He gives us to understand that Mme de Ville-parisis, who had maintained social relations with the great writers of French Romanticism, judged them exclusively from the viewpoint of high society: "When Vigny is mentioned, she bursts out laughing, '...In any event, he was of very humble origins, this gentleman who in his verse has spoken of his 'nobleman's crest.' How tasteful!...M. Molé, had as much wit and tact as M. de Vigny had little of both these qualities....'" The different opinions uttered by individuals about the views of others give witness to the same type of misapprehension. And quite a comedy is played in the Prince de Guermantes's drawing rooms when he takes Swann aside for a long conversation. Since the scene takes place at the time of the Dreyfus Affair, and since Swann is a Dreyfusard, all the guests surmise that the nationalist Prince will expel Swann. Actually, the Prince wanted to corner Swann to tell him that he no longer believes in Dreyfus' guilt, but that he had hidden his opinion from his wife until the day when he learned from the parish's curate that she, like himself, and in the same church, had lit a candle in penance.

* * * * * *

In another form of *quid pro quo*, frequent in Proust, it happens that there are no longer two milieux (the bourgoisie and the Faubourg Saint-Germain) or two different persons who attribute a double meaning to an individual or to his gestures. Instead, one and the same person, placed face to face with the same individual is somehow led by some misapprehension to see two distinct personalities, then to "recognize" his mistake and fuse the two personalities into one, again.

Thus, after some hesitation, the narrator will "recognize" in Rachel — the ideal woman, whom Saint-Loup has depicted to him as his mistress — a prostitute that he had met, several years ago, in a bawdy-house, and who had been nicknamed "Rachel when of the Lord."

Such *"recognition"* scenes are innumerable in Proust's books. In the surprise they cause, he discovers his greatest pleasure: the intervention of the marvellous in everyday life. "I began to find," he writes, "that these moments of 'recognition' would express...an important part of life, if one knew how to go to the very heart of what is truly novelistic."

More often than not, illusion derives from the dual perception of the same person at two different periods, remote from one another. Life passes, and we forget that people change in their external characteristics as well as in their status. Among the friends I have known at the age of 20, one, a Jew, has converted to Catholicism; another, a Sybarite, has turned into an ascetic; the latter, once lazy and indifferent to fame, has become the most active of all stage directors. Thus it is in objective reality as much as in our minds that men are modified into different persons, in accordance with the unforseeable course of life and of circumstances. But our distracted mind is forgetful, or sometimes, when we have lost sight of a friend, it is incapable of parallelly modifying the image we have kept of him so that, when we suddenly meet him again, we cannot adapt our thought to the new image, and hence we often feel compelled to laugh at it.

When Proust learns that Elstir is none other than M. Tiche, an erstwhile "faithful" of Mme de Verdurin's "Wednesdays," he asks himself, "Could it be possible that this man of genius, this sage, this recluse...was the ridiculous and perverse painter formerly adopted by the Verdurins?" And Elstir's example helps him to understand that the evolution of life is precisely, for superior beings, enrichment due to experience, the attainment of wisdom. This explains why Elstir had been in his youth a facetious Bohemian, whose memory he would wish to see abolished.

* * * * * *

Alas! the flow of life is also the aging of human beings. In Venice, which the narrator visits many years after Albertine's death, toward the end of his quest for "Le Temps perdu," he finds it hard to "recognize" in a stunted little old woman devoured by eczema, the Marquise de Villeparisis, whom from his childhood, he had considered an old lady. Time, in the end, is the most active agent in this general modification which human beings undergo in our minds as well as in themselves. How many events have passed since the moment when Swann fell in love with Odette! Swann's death. A new century. A World War. "Recognition" then becomes a sort of hallucination. The mystery which comedy frequently adds to existence, ends in a quasi-tragic vision. Aghast and discountenanced, Proust roams among all the persons he has known as young and very different people.

However, a great joy is going to console him and restore his equilibrium. He has just made a philosophical discovery, which will be the guiding idea of his oeuvre. He understands at last the role, the meaning, the value of time. The study of Proustian comedy will have led us to this conclusion.

3. NOTES ON PROUST'S GIFTS OF COMEDY

Those who were personally acquainted with Proust know that the author of that vast psychological comedy, *A la recherche du temps perdu*, was in no way a wit. He even despised coiners of "witticisms," so numerous in high society, and whom he ridiculed in his work.

Proust was too much interested in real life to waste on trivial language games the precious time he needed for observation and documentation. Of course, as soon as any conversation takes a pedantic or sentimental turn, one wants to abandon seriousness for jesting, but "witticism" soon becomes tedious, since it is a purely verbal exercise.

And yet, Proust showed an interest in the very form of sentences. He found etymologies most exciting. However, when he favored them with his attention, he did so not out of vanity or to obtain a droll effect, but in order the better to understand and use the very instrument of his art.

Unlike the "wit," he attempted to get to the core of thought by way of its form.

* * * * * *

Nonetheless, someone who is not a wit may have a keen sense of comedy, through acute observation.

Observing human beings had become Proust's true passion. Conversations with his friends were in fact lengthy interviews, in the course of which his extraordinary memory recorded the thousand stories he insisted on hearing told in all their details. Anecdotes interested him not for their surprise endings, but for their didactic value, for the psycho-

291

logical insight which they provided. During World War I, while he was more closely confined than ever to his sick room, despite his seclusion, he took notice of changes in feminine dress and in those of the general mentality (the latter having become jingoist, germanophile or hypocritically prudent).

While endlessly questioning his friends, he tirelessly demanded to hear the latest gossip. He closely watched their idiosyncrasies without their noticing it. Thus, he meticulously recorded each of their gestures and tics, the stuff of which his charming "imitations" are made.

It is well known that, in his youth, he took delight in "imitating" acquaintances before the *monde.* In later years, only his chamber-maid Céleste and a few intimates were regaled with his impersonations of Montesquiou or some other typical figure. Thus he mimicked the comedy of his characters before jotting it down in his books. He gave himself a sort of dress rehearsal prior to the *première,* which began when he took pen in hand.

There is no doubt that extremely stupid people, too, have the gift of imitation, but their talent of observation is almost unconscious. On the contrary, Proust, when playing these games, was laying the groundwork for his novel. Even his most superficial entertainments are made to serve his art.

* * * * * *

Proust has been accused of maliciously "caricaturing" those who formed his inner circle. Absurd reproach, resulting from the public's total ignorance with regard to the artist's process of working. It can be asserted emphatically that there is not a single real character, not a single *personnage à clé,* in Proust's work. There are perhaps, I dare say, character traits drawn from real life. Yet, even this is not entirely true. A certain mania, such as, e.g., Mme Verdurin's laugh, is borrowed from the laughter of a variety of personages: it is a composite of several comic types observed and synthesized.[1]

Yet, how often will I still hear these questions: "Who is Bergotte? Is it Anatole France? Vinteuil, is he Debussy? Elstir, Monet? Berma, Sarah Bernhardt?...Is the Cathedral of Balbec that of Chartres or that of Rheims? Did Mme de Ch. serve as the model for the Duchesse de Guermantes? Haas, the Jew, member of exclusive clubs, great aficionado of horse races, of carriages, amateur of true elegance, and in love with every woman — is he Swann? But is Montesquiou actually Charlus? Yet, Montesquiou was above all a poet. In Charlus, not the least trace of the man of letters. Montesquiou was lean, tall. Charlus is obese. His physique would rather remind us of the Baron Doisan, who frequented the same *salons* as Proust. Could Mme Verdurin be Mme M.-D.? Odette de Crécy, Clos Mesnil or Laure Heymann? Saint-Loup, that charming Fénéon, who disappeared during the War?..."

* * * * * *

These questions are meaningless. M. Brunschvicg, who was a classmate of young Proust's, said that he had recognized himself in Bloch. Is M. Brunschvicg therefore Bloch? This deduction would be absurd. He has all the qualities of tact, of modesty, and reserve which the blundering, pretentious, vainglorious, ostentatious Bloch totally lacks.

---

[1] Proust himself has expressed his views on this subject, in a dedication to M. Jacques de Lacretelle, which has been partially reproduced in M. Benoist-Méchin's study. He took this topic up again in the second volume of *Le Temps retrouvé*.

Is it true that the entire conventional aspect of Proust's characters is painted from life? But the author has achieved such associations of traits, and has regrouped them in such a way, that it is in the end impossible to cast any one person in the role of any famous name.

More than that, the majority of the comic characters, as I have said before, also has a distinct psyche, a psyche which Proust alone was able to give them. There is consequently a bit of him even in those characters who seem the farthest from his own personality. To the question, "Is Bergotte Anatole France?" one might rightly answer: "No, he is Proust." Yet time, which ranges writers in the order of their value, with every new century disarranges the scale of these values, just as, every hundred years, the map of the globe is changed by wars, revolutions, discoveries. The failings of our judgment are particularly noticeable in matters of aesthetics: since we need a stable criterion for judging, we depend on the verdict of posterity, the only one we know, although it is fickle, and, if not well defined, of very little significance. The legacies which are transmitted by generations are saved from destruction by mere chance, rediscovered in excavations, or again are preserved for extra-artistic reasons, because of their documentary, historical, or religious interest. As proof I offer the large number of works, which for tradition's sake are held in respect, and which are known, if not always understood, by a few specialists. How many of the titles that one finds in a history of literature correspond to books read nowadays even in classrooms, by students, even by an intellectual elite?

When we honor the memory of an ancient author, this does not prove that he has any real worth. The judgment of posterity is meaningful only when future generations can savor the same pleasure in a book that its first readers had discovered in it. Then the work of art continues to be moving: it remains real.

4. A LASTING WORK OF ART

Two years ago, when I published a book on Marcel Proust, I was essentially reproached for my essay's "Proustolatry."[1]

There are undoubtedly reservations that one must have about Proust's oeuvre, as about any work produced by human intelligence: a remark which is a truism. Thus, certain artists have striven for an impeccable form, like Heredia or Mallarmé, and, sacrificing breadth for quality, have hoped to succeed in writing at least one perfect sonnet. They have always failed in their enterprise, unable as they were to avoid a repetition of words, a weak rhyme, a banality, or some other imperfection. In writing my monograph on Marcel Proust, I had set myself to no other task than to jot down the lively sensations which I experienced while reading his work. That I abstained from determining the limits of the text studied, does not mean that, for this reason, I believed in its perfection, and I never dreamt that my silence would be interpreted as a dithyramb.

It is true that, for certain minds, discussions on the value of a work represent the principal object of criticism. However, I do not believe it possible to rank writers, nor

---

[1] The word was coined by M. René Johannet. On the other hand, M. Paul Souday — one of those rare critics who exercise a certain influence on the public's opinions, and who, consequently, represent public opinion — has found "some èxaggerations" in my book; he also feels that I "do not totally avoid hyperboles."

to grade them like students' compositions. But this is the way the public currently proceeds. Saying, "This author is much greater than that one," amounts to the same as giving the former an "A", the latter a "C". This type of *quantitative criticism* ought to give way to *qualitative criticism* which would define the unique personality of each artist, and rather than judging his work, would empathize to the point of "recreating" it.

If a hierarchical classification of these diverse, delicately shaded analyses were needed, it would develop by itself. Time alone will gradually choose between these allusive documents. Each generation with its idiosyncrasies, seeks food for its own aspirations, for its particular needs, in a work of art from the past that was not made for it. To lend itself to these successive interpretations, a work must contain a *wealth of potential meanings.*

It can also be said that, if a work is of lasting value, this is largely due to a refusal to appeal to superficial and ephemerally faddist notions, but instead to those truly great, primitive sensations which continue throughout the ages in human consciousness. In other words, the work of art must retain a certain universal character.

And the more generations that will have succeeded each other through history, or the more readers that will have multiplied in space across different countries — each of them finding in the same work of art the two essential traits of a wealth of *potential meaning* and *universality* — the more this work will yield profound insights, power, worthiness. Without intending to offer new suggestions here, these are my views on the ranking of works of art by the influence of time.

Will Marcel Proust's works be entered in this category of great books which through the centuries nourish the human mind? How will posterity judge him? Are they destined to last? In other terms, do they lend themselves to a variety of interpretations? What is the measure of their universality?

5. DIVERSE INTERPRETATIONS

My impressions have often varied. I was lacking the perspective that only years can provide. It is certain that, when *Du côté de chez Swann* appeared, those rare fervent admirers of the book — among whom I count myself — had no idea of its importance. It was then believed that the author clung to the most minute details of daily life; it escaped understanding that his analysis was not a scrupulously cut slice of life, of the external world, but that it decomposed reality in order to grasp it in all its depth.

A few years later and up to the present, Proust's enterprise seemed to me one of the greatest efforts to renew the French novel, but destined, nonetheless, despite everything, to remain in splendid isolation, and without any influence. I saw in him, above all, a point of arrival. Proust went, seemingly, too far in depth for anyone to surpass him in the same direction. And whoever cannot be overtaken finds only servile imitators. In fact, to my knowledge, he had no disciples. The handful of writers to whom he was compared were unable to create works independent of his oeuvre; or else they had briskly broken with him. His books remained, for me, without a necessary link to our period.

But today, while I still do not believe in their direct influence on literature, I think that they have made contact with the younger generations. For the last two years I have noticed that they have brought new literary sustenance to young readers whom I had thought hostile, to young people who are considerably different, no doubt, from those who discovered *Du côte de chez Swann* in 1913. The new literary sustenance is itself quite different from the one that has nurtured me up to the present.

This is as good a place as any to stress what exactly separates my interpretation from those of minds who are out of touch with mine. It will be noted that there are no contradictions arising from diverse manners of understanding Proust. It is neither the obscurity nor a lack of precision, but the wealth and depth of content of Proust's novel which explain the constantly renewed sensations, images, thoughts that can issue from it.

* * * * * *

How I Understood Proust

My interpretation of *A la recherche du temps perdu*, it appears to me, is very close to the author's thought. Here it is again, supplemented by the meaning of *Le Temps retrouvé.*[1]

First of all, we must return to Proust's life, which itself sheds light on his books. It is known that his existence was characterized by his total self-sacrifice for the sake of his art. After having passionately worshipped the *monde*, its comings and goings, amusements, love, he gives up everything: he locks himself up in his retreat, to dedicate himself to the work that he bears within himself. In *Le Temps*

---

[1] I apologize for seeming to praise the book I produced on Proust in 1925. I feel, however, obliged to state that I had anticipated the meaning of *Le Temps retrouvé* after reading the first volumes of *A la recherche du temps perdu.*

retrouvé, the author confirms this essential aspect of his life. He tells us how his duties toward his art have gradually replaced his worldly obligations (refusal of an invitation from Mme Molé; dispatch of a letter of condolences to Mme Sazerat). "Even at home I shall not let people come to see me while I am working, for the duty of completing my work takes priority over that of being polite, or even good." Thus he elevates to the highest degree imaginable the artist's sense of responsibility.

To so high a degree that, feeling his novel as a potentiality in his mind, but not yet materialized – it needed "perhaps a hundred, perhaps a thousand" nights – he fears that "an accidental shock" might destroy his body, and that his mind "whence life is withdrawing, would have to lose its grip on ideas which it is embracing at the moment." In *Le Temps retrouvé* he pushes even farther the drama of this struggle between the artist, eager to complete his work, and the disease that is progressively undermining his efforts. In the end, it would seem that he can only envisage artistic creation as something closely linked with the idea of his approaching death. He no doubt does not convert his particular case into a universal model. However, he does think that he can write only once he feels "indifferent towards everything, [aspiring to] nothing but rest, while awaiting the great repose which would eventually come."

The idea of renouncing all passions and joys of living came by degrees to coincide with the idea of death. The latter, writes Proust, "took definitive possession of me, just as a love does. Not that I loved death, I detested it...," but "I could not take any interest in a thing without having it first filtered through the idea of death!" "...The idea of death kept me company as incessantly as the idea of myself."

301

However, at the time of which Proust speaks, when he began to write *A la recherche du temps perdu*, i.e., several years before World War I, the disease which had always tortured his body did not yet threaten his life. The idea of death haunted him not because death, in fact, was near (death came almost fifteen years later, in 1922): it came owing to a disposition of his mind, that had abandoned all yearning for life. Proust himself explains this attitude: it was not a number of mishaps ("impossibility of walking down a staircase, of remembering a name...") "which through reasoning, however unconscious, had caused the idea of death," but it was his mind which "reflected a *new reality.*"[2]

An old problem — nowadays banal, but nonetheless anguishing — has bothered artists for a long time: how to reconcile a taste for living and the need for creating one's work. Life exacts all the energy the individual can muster. A passion becomes rapidly exclusive, allowing the mind no rest. Money that brings with it an ever-increasing lust for money, occupies all our moments of activity, after which we remain little more than mere bodies, tired and impotent. Ambition, which rapidly grows into an *idée fixe*, limits us to the superficial aspects of things and we lack the freedom as well as the indispensable perspective to create an inner life for ourselves. At the age of 20, I encountered an embarassing, somewhat childish dilemma: was I going to be the irresistible lover who, in a lavish apartment, sunk in a cosy arm-chair, awaits the mistress of his dreams? Or would I be the penniless young man who, in a cold, narrow room reads the last pages of a novel of genius to a friend as impecuneous as himself? This

[2] My italics.

question still haunts young writers whom one might believe to be the most cavalier when confronted with scruples of this order. "Today," writes Henry de Montherland, "producing a masterpiece seems to me a waste of time, a *mistake.*" He adds, "Balzac, Flaubert, noble pot-bellies bored at your desks; you have failed your lives." Drieu la Rochelle, taking up the same notion and using the same example, asks himself, "Does it really matter that Balzac, vis-à-vis the Marquise de Castres pushes to the limit the absurdity of which an intellectual is capable, if, later, his Duchesse de Langeais seems more real than the live model?...I found it harder to accept this fact." And Drieu la Rochelle finds himself on the horns of the same dilemma: "Now I wanted to write, now again to live."

Is this conflict between art and action an artificial one? Rich temperaments, like Barrès or d'Annunzio most of all, have refused to opt, i.e., to renounce either one of these two modes of life. However, did they fully succeed? I think not. Did not those nineteenth-century poets, for instance, who were passionately involved in politics, generally cover themselves with ridicule? In the Renaissance a Leonardo, later, a Goethe — only such men of exceptional genius — have achieved a harmonious development of their numerous faculties.

Proust seems to have found an original answer to this disturbing question. The first thirty or thirty-five years of his life were given up to amusements, to laziness, and it is this laziness which, perhaps, saved him from becoming a facile writer. Then, taking leave of social life, he entered the closed domain of art. Thus living successively the one and the other mode, he was spared the need to choose between them. And this all the less, since he had abandoned worldly pleasures for an infinitely higher sphere, that of literary creation. But what is essential and peculiar to his attitude is that, while he gives up ordinary everyday life, while he associates the idea of artistic creation with the notion of death, he does so because he has found yet *another* concept of life. The death that is haunting him is the death of appearances, the death of those ties that fetter the individual, while by his art, he penetrates a new, more profound existence, a *real* existence which endows him with "eternal value."

This reality, so beautiful, and unknown to the majority of mankind, a reality to which he has given himself entirely, this goal of his life, is also the essential object of his research as a writer.

* * * * * *

Proust's principal contribution is perhaps his way of introducing a new psychology into the novel. Not one which goes farther than that of other writers, but a different psychology that uses a modern method: Bergsonian thought. He looked at human life not only from the point of view of social time, of scientific time (where one hour equals sixty minutes, without variation), but also from the perspective of inner duration (where one minute of boredom is the equivalent of one hour, one joyful hour equals one minute). Years, months, days, in other words, recorded *time*, official time, is calculated by the Earth's revolutions around the Sun, taken as our point of reference. This notion of time is an artificial abstraction, a product of intelligence. It is used by humans in their social life, in the common celebration of holidays, in the general observance of a weekly day of rest, in regulating mutual undertakings, in remembering not to miss a *rendez-vous*. This is also the idea of time that scientists use for their calculations and in their projections. In addition, as soon as the individual's

304

consciousness is posited as a fixed point, there exists, however, still another concept of time: this aspect, Bergson calls *mobile duration*; it can expand or, on the contrary, contract, according to our innermost sentiments. It is somehow the continuous gushing out of all our feelings, all our images: our true and deepest Selves in perpetual evolution. Proust was the first author to study this phenomenon in the novel, and to focus the instruments of introspection on it.

By situating man and society in mobile time, Proust lets us catch a glimpse of the hidden reality of life. All studies of consciousness, and in particular the great neoclassical studies of the seventeenth century, may be considered as not being situated in this ever-changing duration, but in fixed time which is assumed to be forever equal to itself. Many writers have doubtless attempted to show that a love is born and dies, that a passion ages. But almost always this passion is studied *in isolation*: an entire character is constructed around it and made out of *one or two* characteristic and simplified *traits*; the character evolves solely at the rate at which this trait or these two predominant traits are modified. The remainder of the self remains unchanged. On the contrary, in Proust the *whole self* incessantly undergoes transformations. Not only is each feeling mobile to such a degree that it becomes almost intangible, but moreover it *blends with other feelings* in the individual's consciousness, which, itself, never remains static for even two successive moments. Proust has "decomposed," "demultiplied" the human personality. He has subjected it to a dual uninterrupted process of aging. In the midst of this universal motion, he is searching less for an analysis of this feeling or that one, than for a way of recording differences. He remarks that his love for Albertine becomes successively sensual desire, annoyance, jealousy, the impression of absence, an obsession...etc. But in those same successive moments, he takes a total inventory of his personality, unable as he is to separate the love he feels for Albertine from the musical impression of Vinteuil's septet, from his desire to pay Mme Verdurin a visit, from his discoveries about Charlus, from the joy he experiences when contemplating the sea's horizon...etc.

Proust's psychological method is indeed original, based on an intuition of duration. He specifies in *Le Temps retrouvé* in other terms — which, however, have the same meaning as mine — his own manner: "a sort of *spatial psychology*," "contrasting with that *plane psychology* normally used" in neo-classical studies which sound the human psyche.

Plane psychology, since time as it was generally considered by novelists before Proust, remains almost always time in the abstract. Their characters indeed can jump from the age of twenty to that of forty without really aging. Within a framework calculated from the motions of stars, i.e., of mathematical time, they pass through different stages, but their consciousness is not aware of these displacements. They have evolved outside themselves, following their calendar, while staying internally *immobile*.

Proust, on the contrary, is concerned above all with the manifestations of this aging process. It is precisely because of his lively preoccupation with the phenomenon of the individual's aging that he is determined to write and to direct his research toward this particular mystery. His decision to write was triggered by a visit he had paid to the Prince de Guermantes, where, after a prolonged absence, he meets again all the characters of his novel, more or less greying or completely white-haired, as though disguised by old age and so utterly changed that they seemed no longer to have anything in common with the young men and women he had once known. (This final scene of *Le Temps retrouvé*, which provides the key to the work, is also one of the most poignant and successful ones.) I make this remark for those who, failing to see the significance of this immense fresco, suggest that *Du côté de chez Swann* contains all of Proust's thought, and that after this book the author has continually repeated himself with less talent: a reflection as absurd as that of a traveler who, after having seen the lateral portal of a cathedral, claims that it is not worth while looking at the façade, since the whole building, uniformly Gothic, can but repeat the same ogive pattern throughout. Proust writes about this extraordinary fête at the Prince de Guermantes's: "Then I, who from childhood on have lived from day to day...perceived myself for the first time in the light of the metamorphoses which had taken place in all these people, over the time that had passed for them; a realization which overwhelmed me through the revelation that time had also passed for me... And now I understood old age...[and thus] the meaning of death, love, the joys of the mind, the usefulness of pain, of a vocation." Upset by this impression and by the suggestive power of these images, he decides to compose his book...

How will Proust express this process of aging, life in its most hidden workings? Precisely through *spatial psychology*, by a multilevel psychology. Since it is impossible to grasp the flux of aging directly in its mysterious flow, a type of lock-gate must be constructed all along the river, at varying intervals, to allow the study of the current and to penetrate down to the river bed. The diverse aspects of the current, all differing from each other, will reconstitute the very impression of mobility, of the aging process itself. Multilevel psychology is based on cinematographic technique, on a sequence of still images which produce by their succession the illusion of movement, i.e., of reality. By contrast, when using "plane psychology," the writer — instead of projecting a movie before the reader's eyes — only presents him with a discontinuous series of single projections, according to the old principle of the magic lantern. Thus, he obtains luminous images, which may have a beauty of their own, but which remain isolated, immobile, "frozen".

When Proust sees again M. d'Argencourt ("the fiercest face, the shapeliest torso was little more than a limp boiled rag, restlessly driven to and fro"), he reflects: "How many *successive stages* of a face I needed to traverse if I wanted to find again that of the d'Argencourt whom I had known..." When Proust wants to resurrect with maximal intensity a character's face — not the schematic design of a face, but the real face which ages, participates in the vital flux — he analyses in depth in different passages of his book, each single one of the principal "successive stages" of this particular face, or at least the most typical ones. This "spatial psychology," used to evoke tangible things, is likewise applied by Proust to a character's mental life, to his consciousness. Thus, he will try to make apparent in every character the most contrasting faces, to make the volume of these faces appear as a solid.

Defining in *Le Temps retrouvé* even more concisely this multilevel psychology, he writes, "Individualities...in this [his own] book were to be made of numerous impressions, which, taken from many a young woman, many a church, many a sonata, were used in the production of a single sonata, church, young woman..."

What is perhaps most striking about this method, is the manner in which these successive aspects act and react upon each other. Every new image of a character that is offered to us recalls a preceding one, which it contains. Thus, each chapter sheds its light on past events, transforms them, rectifies them. In the most recent volumes (*Albertine Disparue* and *Le Temps retrouvé*), the plots, the actions intermingle, move away, draw nearer, alternate continually.

Skillfully and firmly in control of the means of creating a sort of joyous and enchanted excitation, the author precipitates the events, multiplies the sudden changes in fortune at the rate at which he approaches the conclusion. The insignificant Mme Verdurin, who received only a few "queer" characters, becomes the Princesse de Guermantes! Gilberte, whom we saw as a child playing at the Champs-Elysées, marries Saint-Loup, who is suddenly unmasked as the emulator of his uncle, Charlus. Sometimes just a few sentences suffice, phrases which in the beginning would have furnished the subject matter of a volume. And from the marriage of Gilberte is born a girl as enchanting as Gilberte herself. *Coups de théâtre* succeed each other in an ever accelerated rhythm.

In many novels we are brought up to date by a five or six page epilogue which briefly summarizes the fate of the principal characters. But the epilogue is almost always a kind of useless addition. Even if they bear the same names as the novel's heroes, the characters have nothing in common with those whom we treat as familiars; they remain as indifferent to us as people mentioned in a news item, summed up in three lines which may appear to us either curious or laughable, but which do not move us. In Proust, the end is not this sort of banal conclusion that amuses and satisfies the reader's curiosity, but the final metamorphosis is of his fictional characters. From then on, three or four words on their final destinies carry for us almost infinite resonances, evoking, as in a hall of mirrors, a long series of images: their past. Likewise, in everyday life, the gravest news is brought to us in the simplified form of a telegram, a single phrase, or a simple interjection. And these abridgements which overwhelm our consciousness, represent often the most tragic facts of our lives. This is so, because "plane psychology" can only show us the fictional characters in one, or sometimes several isolated moments of crisis, which are relatively unrelated to each other: moments with interspaces during which the personae dramatis no longer really live. In Proustian psychology, it is precisely in the conclusion that the characters become truly three-dimensional: there they stand out with the greatest degree of intensity and depth, thanks to the different simultaneous levels on which we again perceive them.

At the end of the work, the cycles are closed again. The avenues, which in the first tome led in all directions, giving rise to the belief that the work was constructed without any inherent order — a censure which rightly exasperated the author — now meet again, to form a single intersection.

"Life incessantly weaves mysterious threads between human beings," Proust writes, "between events...it interlaces these threads...redoubling them in order to *thicken*[3] the plot to such an extent that between the least point of our past and all the other points a rich network of memories leaves us only with the choice of communications." "Le côté de Méséglise" and, by a detour, "le côté de chez Swann"

[3] My italics.

lead to "le côté de Guermantes." Proust calls this, "to prepare one's book...with perpetual regroupings of forces, as though for an offensive." The traffic circle towards which the diverse roads converge, or where almost all the personae dramatis of the novel meet, is that scene at the Prince de Guermantes's (which I have mentioned already) where the author realizes the existence of internal duration, which here manifests itself as aging, the only absolute notion. In this sense, Proust appears to me, by his life as well as by his oeuvre, above all a "realist". (A dangerous word considered by the public to be synonymous with "naturalist" and one to be easily assimilated to materialist. But this vulgar meaning is but a deformation of this term.)[4] When Proust, in order to characterize his work in a letter to a friend, uses this expression, "It is an extremely *real* book," he wants to say that, beyond customary appearances, which every one of us encounters every day, beyond lazy visions, beyond nominal time registered by clocks, he introduces into the novel true time, that time which gives rhythm to the stream of our consciousness; he enters that reality in depth, irreducible from life itself.

* * * * * *

The quest for "reality" leads Proust to the realization of relativity. If real time, the time which elapses in us, is absolute, then everything else is relative. It is the individual's innermost life which represents the ultimate truth for him, while our superficial sensations deceive us.

In his work, Proust will thus achieve a "transcription of the world which perforce [will be] quite different from

---

[4] "Realism" in this particular sense, is little more than the name of a literary school, whereas the term has primarily a psychological and metaphysical significance.

311

that which is given us by our mendacious senses." And he will try as often as possible to replace their testimony (what he sees, what he hears...) by states of consciousness (by what he experiences). In order to understand that Albertine whom he adores, or in order to explain Swann devoured by his passion, he will not look at them from the outside, but analyze his own impressions. Seldom will he describe Albertine by a series of *notations taken from without* on the color of her hair, her gestures, her way of speaking: instead, he will revive, in certain hours of his existence, those moving memories he has kept of her. Instead of making altogether relative observations, he will resort to introspection, which will bring him — as though in a trance — close to the reality of life.[5]

Proust himself writes that he is led at times to put onto the face of a female passer-by, in the place of her nose, her cheeks and her chin "...an empty space on which plays at the most a reflection of [his]desires." Then again, he is tempted to consider the body of a beloved woman as consisting only of sexual *memories* which prolong "[this] cherished body into the order of time." And this is so true that, once the body perishes, the lover's memories, too, will soon perish, and it is because this female body will cease to exist in the lover's consciousness, that it will absolutely cease to exist. When Proust, at the end of *Le Temps retrouvé*, retires within himself, he will find that "man's length is not that of his body, but that of his years," in inner duration. By means of all these images,

---

[5] When Proust, instead of engaging in psychology, concentrates on the comical aspect of his characters, he proceeds — as we have seen — exactly in a reverse manner, and, abandoning introspection, he then contents himself, on the contrary, with observing the significant gestures and aspects of people.

he explains that the individual as a whole is real only in as much as he lives on in our memory.

When Proust, in a work of art, relies all the same on his senses, in order to compensate for the relativity of his perceptions, he superimposes on the same face (as I have said) "a hundred masks" in succession: according to his vision, the particular moment in time, the direction of his focus.

Thus, Proust has discovered "relativity" on the level of psychology. Once this relativity is recognized, its importance and scope must not be exaggerated. Einstein's formulae, for instance, help us to understand the mechanism of the universe and its vertiginous problems; Newton's laws, applied to the solar and terrestrial systems alone, remain nonetheless valid for our ordinary calculations. Likewise, traditional psychology, with its fixed values, continues to be true, as far as man in general is concerned, as he goes through life remaining practically identical to himself, while Proustian mobile psychology attempts to explain him, as he appears in ever changing moments, in the unfathomable mystery of his self.

* * * * * *

Proust applies this new psychological method to the individual as well as to the social consciousness, which, in fact, still nowadays remains little explored.

Thus, I see still another contribution, which I wish merely to point out, a contribution that is more specific and more limited, but equally profound.[6] Proust was the first to point out the totally unsuspected or unavowed extent of sexual and secret passions in society. If he limits

---

[6] Indeed, I cannot take up again here the chapters which I have already written about *Sodome et Gomorrhe* and *Les Salons*.

313

himself to the simple statement that homosexuality today is a mysterious human disease, he assigns to it, on the other hand, an important role in collective life: it extends its effects throughout all layers of society, into politics, into the arts, into the *salons*, into marriage. Nobody, since the Marquis de Sade, had dared lift that hypocritically veiled side of human activity. Proust's boldness was all the greater, since he brought to light a little known aspect of the human heart, while simultaneously explaining the social impact of these passions.

In *Le Temps retrouvé*, Proust courageously even enters upon a study of sadism. We see Charlus in a specialized establishment, chained, and attaining orgasm by the same psychological process which an adolescent undergoes with a girl. Proust believes that, through no matter what sexual deviation — abnormal, bestial or ridiculous as it may be — man always instinctively proceeds to the same idealization of the object of his desires. Whether it be the bell-boy of a hotel or a princess, a brute armed with a whip or an animal: the lover will always endow the beloved with charm and radiance. What matters is the transformation that we impose upon reality, to the point of re-creating it completely; to the point of turning a monster into a ravishing beauty. Thus, if our own thought, our inner life, did not constitute almost all our desire, these passions would be inexplicable.

Here I would compare Proust to Freud: the Viennese scholar, by revealing the role of sexuality, has opened new avenues to psychiatry. Likewise, Proust, by insisting on the moral and social importance of homosexuality or sadism, has widened the domain of literature. In his various disquisitions on Proust, M. Edmond Jaloux has grasped and made comprehensible all the consequences of this innovation, all the psychological undercurrents it reveals, and how, by overturning this first barrier, the study of the human heart can take an unexpected, marvelous, thrilling turn. Is not literature destined, like the ocean that gradually encroaches on the cliffs, constantly to appropriate new terrains to the detriment of blindness and ignorance?

A New Interpretation

These are the discoveries which I made in Proust's work. I admit that I was fairly surprised when other readers recently communicated to me findings entirely different from mine.

The diverse generations of contemporary youth have at least one tendency in common: a mysticism stripped of any religious faith, or even antireligious. From Rimbaud to surrealism and certain still younger groups who are just now beginning to express themselves, a reaction is voiced against the great current of nineteenth-century scientific fervor, which leads, via Taine and Renan, to the skeptical intellectualism of an Anatole France. Denial of traditional forms of beauty, disorder of the mind considered to be sacred, dream images and images suggested by the unconscious declared to be the only source of art: all these judgments imply, on the part of their promoters or their adepts, a hatred of reason and of clear ideas and a taste for inspired quests ("Oh, thinking is unworthy," exclaims Rimbaud!). These various disciples of Rimbaud ought to feel quite remote from Proust, who only experiences complete satisfaction when he has brought the light of analysis to illuminate a confused feeling, and when he believes that it has been exhaustively clarified. In fact, today's young mystics hold all "psychology" in utter contempt. Those who love vagueness, the ineffable, the absolute, can hardly savor any relative results, of which Proust's books undeniably represent the prototype.

But it is precisely the character of great books to accomodate the most contradictory interpretations. They bring nourishment even to those who do not understand them: they force their admiration.

What the new contemners of reason discover at first in Proust is his poetry. What they admire above all is his gift of transposing everyday aspects of life into an unreal atmosphere, his eminent skill in re-creating things or elevating extremely banal events onto an epic level. Thus a walk on the Avenue des Acacias, a season in a Palace Hotel, a reception in the *monde* of the Faubourg Saint-Germain become, through the "recherche du temps perdu," events in fairyland.

The Romantics and the "naturalists," who at times are Romantics, too, have no doubt poetically enhanced certain aspects of the external world. In *L'Assommoir*, Zola transforms a still into a monster with tentacles; Victor Hugo succeeds in depicting a small house, lost in the night and where there is a wake for the dead, in such a sinister light that it becomes an immense monument. But by this procedure, Zola as well as Hugo attempt to lend a soul to inanimate objects, and, above all, to endow them with human intelligence, evoking by the still a symbol for alcohol-poison and for intoxication-decadence; by the isolated hovel the symbol for death. Hence, their amplification serves a moral or sentimental end, which lies outside the object under conideration; it is a means: poetry is here merely added.

Proust's manner of re-creating the world is quite different. He wants to give a profound and exact representa-

316

tion of it. He is concerned with the object in itself, nothing but itself, and if he carries it to the level of the fantastic, he does so in order better to apprehend and to depict it. The poetry which emanates from it, then, is gratuitous like contemporary lyricism. Proust becomes the creator of a truly modern epic.

Nothing is more striking, for example, than the description of a dinner of his hero with Saint-Loup, at Rivebelle, in a fashionable restaurant near Balbec. The narration sounds like a fairy tale: the tables figure as planets: "...an irresistible magnetic force played among these diverse stars... The harmony of these astral tables did not impede the incessant revolution of the countless waiters...their perpetual race...ended by revealing the law of their vertiginous and regulated orbits." The entire evening takes place in this unheard-of and supernatural setting. On rereading Proust, I notice that the author enraptures us continually with the preternatural, which becomes one of the most important aspects of his work: the hero went to the theater to see a performance by la Berma; while waiting for the curtain to rise, he watches the audience: it is metamorphosed into a sort of legendary arch. On the first balcony, ladies in low cut gowns with brilliant and spangled bosoms, but whose lower body is hidden by the front wall of the loges, appear to resemble those oceanic nymphs whose tempting busts are complemented by a fish's tail concealed by the waves.

How is it that this psychologist, fond of concise observation, can leave the impression of being a kind of surrealist, a creator of dreams? Because, at the depth where Proust explores the world, reality is no longer that cohesion of conventions which common sense accepts without hesitation: it forms a world apart, singular, strange, mysterious, which varies with each individual, and which, when revealed, achieves stupefying images, often close to hallucinations.

* * * * * *

These remarks become even more forceful when Proust speaks of his own emotions; be it by describing the mirages of somnolence, of brusque awakenings, of nightmares; be it that he entrusts us with the surprising effects of his affective memory, e.g., in the classical scene of the "madeleine" or in the chapter on the "Intermittances of the Heart," be it while he is stooping to tie a shoe lace, when he realizes the vacuum left by the death of his grandmother, and when he feels for the first time the reality of suffering; be it that he tells of his love for the "budding" girls, and that, playing "who's got the button" with them on the cliffs, their simple presence rather than a conversation about art with Elstir, endows him with the richest, the fullest, the truest instants of his life; be it, finally, that he narrates his extraordinary ravishment with the flowering apple trees in spring, where he experiences Nature as a whole. He might compare this joy with the aesthetic happiness which he felt before a masterpiece of painting or while listening to Vinteuil's music.

In their wide diversity, all these emotions have essentially one common denominator: they cause the individual to participate in a hidden and intuitive reality. It is in such moments, that today's youth feel for a second time close to Proust; it happens when the author seems to commune with superior forces that surpass him. These instants are the summits of what might perhaps be called his mysticism. Thus, Proust succeeds in satisfying by other means than poetry, those who are fascinated by a sense of the ineffable.

This time, again, there is no contradiction: personally, I was mainly interested in his analytical method which cuts out and fragments the outer shell of things. But I understand perfectly well that others might rather cling to his results which aim to seize sentiments *in nuce*, in their irreducible essence. As to Albertine's love, for instance, I was first captivated by its successive phases, so marvelously described. Now I can concentrate on the intensity of this passion which transports us beyond ourselves to a point where we experience the absolute. Generally, I had looked at Proustian images from an aesthetic distance, reuniting them in my mind and comparing them to a magnificent storied cathedral, each level lit by rows of windows. Today, I see this cathedral with a thousand precise facets as it towers toward the heavens. No longer earthbound, it is detached, as it were, from the ground daily trampled by our feet. With its spires, it touches mysteries of infinity.

Scholars like Berthelot, philosophers like Renan, Taine, Le Dantec, Ribot, believed that the world resembles a vast machine. They have envisaged it as comparable to certain church clocks, whose gears in all sizes keep in motion minute ships' planespheres, human automats, and reproduce on a reduced scale, and very faithfully, the tidal system, the movements of the Earth and the stars, foresee leap-years. For these minds (who have been called "scientistes") there exists no mystery that would not be solved some day. They feel no anguish, since they hope that some time in the future they will leave their present ignorance behind. Consequently, no mysticism is possible for them.

Proust's attitude is almost diametrically opposed. He admits the existence of the soul and the mind. He believes that there are more things in heaven and earth than we can dream of. He thinks that existence itself is full of the un-

319

known and the forever unknowable. And it is the unknown that attracts him...in all its forms: in nature, in the joy of love, in the shock of involuntary memories, in the extravagance of dreams. Those "scientistes" had assumed the universe to be an immense house made of transparent glass. Proust imagines it as a garden filled with shadowy shrubs. He stops in front of them. He allows himself to be carried away by all those spectacles whose mystery inspires him, uplifting him, in a way, to a state of inner, sacred trembling.

In *Le Temps retrouvé*, he writes that he wants to create a world *"without leaving aside THOSE MYSTERIES which can only find their explanation in OTHER WORLDS and whose life is in art."* A mystical interpretation of the Proustian oeuvre is perhaps not altogether excessive, since the author himself seems to confirm it.

However, it is not without extreme caution that one may move from the mystery which permeates his books, to the concept of mysticism. One may wonder, for a while, what is meant when Proust speaks (in the above quotation) of "other worlds". But this allusion to the beyond of past metaphysical systems comes to him with lightning speed and like a vague possibility. At no time does he develop this unexpected appeal of the "infinite" which remains so alien to his way of thinking. He posits a hypothesis. He neither accepts nor rejects it, but passes by with indifference. It is his intellect that dictated this sentence to him.

In fact, it has to be admitted that he never pronounces the word God. The religious anxieties of the individual soul leave him as indifferent as any established religious cult. For all religions appear to him to be pure creations of man, since they do not reach out for the profound realities of life, but instead yearn for a beyond. Now, death and

320

whatever may come after death are problems that never preoccupy or frighten him. He is anguished by life, never by the after-life. Immortality worries him so little that he hardly sees any other form of after-life than immortality on earth, than that of the work of art and of the artist's survival in his works.

Thus, if Proust is really a mystic, it must be clearly stated that his mysticism is that of life in itself, that is to say, a psychological mysticism. If it has been said that he wanted nothing else but to understand God, then it must be made clear that by the word God is understood actual time, the ideal gushing forth of consciousness, existence in depth. Hence, he has never sought to assay the mysteries of those Pascalian infinite spaces, but only finite ones, never the beyond, but only the present and the immediate. Beside this, he has chosen as his task much less to communicate with the unknown factors of life than to understand them. Not communion but the analysis of communion is his goal. If he feels and insists on sensing in the smallest events what is at first sight irreducible to thought, it is not for the pleasure of the impression, but for those events to count in his work and to give his work the character of immortality. And it is precisely this faculty which enables him to talk about any insignificant topic without sounding trivial or boring. If at the moment when the ocean, Venice, a piece of music vibrate in him with the mystery that emanates from them, he fails to analyze his impression to retain it in its plenitude and to recreate it in himself and then in his book: he then feels regrets which rapidly turn into intense suffering. There is joy for him only when the results of his observations are introduced into his art, when a state of affective intoxication is transformed into logical terms. Even at moments when he seems to surrender himself to Vinteuil's music, he observes his reverie: at every detour of his thought's flux he installs those lock-gates which I have mentioned, stopping points where he is obliged to control the rush of inner inspiration. In short, by slight alteration, he could have adopted Socrates' phrase to his own needs, and could have said, in life's most beautiful moments: "Forget thyself, but at the very moment of forgetting, know thy innermost self transfigured in art."

And art will never be pure surrealism for him: he does not believe that inspiration alone justifies the writer. He wisely blends sensitivity with reason. Proustian mysticism is counterbalanced by a strong passion for the intellect.

* * * * * *

The true mystic, on the contrary, only seeks the purely ineffable. If it is only a matter of ecstasy, where thought has of course not disappeared but has less and less value, there are a thousand ways of obtaining it: any intoxication, that of love or of hashish, of flagellation or of alcohol can procure it. Devotees of beatitude do not always reject such artificial means. If they avoid them, they do so hypocritically in order not to diminish the quality of their ecstasy. What does it matter if the latter is induced by drugs, or whether it arises spontaneously from a nervous excitement or from a physical infirmity? They obtain essentially the same ecstasy.

I would not condemn ecstasy as a momentary step backward toward a state of animality. On the contrary, I consider it a flight from consciousness and from the perpetual cares of life, as a moment of sleep without dreams, without hallucinations, without visions of Paradise, without expectations of a beyond. For me there is no true joy other than negative joy, that joy which gives us a foretaste of death, that is to say, of non-being. "Consciousness is an unchangeable function of distress," as Lessing puts it.

Proust categorically rejects all stimulants. If he speaks here and there with indulgence about the metamorphosed universe lightened by alcohol, of the joyous facility which alcohol brings him; if he contemplates lovingly the small phial which will provide sleep and forgetfulness, it is because he is instinctively attracted by these artificial pleasures, but he regrets them the following morning, and he disapproves of them morally. This condemnation is understandable: he is hostile to everything that suppresses consciousness and the possibility of analyzing it. He tells us, for instance, that he scorns drunkenness since it leads to "a purely subjective nervous tension which isolates us from the past." On the contrary, he wished to attain a "broadening of [his] mind in which the past would shape itself, actualize itself and provide — but alas! only momentarily — an eternal value."

Thus, what Proust seeks to achieve with ecstasy is the experience of intellectual lucidity. And we note once again, in speaking of his mysticism, to what an extent it is connected with his will, his thought, with life. If Proust likes obscurity, it is in order to enlighten it, to give it clarity.

Diverse Meanings of "Art" in Proust's Work

There is in Proust's work a particular domain, that of art, where the author's constructions offer, more than elsewhere, all sorts of modes of comprehension. Art, after having been the explanation of his life, provides the ultimate key to his novel.

Its significance appears distinctly in *Le Temps re-trouvé*. The call of the unknown which provokes in the author's mind the short phrase of Vinteuil's sonata or the "small expanse of wall painted yellow" in a canvas by Vermeer, in my opinion, is a divine call. Art replaces the absent idea of God in Proust's thought; it represents for him, in the midst of the universal flux of phenomena, the only absolute towards which the individual may aspire.

But the younger generations find an interpretation for Proust's art not only very different from my own, which I believe to be the one the author would have preferred, but, in addition, what is even more curious, a meaning which is almost contrary, almost hostile to his own.

For Proust, art, while expressing reality, simultaneously represents the only source of joy: of the only *true* joy, both human and superhuman. By the example of his life he has taught a great lesson, a *raison d'être*; likewise, he represents in his work a motivation for action, ideal action. He wasted his youth frequenting *salons*; he never believed in reciprocal love, except when he was watching Albertine sleep, immobile like a dead woman. But he discovers that life can be meaningful when he reads Bergotte, when he seeks to penetrate the secret of the beauty of Elstir's canvasses, or when, over many years, he deepens through Ruskin his understanding for the aesthetics of cathedrals, resuscitating them in the description of the church of Balbec.

Thus, I aver that Proust has used art both as the basis of his concept of the world, and, above all, as the foundation of his ethics. If he remains indifferent to, and does not revolt against the traditional laws of religious, bourgeois or social morality, nonetheless he creates for himself a personal set of moral values: the only moments worth living, he gives us to understand, we owe to art. Here, then, is a *raison d'être*, which may serve as a general rule.

This aesthetic morality is, with its respective nuances, that of most artists who today are roughly forty years old, and in particular that of the symbolists. I am thinking of Valéry, André Gide, Valery Larbaud, who, each recreating for himself his own morality, is fairly close to Proust's concept of art.

* * * * * *

But then came "dada" in 1917 and 1918, which destroyed the idea of Beauty in itself, just as the scientific hypotheses of the nineteenth century had already tumbled Truth in itself and sociology had dethroned commonplaces about Good and Evil. Art with a capital A was overturned as the last contemporary idol. However, since a void signifies nothing, a new concept of art took the place of the preceding one. Art for art's sake was succeeded by art of the unconscious. After Ruskin, Freud. Nihilists like the dadaists are not destructive: where they have undermined, they build scaffolding.

"Why do you write?" This question was the subject of a survey at the period when the little magazine called (by antiphrase) *Littérature* made its debut. At first, most of the interviewed writers were surprised, but in the end they justified themselves at length: art is our *raison d'être*. The dadaists wrapped their generally ridiculous and pretentious answers in sarcastic and insulting commentaries. I suspect that the young writers feel almost ashamed when they think about their artistic activity. "Forgive me for writing," implores Drieu la Rochelle.[7] "I write as fast as I can, and

---

[7] *Le jeune Européen.*

get a move on," shouts Philippe Soupault,[8] who at the moment of writing believes he is in a sort of prison. They all are obliged to admit that they write, that they can do nothing else but write. They are not proud of it, except if they make money, which, to their minds, justifies their authorial activity. Let it be well understood: it is not a matter of greed. Money becomes a moral justification. It is the exact opposite of the situation as it existed in the nineteenth century where an author felt dishonored if he composed books or a painter painted with lucrative ends in mind.

If art henceforth no longer appears to be the superior and unique end of the young writer's existence, it continues to be a means, the equivalent of many other means, which leads to an escape from the self. For them, art is not the only way, but one of the ways which lead to oblivion — a forgetting of ordinary life — and often to a kind of true ecstasy.

Thus, while the young literati debase art to an ordinary activity, Proust elevates it to the highest rung on his scale of values. The contrast seems total. However, we know that the riches of a work like *A la recherche du temps perdu* are such that the new destroyers of art find in art's greatest admirer impressions they can feel and accept. They neglect the idea of virtue which Proust attributes to art, the superiority he accords to the artist, the concept of beauty which he places on a supreme level. In short, they reject the author's moral attitude, but they accept, if I may say so, his use of Bergson's philosophy which guides him in his artistic quest.

When Proust concentrates all his strength on reaching beyond the daily routine and deceptive appearances for a

[8] *Le bon Apôtre.*

sort of "noumenon," the true substratum of things; when he does not imagine art without mystery, as a deep notation which touches upon an unknown reality, the young neo-Romanticists, surrealists or mystics of today sympathize with him: they find the way to the abolition of the Self, the great road that leads to the unconscious and to all experiences liable to result from it.

* * * * * *

Doubtless, I am mistaken when strictly limiting the notion of art to only two interpretations, one being essentially rational, the other, mystical. The generations that succeed each other in time, just like the minds that are distributed in space, present a greater diversity of trends and nuances.

Here are, for example, two small books, each of which expresses a personal appreciation: *La musique et l'immortalité dans l'oeuvre de Marcel Proust*, by Benoist-Méchin and *Le roman d'une vocation*, by Auguste Laget. The titles of these studies show no interrelationship, nor do the authors, who published, one in Marseilles, the other in Paris. The limited topic is different in both monographs, and so is the tonality, a trifle obscure in the former, very simple in the latter.

However, both of them arrive at the same discovery, which does not lack originality. Art represents for Proust, as I have said, a moral purpose, an ideal way of living. It also leads to an escape toward the realm of mystery. Laget and Benoist-Méchin see in it still another meaning. They remark that art, central to Proust's work, constitutes not only the very basis of his ideas, but the unity of the narration itself. It somehow intertwines with the entire plot. Events would reveal their true meaning only through reference to the idea of art, just as the colors of a painting would reveal their exact hues only when contrasted with the dominant background color. Let us take, for instance, the concept of love in Proust: Swann is really in love with Odette, his love is sincere and profound, only at the period when he savors and understands the famous short phrase of Vinteuil's sonata, when music exalts him. Later on, when his life is reabsorbed by the *monde*, he is no longer capable of being moved by Vinteuil's music; from then on, he is no longer able to love. Odette has become his wife, but this union is only the result of a weakness, almost a lapse; it has nothing in common with the former violent passion.

Thus, all of a man's actions can be judged by his attitude towards art — the true touchstone and talisman. The more a person is burning with artistic fervor, the more the other passions intensify by contagion, the more elevated he becomes by this very fact in other realms of activity. Miraculous potion of youth, beauty, life: art renews love, intelligence, work, nature, travels, desire...

* * * * * *

Is the demonstration I attempted to make definitively convincing? I could not affirm it.

Proust's books have been published too recently. *Du côté de chez Swann* appeared fifteen years ago, but *Le Temps retrouvé*, the necessary conclusion, has just reached the book market. The few successive generations, who, each in its own way, have given the totality of this long novel a personal meaning, are still too close to each other. Only after a longer space of time, when the readers' sensitivities and intelligence, modified by unforeseeable upheavals, continue to show an interest in a book which has preceded these changes, and still find in it a source of pleasure: only then can one feel certain that this work embraces material rich and general enough to endure.

However, the diversity of modes of comprehension which at present are awakened by *A la recherche du temps perdu*, the passionate nourishment which this vast series offers to curiosity in all countries, seem to prove already today that Proust's work will be long-lived.

6. UNIVERSALITY OF PROUST'S WORK

Without resorting to an objective critique, based upon the reception and interpretation of the reader, one may rely on another way of studying the value of a book; that is to consider it in itself and to examine the extent to which it reaches the commun fund of human feeling. The two methods complement one another: it is probable that a novel like Proust's, which satisfies the demands of greatly differing temperaments, encompasses precisely some of those general traits that are characteristic of masterpieces.

There is no truly powerful work that does not touch the psyche's essence, which is formed by primitive and simple passions: filial love, the maternal instinct, devotion, sexual jealousy, compassion. A drama, an epic, a novel, a study which does not cause that part of the self, common to all men, to vibrate, can of course be curiously original, or even technically perfect, but it will never be more than a tentative model, new in a very limited genre, and it will not belong to the true, aristocratic patrimony of civilization. Any real masterpiece, despite its philosophical or esoteric underpinnings, will succeed in moving the simplest readers, even a child, because it will have frozen a very general feeling in an artistic form. The *Iliad* touches us, because Homer sings about Achilles' faithfulness to Patroclos in the midst of the heroic furor of combat. Antigone moves us with her love for her family; Cinna with his generosity; Don Quixote, by his sense of sacrifice, although pushed to the extreme of absurdity.

Without attempting to establish comparisons between these works and *A la recherche du temps perdu*, one must concede that in Proust's work are found similarly vast currents of universal feeling. With the learned apparatus of the novel, Proust scrutinizes the simplest movements of the heart: the hero's love for his mother and grand-mother, his passion for an Albertine that absorbs all his thought. It is precisely through the portrayal of these elementary feelings which are at the roots of our nature, that the book has such vitality in its vast scope. If its import is not more widely felt yet, it is due to the fact that Proust hitherto has only touched a limited number of our heart's strings.

In fact, he has almost exclusively limited himself to the analysis of love, which he considers to be a sort of anxious need and which he sometimes compares to the child Marcel's anguish when his mother refused to kiss him. Moreover, in his diverse portrayals of passions, he neglects, for instance, the women in love. In his novel, only men love sincerely, forcefully, with pain. Perhaps Proust judges that mundane life becomes rapidly all-absorbing and that love is only possible between indi-viduals who belong to thoroughly different classes. This being the case, men alone have the facility to enter into liaisons with whores, peasant women, working girls, servants. Nonetheless, the gap left by the omission of women's love subsists.

Next to emotions common to all humans, what moves us most in great books is less the quest for a goal, for an ideal, than man's weakness vis-à-vis this ideal. A writer reaches the climax of pathos when he has us witness the failure of all the hopes of a hero whose ambition had been to act in conformity with a moral rule. There is nothing more beautiful or more striking in *Faust* than the moment when, in Gretchen's prison, Faust, torn by remorse, in vain calls the name of the woman he has abandoned; in *Hamlet*, the scene where, moved by pity before the king kneeling in prayer, Hamlet can no longer muster the courage needed to accomplish the mission with which his father's ghost had entrusted him; in Balzac's *Splendeur et misère des courtisanes*, the death of Rubempré who succumbs, not through ambition, but for having given in to all temptations, to all his desires, without taking social hypocrisy into account.

Proust takes only a fairly remote interest in these kinds of moral questions. For him, the duty which has priority over all others, is always that of the artist towards his work. The hesitations and the laziness of his hero, before he takes the decision to write, do not suffice to excite our emotions. In his books, Proust views all morality with indifference. This heedlessness somewhat lessens the humanity of his novel.

* * * * * *

It is worth noting that these general traits (great primitive impulses of the heart, man's attitude and debate vis-à-vis morality, whose presence seems to me the distinguishing mark of valuable works), are seldom to be found in so-called modern literature. The latter abandons more and more the study of emotions and passions, seeking instead extraordinary states of the mind at the very limits of consciousness. The younger generations attempt to find in desire, in hatred and revolt that which is so unnerving, creating such tension in them, that a point is reached where these feelings appear like kinds of reflexes; they become movements of fear, of horror, that translate into obsessions.... Today's psychology does

its utmost to put aside everything that is motive, or reflections, in order to concentrate on the most pathological
states of mind, and, by the mechanical interplay of images,
on naked instinct. It is positioned on the boundary which
separates reason from madness. It no longer sees anything
well-balanced in man.[1] It is also true that this new literature which seems to have reached a sort of culminating
point both in the subjects treated and in the form it uses,
is evolving at the same time towards a pure, ineffable,
prophetic poetry and towards a vast metaphysics. Will
this extremist movement serve as a point of departure for
a reaction which, while being inspired by what it will
destroy, will lead us back into the plenitude of literature?
Or will it continue for a long time to proceed on its present
course, as in the past, in, for example, the Byzantine movement?

This, however, is not the question. Let us simply note
that modern books show little interest in intellectual or
moral problems. For authors whose states of the mind are
confined to madness, there exists no longer any moral or
intellectual discussion; there is even no longer any duty
toward the authorial self; there is no longer any question
of strength or weakness of the will. On the other hand,
since a book must, after all, touch our sensibility, we find
that the new literati sometimes devote themselves to the
study of social problems, the class struggle, and racism. In
these studies, one discovers above all, developed in the
most varied forms, a woeful feeling of disquietude (Why
is man on Earth? To what dilemmas will civilization lead
us?). A goodly number of contemporary novels simply
mark a return to questions which beleaguer the fifteen-

---

[1] *Cf.*: Rimbaud in part, Lautréamont, Blaise Cendrars (*Moravagine*),
Ribemont-Dessaignes...

year-old adolescent when he enters adult life. Anguish is not a discovery dating back to the First World War, or even to the years preceding that war: what is novel about it is the intensity with which it is felt these days; it is no longer this or that manifestation of love, of friendship or ambition that is accompanied by anguish, it is anguish itself as a dominant force. Anguish is examined in itself, as a topic sufficiently vast and deep to serve as a source of inspiration and interest. Anguish is explored to such a degree of asperity and suffering that the handful of successful books will again by this very fact take on a human significance and tragic character which will lend them a grandeur that they will share with other, more classical works.

* * * * * *

I notice in Proust's novels some of the characteristics of modern fiction. His work draws its inspiration from the canon of classical literature, as well as from today's literary production.

To begin with, to a certain point Proust tackled social problems. The different classes perform in his novel within the framework of broad canvasses, not as entities, but with a life all their own. The bourgeoisie, the nobility, and farther down the scale, the domestic, constitute masses in constant movement. The great events of the century, the Dreyfus Affair among others, stir these *milieux*, displace their boundaries and their interrelationships and cause them to evolve. But since Proust envisages all these grave problems in the frivolous environment of the *salons*, his work seemed to be only that of a member of the leisure class. It is through a misunderstanding of the same nature that he was accused of being merely a *boulevardier*, mainly because he wrote for the *Figaro*. Forgotten is the Herculian labor he performed when confined to his room by his illness. In order to be convinced of it — not to mention the physical effort represented by the production of the twenty volumes of his novel written in less than ten years — it may suffice to peruse his translations of Ruskin; one can see the formidable *labor* of criticism and compilation involved, just by looking at the footnotes on each page. A mind as open as Proust's could not have misunderstood the meaning of "work". The daily routine of work is, no doubt, one of the means of better enduring life. Transformed into a mechanism and into reflexes, it allows us to fall into the numbness of oblivion, into a state of stupor; it causes us to lose the awareness of painfull consciousness. On the contrary, when one is driven to the point of feverish activity in artistic creation, or simply in strong action, it opens up the innermost depth of the individual, it becomes a means of escape from conventional habits — perhaps the surest and the most beautiful of all means of escape. In his novel, Proust has brought out some of the idiosyncracies of work, the professional imprint left upon the individual (on Dr. Cottard, or on the university professor Brichot, for example); its importance and its role in society (Cottard, petty-minded "petit-bourgeois," is transformed when he becomes a university professor, into a "grand-bourgeois," accepted and welcomed everywhere).

But there is one aspect of the question which Proust, in fact, does not cover: the "forced labor" of those who would starve if they remained idle. There are no manual laborers, be they workers or peasants, in his book. This absence is all the more striking after the First World War, when the necessity to earn one's living has now become a common concern for all of us. Yet, poverty and class struggle existed when Proust was writing, but they had not reached today's urgency. On this point, his novel remains partly situated on this side of an epoch where social instability, anguish and malaise could be ignored. Europe had then been living on its savings for a hundred years, had become rich and believed that it had prepared itself for an old age without financial troubles.

And yet, Proust has completed the last volumes, whose action takes place during and after the war, with considerations which liberally display irony on the topic of patriotism. He would doubtless have examined more thoroughly moral and social problems if death had not prematurely overtaken him on his work bed. Through the cork-lined walls of his bedroom, he would have sent out vibrations echoing the troubles of today's world, and his oeuvre would have been richer for it.

* * * * * *

On the other hand, I feel in every page of Proust's work a very modern anguish. From childhood on, the hero is tormented by nervous needs which his mother tries to calm by kissing him; he grows up and ages throughout the novel, in perpetual instability, whose painful nuances are certainly those of our day. Just as there is no minute fact in which the author does not introduce a sense of "mystery" with its extension into the infinite, so the slightest event is accompanied by an anguish which transforms the insignificance of a topic into a moving story. A project to travel to Venice, an arrival at the hotel in Balbec, an unknown beach, a short carriage trip with his mother and the Marquise de Villeparisis, a discussion with Brichot on the etymology of names of cities, an account of strategic theories by military men who are friends of Saint-Loup, no mattter which conversation, visit, or encounter is always linked at some point to that great human anxiety, the misery of living.

The words *"mal du siècle"* have been much misused in the last few years, and for a century now. Anguish is timeless; it takes on colorations particular to each specific period. I find in Proust the anxieties of love carried to such a degree of tension that these analyses of passion reveal above all our inability to love, our nearly total incapacity to escape from the closed system of the self, our solitude, our sad impotence. Besides this anguish of unhappy passion — the romantic type of anguish — Proust, the permanent invalid, the neurotically "anguished" sufferer, seeks at the very limit of psychological exploration, in sleep and in dream, in the most secret instincts, to question our ready-made ideas on the spectacle of the world and to plumb our continuous and miserable state of insecurity.

Thus, Proust's novel offers its wealth to yesterday's, today's and tomorrow's generations. Limited but durable, it proves to the scorners of our times, to the eternal Cassandras who, since mankind's beginnings, have been preaching its approaching end or decadence, that literature in our day is still widening its domain, since the last volumes of *Le Temps retrouvé* were only published yesterday.

PART FIVE

A NEW READING: TEN YEARS LATER

1. IMPRESSIONS FROM A NEW READING

For the past nine or ten years, I have not reopened a book by Marcel Proust. After having published the present monograph, I felt that I had sufficiently dealt with this subject; I admired the author as much as I had in the past, but I no longer thought about him.

One loves a book like a landscape or a human being; to live for a certain length of time with it is sufficient for the love to die down; its mystery has been dissipated. Then, once some time has passed, the desire is reborn to find the beloved again, to return to the scenes of our childhood, to confront old impressions of reading which have never ceased to change in us, with new impressions we may gain.

* * * * * *

It is not without apprehension that I re-read Marcel Proust's books: I felt at first embarrassed by the indifference of a part of today's youth for a writer who was uninterested in social problems, and I asked myself whether the younger generations hold too narrow a view of art, or whether Proust's work is lacking universality.

On the other hand, the criticism which has been levelled against the man, especially after the publication of his correspondence, it seems to me, cannot remain totally unanswered. At the beginning of this book, I have traced a portrait of Proust, focussing above all on the artist in him: his abnormal and irregular existence is explained by his disease; his difficulties with regard to practical action, his exaggerated politeness, the oddities of his character find

341

their explanation in the natural complexity of his mind and in his continually vulnerable sensitivity. The result is a sorrowful, immensely generous Marcel Proust who has little by little sacrificed all pleasure to his art.

I continue to consider this portrait as a fair likeness, but I realize that it is possible to draw another, perhaps equally true one. One can observe an author shut up at home with his work or, again, "in slippers" in his bathroom; through his work, or as his butler sees him. Must we interpret his excessive amability as a defence mechanism, as his means of escape; his all too flattering compliments not as a form of poetry but rather as a vain and perpetual "niceness"? Phrases which are recurrent in his letters: "Don't repeat that..." "Don't say that I told you...": his expression, "tomb," meaning "be quiet on this topic" – are such mannerisms the signs of a mind twisted by life in the *monde*? It is certain in any case that the secret which has weighed on him, from adolescence and throughout his life is on the order of those, as Proust himself has expressed it, which oblige the descendents of Sodom "to live in mendacity and perjury," "to disown [their] God," to lie to society, to their friends, to their mothers "even at the moment of closing her eyes forever." If Gide felt the need of proclaiming publicly his "corydonism," he did so because he felt his life being stifled by Tartuffery. Henceforth, can not certain of Proust's gestures, for instance his legendary tips, be explained independently of his generosity, by the pathological side of his nature, by his habit of buying inferiors, by his need to dominate and seduce them? If the already enormous tip seemed to him still not high enough, it was because he overestimated their value, and, considering himself their debtor, he added another sum of money in order to achieve the impression of "ownership" and peace of mind...

All the same, if these faults: snobbism and an unbalanced sexual life, characterized Proust, the man, they are of interest to the critic only inasmuch as they explain his work. It is first from this viewpoint, I admit, that I have re-read *A la recherche du temps perdu*. I picked up this work again, not as I ordinarily take a book off the shelves, with a preconceived sympathy, which is a promise of happiness in reading, but, on the contrary, with the prejudice of an adversary. I must hasten to say that the test was, once again, conclusive: my feelings of hostility could hardly resist Proust's extraordinary poetry, the depth of his analysis of sorrow, which seems to come close to the boundaries of life...

* * * * * *

Having depicted fashionable society from 1890 to 1920, Proust could not pass over the most poignant political events of that epoch: for example, the Dreyfus Affair and the war. Generally, it is only as a novelist that he studies their repercussions on the individual lives of his characters. But the War of 1914 occupies an important place in *Le Temps retrouvé*: now his personae dramatis approve – in the terms of the period – of the slogan: "to the bitter end"; then again, placed "far from the madding crowd," they heap ridicule on this cliché.

When the aristocratic officer Saint-Loup writes from the front that it suffices for wounded soldiers to learn, before dying, that the enemy trench has been taken, and they will expire contentedly with a smile, Proust declares seriously that he finds himself "in full sympathy" with this letter. If he has Charlus speak at great length in a "defeatist" spirit, he immediately adds that Charlus is "Germanophile," i.e., that he does not love France. The whole country is mobilised. There is unanimity in the people's feelings:

343

Proust bows to them, just as he would bow — as a matter of good manners — to a duchess. Patriotism is to his way of thinking something on the order of a true instinct of conservation, which every "living member" of a "nation" must naturally experience. I am not certain that Proust himself felt deeply patriotic, but since he found it suitable to be accepted as a participant interested in the conflict, he at least confirmed his patriotic feelings.

The forms and formalities of social respect thus being safeguarded, Proust has dared to deepen his analysis further: he establishes that patriotism, truly a passion, troubles our reasoning power and falsifies our beliefs. Affected by this blinding force, every Frenchman and every German thinks, in that broadened quarrel which is war, that right is on his side; he treats his adversary without scruple as "beast of prey," and he has been hoping daily, for two years now, that "the barking beast" (France or Germany) will tomorrow be "reduced to impotence." By contrast, the author believes that a Charlus, thanks to his detachment, is closer to judging the events with some degree of wisdom. And the reflections he lends him, (precisely because they are devoid of patriotism) seem to him closer to the truth.

For Charlus and actually for Proust, the war is a vast, generalized deception: has not Briand, Minister of Foreign Affairs, himself declared that in 1914, *all* countries believed they were attacked by their neighbors, and that they *all* fought only in defense of their illusorily threatened existence? This is what makes the war so absurd in the eyes of reason. Nonetheless, in the press, every day, states Charlus, brilliant chroniclers like Brichot and Norpois try to find new rationalizations for the onslaught which are lies and commonplaces: propaganda, this school of conformism, seems to have been born, in fact in its systematic form, during the first world-wide conflict. And Proust, choosing Charlus as his mouthpiece, proclaims: "The truth is, that every morning, war is declared anew."

The author's view of the "home front" is full of bitter irony. From the first pages on, Proust shows us the women transformed by their short dresses and their turbans, preoccupied with fashion and finery to "please the eyes of the warriors!" Mme Verdurin's *salon* has become one of the most elegant ones in Paris: "You will come at 5 o'clock to talk about the war," dictates the "patroness" to her guests. She considers the war as a "great nuisance," since it takes her "faithful" away from her. The presence of the Germans only 70 kilometers from Paris has changed nothing in the daily routines of most civilians. When Mme Verdurin learns during her breakfast in the morning that the *Lusitania* has been sunk, her face expresses first of all (though she exclaims, "What a horror!") the "sweet satisfaction" caused by the "savor of her *croissant*" dunked in her tea. The "horrible" event, of which she took notice only in a purely intellectual way, and which does not touch her directly, cannot, explains Proust, have any hold on her.

Such is the author's viewpoint on the war. Despite all declarations to the contrary, which he made in his letters, in order to remain a "gentleman," the war does not interest him; it does not count in the eyes of Proust, the artist. He sees it "on the scale by which...a tall man" would measure "infusoria," of which billions are needed to fill one cubic centimeter. The struggle between the French and the Germans is as far from his mind as would be that of the Frogs and the Rats in the Batrachomyomachia. He considers the grotesque little eddies of heroic combats in their relationship to the infinity of the universe and

345

concludes that men "are mad enough to pursue... their vain wars..."

Proust is not very sensitive to the profound reality of social life. The individual plays so important a role in his mind that he imagines nothing outside it. He believes that a nation is composed of a "sum" of individuals; he does not realize that, when men are grouped together, a new, collective consciousness, different from that of each of its members, arises, refracts itself in them, is added to their own individual consciousness, and imposes upon them moral obligations. Certain minds, leaders of nations, social reformers, are more moved by the realities which are represented by a nation, by a social class than by particular human beings or by specific aspects of nature. For Proust, on the contrary, the memorable dates of the Revolution or the Empire entailed of course a number of historical consequences, but they are much less important than the song of a bird or a breeze which have inspired Chateaubriand to write certain pages of his *Mémoires d'outre-tombe.*

Hence there is no reason to be surprised that Proust remained silent on the economic causes of the war, on the new rich, on inflation, on poverty, on the wounded, the amputees. He discusses strategy in the abstract, but one does not find in his novel the foreboding of the heart-rending horror of the front, nor true compassion for the lamentable herd of combattants. It is in solitude that Proust experienced so intensely the infinite sorrows of mankind. One is led to believe that personalities are rare who would be equally sensitive both to the problems of the individual and to those of a collective body.

* * * * * *

The same holds true when we enter fashionable *salons* with him. Having opened at random one of the tomes of the novel, I was struck, like many other readers, like Gide at his first reading of Proust, by the superficial agitation and inanity of the utterances of all these princes, these dukes and these duchesses. How many hours wasted over questions of protocol and precedence! How much ado about nothing!...Did the author really admire these useless members of the nobility? Was he a snob?

It is true that, from childhood on, Proust had enveloped names of great aristocrats in a dreamy type of poetry. He re-created an ideal Duchesse de Guermantes and linked her image to that of her illustrious ancestors, as he saw them in the stained glass windows and tapestries in the church of Combray. Even a touch of masochism entered into this frantic admiration; the Duchesse de Guermantes, he said to himself, "does not know, nor would she consent to know any of the persons who are here." Mingling with the bourgeois, he felt voluptuously that he was disdained, and when he recalled that the Guermantes had formerly had the right to decide "the life or death of [their] vassals," he felt that he was losing all will of his own, and that, as an imaginary slave, he threw himself at their feet, "...an earthworm in love with a star."

But when Proust had reached the age of 16 or 17, this feeling was translated into intense worldly ambition. He had a frantic desire to be admitted to a *monde*, which appeared all the more prestigious and delightful to him, since it seemed quasi-inaccessible. His novel shows frequent traces of that period of his life: he considered it a sign of meritorious superiority to become initiated in certain worldly rites; he mentions his "first highness"

347

— the first one to whom he was introduced — and his entrance at Mme de Guermantes's as "exceptional" events — or again he speaks of "tact," "taste," "distinction" as of qualities essentially linked to a person's rank on the social ladder. Wouldn't it be the view of a progressive democrat to believe that distinction can be acquired by anyone at all?

Proust felt himself unable to resist the magic attraction of the *salons*. As is always the case with weak and nervous persons, the quest for a particular pleasure rapidly took on, for him, the form of an obsession. To attain his goal, he was willing to attempt anything, ready to make exceptional efforts, to make sacrifices he later regretted, to overcome all sorts of obstacles. This attitude of Proust as a young man explains his correspondence with Montesquiou, which, it is said, has done a disservice to his memory, for Proust exhibited embarrassing weaknesses in these letters. But the Comte de Montesquiou could open for him the most closely guarded doors in Paris. It must be added that relations were always difficult with this tyrant, before whom, inexplicably, all socialites trembled. Proust, the simple, still unknown bourgeois, necessarily felt like a little boy vis-à-vis this distinguished nobleman, whose arrogance, wit and elegance he must have admired somewhat naively, but on whom he later modelled the extraordinary figure of Charlus. Having successfully entered a relationship with him, Proust unhesitatingly submits to his caprices, "scrupulously" obeys him. For his neckties, his witticisms, his poems, he has hyperbolic expressions of praise, like a courtisan of Louis XIV. When Montesquiou has one of his legendary fits of anger which always ended in a series of gross insults, Proust responds humbly, "One is not angry at lightning,

348

even when it strikes us, for, after all, it comes from heaven." In order to have Montesquiou attend one of his *soirées*, he is willing to exclude, on that particular occasion, his most intimate friends.

But as one turns the pages of this correspondence, the letters change their tonality: Proust gradually grows with them. He has brought to light all that is mere artifice in Montesquiou's grandeur. "I know you better than many other people," Proust writes modestly but with the self-assurance of a protector. Proust has gone to work and he thinks of his novel as of his life's sole duty. Montesquiou has remained *homme du monde*. In one of the last letters, it is the nobleman who asks the now triumphant writer for his support in solliciting a column of art criticism in a magazine! The reversal of roles is complete. Now, Proust has stated the absence of culture in the majority of the noblemen whose names had seemed so beautiful to him; he now recognizes their intellectual emptiness, their pettiness, their vices, and often their nastiness. There is nothing more sincere than his immense disappointment. There is no contradiction between the boundless snobbism of his youth and the severe condemnation which, in his maturity, he has pronounced upon the socialites; all one has to do, to resolve this apparent contradiction, is to see it in the perspective of time.

It is his personal experience as a "snob" that enabled him to bring the *salons* and those who frequent them so convincingly to life. Proust has endowed them with his own mundane ambition, an ambition which becomes their unique obsession: everyone only thinks of climbing socially by acquiring ever more elegant connections, to the detriment of those who are judged inferior in rank. An exhausting quest which leads, below the apparent

349

show of polite manners, to astonishing cruelties, to cow-
wardice, to the most ferocious expressions of selfishness.
Gilberte, now Mme de Forcheville, does not dare to
pronounce her father's, Swann's, name before the Duchesse de Guermantes, whose best friend he had been to his
dying day; in the end she disowns him who had hoped,
on the contrary, to survive in his daughter. This scene
— chosen at random — recalls the most poignant pages
of Balzac's *Le Père Goriot*. Snobbism has become here
a true passion, violent and tyrannical: in the midst of the
perpetual excitement which whirls these socialites from
visit to visit, from reception to reception, the most tender
feelings are sacrificed; the friends who cannot keep up
the pace are doomed to oblivion; no one has time to think
of those who disappear; there is no place for death in the
midst of these *fêtes*. Proust is not wrong in thinking
that, considered from this point of view, which is that
of the artist, the lives of these idle rich — though they
belong to a doomed environment — deserve no lesser
interest than the harsh and tense ambition of persons
who want to dominate in the world of finance and indus-
try, or to become managers of a corporation, union
officials or politicians.

However, what Proust has depicted is less a particular
social milieu than a certain number of individuals, taken
in isolation and each animated by a frenzied passion:
the pursuit of snobbism. A closer look at one case in particular, the evolution of Mme Verdurin's *salon*, will help
us to understand how the upper middle class gradually
rises to the level of the aristocracy, tending to absorb
or to replace it. But at no time do we fully grasp the
useful or useless role which this fashionable elite plays
in the country as a whole, which it no longer leads, and

from which it feels cut off. Proust never studies his characters in relation to their social function: with the rare exception of a diplomat and a physician, seen outside their professional framework; none of them work, yet all are wealthy. Apparently, in Proust's novel, money can only be acquired through marriage or inheritance, speculation on the stockmarket or prostitution. We are not told the true origins of the riches of these socialites and why their perpetual idleness seems to endow them with superior power... Such questions, as a matter of fact, do not even occur to the author. The fact is, that he seems to consider the privileges of this elite as unquestionable and existing from the beginning of time; this has led to the belief that there is on his part a sort of prejudice in favor of the aristocracy, a masked and hidden snobbism (while actually, in his artistic ascesis, he condemns them as outlived, as anachronisms). Actually, communal life, it must be repeated, has no real existence for him.[1]

---

[1] However, Proust's genius had obscure forebodings of the epoch's social malaise. He understood that the nineteenth century maxim: "Get rich!", a maxim that was so successful that one was led to believe in a natural order exclusively established on the principle of profit, no longer corresponds to the realities of the present. He had at least one opportunity to express this abstract finding in a magnificent image: three rich celebrities and the mistress of one of them were dining at a hotel, "where electric sources made waves of light well up in the large dining room; the latter becoming the equivalent of an immense and marvelous aquarium, before whose glass wall the working class population of Balbec, the fishermen and also the families of the petty bourgeois...pressed themselves against the windows to catch a glimpse, slowly wafted in the golden eddies, a glimpse of the luxurious lives of these people, as extraordinary for these paupers as those of fish or strange molluscs (an

However, in his representation of the individual, notably in depicting love, the question of sincerity cannot be raised either. On the one hand, he considers Sodom and Gomorrha as a Dantesque circle of hell; but on the other, he envisions the character Albertine — though the product of a transposition of sexes — as having awakened his best and innermost self.

Proust has proceeded in his intimate consciousness to a true dissociation from his sexual emotions: on the one hand, he has extracted from them all his knowledge about passion; on the other, all he learned about deviations from the sexual norm; he has studied, on the one hand, the general characteristics of love, and, elsewhere again, love's abnormal and exceptional aspects. Thus, he has devoted a certain part of his book to his feelings for Albertine;[2] other parts, which are almost independent of the former, are built around Charlus and his likes.

If Proust presents, as the object of his passion, not a young man, but a young woman, he does so in order to give his work a general scope, following in this the example of other writers before him. Since a Sodomite, in order to experience emotions in the course of reading, substitutes a male image for the novel's heroine, a "normal" reader would have been obliged, when reading Proust, to proceed to the opposite transposition, if the author had not himself made this effort for him to begin with.

important social question: it remains to be seen whether the glass wall will forever protect the feast of the marvelous beasts, and if the obscure people who are staring so avidly in the night, will not come and pluck them from their aquarium and eat them)."

[2] I wish to point out that Albertine is composed, like all of Proust's characters, of memories involving several persons of his set of acquaintances.

And this effort seemed all the more natural to him as the depth of the passion, its broad psychological laws (crystallization, anguish, jealousy) had always appeared unchangeable in man, no matter what might be the sex of the beloved. Only the social framework and circumstances external to the environment where a passion evolves are different, when a young man and a young woman or when two young men are involved. Through carelessness, no doubt, Proust has not avoided certain improbabilities in his narrative about Albertine, when he has her come to see him at midnight, or has her stay for weeks in the apartment which he inhabits together with his parents. But these details are so unimportant that most readers do not even notice them and that a distinguished playwright was unwilling to believe that Albertine could be the product of a transposition, because, to his mind, the author has spoken with authority and depth about women. (Not about women, but about love.) And it is true that into the narrative of this love, Proust has put some of his purest, freshest and most tender memories. He has attempted to associate the passion for Albertine with the idea of youth, with youthful enthusiasm, with its puerile gravity, with its unquenchable laughter. Hence the translucid and almost nacreous pages of *A l'ombre des jeunes filles en fleurs* with its young women who offer him the spectacle of "incessantly changing forms," of a "perpetual re-creation of the primordial elements of nature." Love in communion with youth becomes for him, at certain moments of exceptional happiness, a sort of mystique, which allows him to attain the highest realities in life.

When, however, he portrays Sodomites, he confines himself to studying the fatal calamity of their desire and its social consequences. Proust compares the Sodomite to a thief, a spy, a madman, a pedlar tracked down by the police. He shows us how Charlus is obliged to throw us off the track — and this is what makes his first appearance so impressive — with each one of his sidelong glances, with each one of his verbal mannerisms, each one of his gestures. But the author does not revolt against the persecutions suffered by the Sodomite. And this is the reason why he does not feel the need to drop his mask personally. Speaking in the first person singular, as "je," signifies taking a position as an individual and against society — an attitude which seems almost indecent to him. He has always accepted, like rain or good weather, mores and customs, arbitrary as they may be. Sexual deviation doubless appears to him a "poorly understood" and "uselessly blamed" phenomenon. He knows how vain are the laws that try to quell it. But his protest is not directed against these laws; it is expressed along different lines; it derives from the Sodomite's very sufferings and from the degrading lies to which he is perpetually constrained. It is precisely the painful character of the question which causes the reader to accept an otherwise shocking topic.[3] But Proust went farther: he has stressed the comic, grotesque and often repugnant aspects of homosexuality, comparing, for instance, these lovers to criminals who seek to wash away with water the traces of their crimes, as in the famous scene where Charlus enters in "conjunction" with Jupien. Never is Proust more sincere than in these pages, for he feels a sort of repulsion for his own

---

[3] Let us not forget that Proust was the very first one to treat this subject openly in literature.

desire, and, realizing his pathological state, he wants in this way, to condemn himself.

Gide, who has tried, on the contrary, in *Si le grain ne meurt* and in *Les Faux-monnayeurs* to link homosexuality with the ideal Greek love of beauty, found Proust's Sodom distorted and all too atrocious. To his objections, one day, the author replied, "I have infused my girls *A l'ombre des jeunes filles en fleurs* with all the grace of youth that I find in my memories, I have given them all the poetry that was in me, so there was nothing pure or delicate left for the portrayal of Sodomites ..." And indeed, Proust never shows them transfigured by love's magic.[4] All that is left for them is the brutal pursuit of pleasure. But, this way, he has hardly ever exaggerated the portrayal of his homosexuals. The dissociation of passion and desire which he stresses indeed conforms fairly well to the manifestations of their nature under the impact of social constraints.[5] Mutual love, already rare in normal beings, becomes for them something so exceptional, that they are reduced to seeking illusions in the environment of prostitution, illusions which, despite everything, quiet their need for sentimental effusion. The habit of resorting to venal love, because of the facilities it offers, progressively effaces in them the very possibility of a passion, and one sees the Charlus — more and more devoured by their sexuality — buy all sorts of

[4] There is only one exception: that is the love which Charlus feels for Morel, in effect hardly analyzed by Proust.

[5] Note that, for Proust, passion and desire both are dependent on physical pleasure, whereas for Gide, who proceeds to an analogous dissociation, passion always remains Platonic. Gide's dissociation goes much farther, since it succeeds in totally separating sentimental from sexual life.

creatures, glimpsed for an instant in random encounters, or in the street. Money becomes the natural mode of satisfaction of their lust; with the aid of money, they satisfy their desires, which soon become more and more abnormal. Toward the end of the novel, sadists, masochists, men of the world, men of the people, a priest, an alcoholic, all without purpose, brush against each other in a house of flagellation, where the follies of vice, its most repugnant "demands" are satisfied: where even a mutilated ex-serviceman is provided at request. This is where Charlus ends up after having established Jupien as manager of this house of male prostitution.

Such is the atmosphere, hallucinatory in its horror, which pervades Proust's cursed Sodom. But this atmosphere seems gradually to contaminate all scenes of the novel, at the rate at which one progresses in it: the characters are almost all revealed, Saint-Loup, M. de Cambremer, Bloch's uncle, under their new aspect as Sodomites; the women, Mlle Vinteuil, Albertine, Andrée, Bloch's niece as Gommorhans; whether they are normal or abnormal, the men only cling to inferior beings: to floozies, whores, valets that can be ordered sent to one's home at any hour, or that can be kept "captive" for weeks. In society as depicted by Proust, love felt between two equally cultured beings is an unknown phenomenon. In the end, does not this tendency in his novel, to generalize certain pathological types of desire, distort Proust's vision?

This is a question which is raised by the works of most great writers. Almost all of Dostoievski's heroes are epileptic, like himself. But by this very fact, they reveal depths of the unconscious hitherto unknown; Baudelaire had a taste for gamy and monstrous women, which, however,

incited the poet to develop a magic aesthetics of ugliness. A certain nervous unbalance, deforming the writer's
perception in some particular way, allows him to notice
new aspects of the external world, which remain hidden to
normal people. It is because Proust, who, by the fact of his
inversion, has suffered more than ordinary men from un-
requited love for morally low partners, has conceived of
passion as a purely individual creation which only feeds
on nervous anxiety, thus throwing light on an unknown
psychological law, whose scope is general. If he has driven
his jealousy to a quasi-morbid and masochistic degree,
going so far as to interrogate Albertine in order to re-enact
in his imagination pleasures she experienced with others,
by its very existence, this jealousy augments the depth of
his universe.

Of course Proust realized, in a general way, that a work
of art is often born in the midst of the most immoral circumstances: in an act of sadism, Mlle Vinteuil and her
girlfriend voluptuously defile her deceased father's photograph; later the two women will work day and night pious-
ly to reconstruct the notes for the septet which Vinteuil
had left unfinished and which will become a musical
masterpiece. Vice can cohabit with virtue, and sublime
feelings can grow out of the basest instincts. The morbid
traces, which we may find embarrassing in Proust's books,
are in some manner the price he pays for his genius.

* * * * * *

Thus, we reach this general conclusion: only a narrow
and superficial critique would find Proust's work vitiated
by the presence of pathological characteristics or by traces
of hypocrisy; these aspects are clearly apparent, but they
almost always conceal the author's insensitivity to collective life.

However, Proust has attempted to justify his views. Like Gide in *Les Faux-monnayeurs*, he has interspersed his novel's narrative with a sort of "Diary" of the novel, explaining how he succeeded in writing a certain scene, how he made such and such a discovery, thus little by little revealing to us and entrusting us with his aesthetic concepts. He starts with precisely this assertion: the writer must not leave his ivory tower; there should be no place for social, moral, religious or political questions in the work of art.

These questions, Proust maintains, can only be the objects of abstract theories, of endless discussions; they never cause us to leave the domain of formal intelligence — a domain which the artist must surpass. If diplomats or financiers suggest that such abstract theories and discussions are the only ones to be taken seriously (while actually they are the only frivolous ones), it is because they totally misunderstand the true nature of art. If otherwise they excite an immense public and fill most magazines, it is because they concern the practical side of our lives, which is of interest only to our superficial and lazy selves. The novelist, Proust says, who prefers to depict a worker's movement rather than a few idle rich, almost always succumbs to the attraction of facility: a considerably more intense effort is needed for the analysis of a minute emotion which is hidden in the dark background of our unconscious than for the agitation of humanitarian ideas or union problems: in a conversation, anyone can easily surrender to this kind of intellectual exercise, to this facile game. The artist who evokes a strike or an armed dispute is led to "speak" like a journalist who writes about an insignificant song: "It makes us *weep*...," or about his meeting with a sovereign, "I have had an *unforgettable* experience," i.e., he is not emotionally touched by his subject. The social novelist arrives in the end at a point of pure description, of producing mere nomenclatures of facts. Certain critics will admire his objectivity. Proust calls it "false realism."

As a matter of fact, like almost all great artists of his time, Proust believed that religious, moral or political topics are always and necessarily limited to simple intellectual "problems": that they cannot give rise to emotions which are as profound or as "real" as those of the life of the individual. Perhaps he has thus imposed certain boundaries on his work.

On the other hand, what constitutes the author's true greatness appeared to me more than ever before in the course of this new reading. Proust himself became, in fact, aware of it, witness the "Diary of [his] novel," and he gives an account of the nature of his art with a lucidity which is seldom found in other novelists.

Rightly considering that pure ideas never penetrate to the heart of a subject, he thinks that the writer should attempt to make his way through the layer of abstract speculations, ready-made theories and images, conventions and habits, and instead to seize from within the objects of the tangible world, their supreme reality. Proust's entire work is one continuous effort to retain in the most intimate realm of his consciousness, the very essence of things, i.e., emotions in their primordial purity. When he has fully understood them, then and then alone, he turns them into the objects of an extremely searching intellectual analysis. It is in this manner that he has succeeded in giving us the vision of a universe which has practically nothing more in common with our everyday views of life. It can be said that his flowers, his pleasures, his amorous intoxication are as different from our daily impressions as an ordinary table is remote from a table as conceived by the scientist: a collection of atoms spaced by the void.

Most remarkable is his method in itself, which he has so well described in *Le Temps retrouvé*. For Proust, the impression of the absolute which he seeks at the heart of his emotions is never found in moments of the present, or, at least, the present alone is nothing for him if it is not linked to memory — if, thanks to an association of his affective memory, he does not succeed in resuscitating past emotions. What happens is, as in the scene of the "madeleine" and in many others, the association of an immediate perception with a past perception, which is enlarged by memories. When he succeeds in this way in establishing a sort of identity between a moment of his past and the present, it seems to him that he has placed himself outside time, in eternity, that he has wrested this emotion from duration, from death, thus rendering it imperishable.

His style directly derives from this method of research. Proust tries constantly to establish analogies between two objects, or to discover a quality that two sensations have in common and thus to join them together by way of an image, which, properly speaking, is a metaphor. Proust's metaphors are doors which open immediately onto mystery; they create in depth truly fairy-like perspectives. If there is seemingly excessive length in the structure of Proust's sentences and unnecessary repetition in his work (as in most powerful writers), if I have detected stylistic affectations which, going back to the epoch of symbolism, sound dated, one forgets all these weaknesses thanks to Proust's metaphors. Aren't they the source of a perpetual poetic transfiguration of the universe? In this manner, Swann's estate and the castle of the Guermantes, associated with the quasi-mythological characters who inhabit them, and to the blossoming landscape that surrounds them, become for the child Marcel supra-terrestrial worlds: *Du côté de chez Swann* and *Le côté de Guermantes*. Here Odette's image is likened to a "Florentine work"; Albertine, to a Balbec seascape; love, to a given framework in nature or to Vinteuil's little phrase... These metaphors, too, have a distorting power; the most familiar things appear to be other than they are: a floozy or Mme de Sainte-Euverte are transformed into "a pink lady," respectively "the wicked fairy"; women seen in the proscenium of a theatre are metamorphosed into water-nymphs, whose busts alone appear above the balustrade. People and objects are sometimes so disguised, that, at first, one does not "recognize" them without surprise or quid-pro-quo. In Paris, one morning, half awake, Proust believes that he is transported to Balbec, and his room, his bathroom, suddenly seem to him those of the Grand Hotel; in *Le Temps retrouvé*, the Duchesse de Guermantes's famous *fête* seems to take place in a strange, dull, slow, snowy, fleecy atmosphere: one could be led to believe that the participants, like those of a masked ball, had put on white wigs, false double chins, lead soles on their feet; Proust gives us the unmediated impression of their aging, which, through its directness, deals a stunning blow to our hearts. Each metaphor brings us a different sensation, from which we can learn an intellectual lesson.

Often, the development of the metaphor (and the idea it represents) extend over several pages. Part of a primary observation, one might say, it gradually communicates its impetus to the surrounding objects: the small tables of the fashionable Rivebelle restaurant, at night, are seen as astral tables, like planets in a harmonious celestial system; the

361

waiters in their dizzying activity, are carried away by an incessant revolution, and, since they are standing, they evolve in a superior zone; the two horrible female cashiers are two magicians busy in this celestial vault — the image is even more striking when the author shows us Charlus at a ball, enthroned in the midst of women, giving the impression of an archbishop in his ample purple cassock, cross in hand. These are never, as it is sometimes the case with Giraudoux, bravura pieces, literary exercises, jokes perpetrated by *normaliens*. Every phrase reveals a secret; each stroke of the pen, a new, mysterious peculiarity of a being or a thing.

Finally, Proust's metaphors take on the power of hallucinations. Like modern poets, like Rimbaud who sees "a mosque instead of a factory, a *salon* at the bottom of a lake," Proust seems to be haunted by a perpetual dream. We ourselves no longer distinguish clearly the borderlines between dream and reality, between sleeping and waking. Conscious life becomes enlarged by the world of the unconscious, endowing the work with a quasi-unlimited power of suggestion.

* * * * * *

The philosophical conclusion of the work is based upon a generalized relativism and idealism. Outside the world of poetry, there seems to be nothing real for the author. In the perpetual flux of appearances, in the constant renewal of forms, there seems to be no fixed point of reference on which he could focus. The views of the child, of the adult, of the old man, differ so greatly from each other, that one might believe that he is confronted each time with another world, that at every moment one is presented with a different universe. The Albertine whom Proust had loved is not today's young woman whom he no longer desires; nor is she the same girl that his friend Saint-Loup may know, as he looks dispassionately at her. As I have pointed out elsewhere in this book, Proust has insisted on the closed character of our personalities, on our irremediable solitude. He finds it hard to perceive, at the heart of our consciousness itself, the nuclear *self* that remains; he only sees a succession of instant personalities...; when he is about to kiss Albertine for the first time, he wants to retain in his memory, be it but for a fleeting instant, this face which, as he says, will presently disappear forever.

Our beliefs are equally erroneous and deformed by our passions. "What criterion [is one to] adopt for judging humans," even if one bases his judgment on reason? Everyone is mistaken about his neighbor; views held by members of one social sphere about those in another are always fallacious, the results of incomprehension, disdain, ignorance. Having received an anonymous letter, Proust attributes it successively to each of his best friends: how is one to guess an individual's feelings when he wants to conceal his sentiments? If this one or that one were to confess, a new being, and, consequently, an unforeseeable person would suddenly be revealed. In this order of research, intelligence is of little help to us; as Bergson has said, it deals only with abstractions which are useful to us in practical life; it fails to attain truth in its fullness. In the end, only those few impressions are valid for the author, which from his sickbed he attempts to resuscitate at times in himself, through the power of memory.

This negating pessimism which recalls Ecclesiastes, may be discouraging. Why act at all, if all except art is illusion? Is there really in ordinary life no justifiable form of activity? By his disdain for the circles in which he moved, Proust was forced into a sort of dualism: he has severed the appearances — from absolute reality; the mobile and ephemeral images of the world — from the profound vital impetus. Nowadays, certain philosophers, like Emile Meyerson, show, on the contrary, a tendency to bring phenomena and "noumena" more closely together: they think that through science our intelligence penetrates the real universe every day more deeply (even if it will never understand it in its totality).[6] They oppose Kant and the Kantians as well as positivism. Science and reality reconciled achieve a monist view of the universe, upon which a new and solid morality of action can be founded.

Proust's position is more traditional: by disgust for the world of appearances, it can fill man with a desperate desire to turn to a God and to throw himself upon his bosom. Thus, towards the end of his life, Bergson identified the vital impetus with Roman Catholic mysticism. Proust, it is true, haunted by all types of anguish, has at least escaped one of them: anguish about the after-life. Preoccupation about any "beyond" was alien to him. The German critic Curtius has pointed out in the scene of Bergotte's death and in one or two other passages, some sentences about "other worlds," and although these allusions to the afterlife are buried in the immense text of Proust's oeuvre, Curtius thinks that he can conclude on their strength that Proust was a Platonist. But I believe, on the contrary, that these incidental remarks by Proust on "other worlds"

[6] The laws of science, says Meyerson, are not just arbitrary conventional interrelations; they have a *real* foundation, because otherwise, they would become true metaphysical entities. The world of quantity can lead as far in profound knowledge as that of quality; scientific intuition has its illuminations which are as extraordinary as those of artistic intuition.

correspond to hypotheses of his abstract intelligence, cast at random by the author who failed to attach any importance to them. It would be absurd to deny the existence of a beyond. Why not? Everything is possible. The soul's immortality — Bergson is said to have once answered a lady who during a dinner had interrogated him on this topic — "the immortality of the soul is a possibility which has nothing contradictory about it." But this "possibility" did not enter into the system of Proust's living thought. Certainly, he believes, like Bergson, in spiritual life, but in a spiritual life which finds its perfect expression in art. Art becomes part of duration. By means of the creative work of art, we can have the impression of hearing replies to certain "questions," to certain "interrogations," of reaching the outer limits of the entry way to Mystery. (Read the pages on Vinteuil's septet, which figure among the most beautiful texts of the author.)

But Proust assigns a place to the absolute here below, on Earth. This absolute, which endows life with meaning, does not necessarily make life desirable. Toward the end of his existence, Proust called for the coming of death; having no religious ideal, he only wished to leave the universal chain of illusions, to escape from pleasures and pains, which are nothing but aberrations of our senses, to attain the moment when he could at last cease to be agitated, cease to desire; he asked for no more than the absence of movement, for disappearance, fusion with an inconceivable non-being.[7]

---

[7] I have described this, the writer's state of mind, below, in *Remarks on the Last Months of Proust's Life* (p. 378 ff.).

2. PROUST AND TODAY'S YOUTH

What can the writer, whom we have just portrayed after a renewed reading, contribute to today's youth, so totally committed to solving social questions?

Here is a man who seemingly does not care about civic affairs. Obviously, Proust has taken a position in the Dreyfus Affair; in 1898, he even signed the demand for an appeal, presented by *L'Aurore*, guided by a call to reason. But rational views — as we know — appeared arbitrary and conventional to him. On the other hand, he protested, for instance, like Maurice Barrès, against Briand's project of the "separation" [of Church and State] which he thought susceptible of bringing about "the death of the cathedrals." He maintained close ties with Léon Daudet [of the right-wing and anti-Dreyfus *Action Française*] and with Gaston Calmette, manager of [the pro-Dreyfus] *Figaro*, to both of whom he had dedicated copies of his books. He did not discuss, as a matter of principle, the necessity of duels; he even declared constantly, for trifling incidents, that he was offended and wanted to fight a duel...Altogether, he considered laws which derive from public life as a simple matter of custom that a man of breeding accepts without question or discussion. He bowed to the hierarchical division of classes, to time-honored abuses, so gracefully that he made the impression of believing that society had always been the same in the past, and would never change in the future. This is the only social morality practiced by men which, in the end, he judged not according to an idea of what he perceived to be quite relative concepts of good and evil, but by proclaiming that certain gestures are attractive or unattractive, in accordance with a vague inner feeling about moral conventions. Yet, he believed that, from the viewpoint of intelligence, kindness is superior to cruelty. Why inflict useless suffering on anyone? Man left to himself is a vicious animal, easily capable of theft, murder, coarseness. To keep him from giving way to his instincts, it is consequently preferable to submit to rules and regulations, whatever they may be, of established conventions of politeness, on which rests what is called civilization.

To our contemporary youth, Proust thus looks like a solitary outsider who behaves as though he lived outside society, while respecting its formalities. Even the family group does not seem to exist for him, and if he adores his mother, he does so out of passion, but not out of a sense of duty. The only true morality he conceives of is that of an individualist.[1] No principle that is alien to him occupies his thought; nothing of a practical nature constrains him, since he is financially independent. An immense anxiety seizes him: he fears that his life will be a failure. Questions which anguish everyone during adolescence never cease to haunt him: he asks himself whether existence has a *raison d'être*, and what this *raison d'être* might be; why we are on Earth, and what exactly is our role.

---

[1] Morals similar to those of Gide, of Valery Larbaud, of Valéry and of the majority of great artists of this epoch; morals which signify the individual's duty to make the best of his potential in an effort to surpass himself, to reach beyond himself for something more vast.

In fact, he is engaged in a quest for pleasure — in the noblest sense of the word — with all the strength of his youth. The pursuit of pleasure becomes his one and only duty; sometimes the most insignificant rendez-vous with an unknown creature of easy virtue (Mlle de Stermaria, for example) provokes an agitation, an excitement that seem disproportionate to their cause: he does not hesitate to remove all obstacles, refusing, on that particular day, to come to the aid of a friend, or to keep his mother company, although she beseeches him to do so. It appears to him that to renounce this rendez-vous and not to benefit from this unique instant, susceptible of bringing him a true and profound joy, would be a crime which he would never be able to forgive himself.

However, having soon noted the inanity of all pleasures, having gradually exhausted the charms of life in the *monde*, the attractions of travels, the beauties of nature, the power of glory, the intoxication of love, all that remained for him was the joy of literary creation. Here, individualism seemed to him even more necessary: the artist must not let himself be distracted from his work, be it by intruders, be it even by disciples, be it by articles of propaganda, even for a good cause. "Human altruism," Proust proclaims, "which is not selfish, is sterile." It is true that in art he found those few minutes of ineffable emotion, of supreme happiness; these few minutes which are worth the sufferings of a lifetime; these rare instants which Faust has sought during his entire existence, these instants which one could invoke with these words: "Oh Time, arrest thy flight! Instant, prolong thyself!" Yes, it is finally in certain memories relative to painting: one day, Bergotte returns to the museum to see in Vermeer's *View of Delft* the precious "small expanse of bare wall so well painted yellow," and, suddenly struck by an attack, he dies, focussing his gaze on that color, which is of an almost absolute perfection, communing with it in a sort of ecstasy, before definitively losing consciousness. Or again, it resides in remembrances of music: one day, Proust heard the famous little phrase of Vinteuil's sonata, giving him the impression of entering, thanks to this phrase, into unexplored worlds and revealing to him, so to speak, the ultimate key to existence. It is in such moments that Proust perceived "le temps retrouvé," total happiness, a *raison d'être*.

Now, nothing could be farther removed from today's young man than this type of attitude towards life. When, as a consequence of the present economic depression, an adolescent finds all potential jobs taken, and is reduced to a sort of forced idleness without unemployment insurance, with a choice only between begging and voluntary service in a military work camp, he would not think of asking himself universal questions on the meaning of life; not only does he lack metaphysical disquietude but he has no disinterested terrestrial anguish either; he does not inquire: Why should I live? but: How could I live? What interests him is not the quest for a *raison d'être*, but a society adapted to his needs and basic necessities. His ambition would not be to enter this or that *salon*, but rather to join a certain social organization, a certain league or movement. Proust's work stands at the opposite pole of such preoccupations...

But I doubt that any great artist could answer questions of this nature, which are predominantly dictated by cares of a material order. A novelist committed to social concerns, who sympathizes with the oppressed masses, does not discuss in his works the future organization of a new society; he even distances himself from the present, seeking under surface images, a more profound, perhaps remote, but also more lasting reality; in other words, he places himself above all on the levels of form and creation. This is precisely why art, which, partly at least, demands a detached attitude, never manifests itself during periods of great social upheaval. When a person's safety and possessions are threatened, when his mind and heart are absorbed by daily political life to the point of only living in it and through it, being obliged to foresee, to decide, to act, he will be totally incapable of creating, or, if he is part of the audience, unable to understand the work, to receive the creator's productions. While they were taking place, neither the French Revolution, nor the War of 1914 saw the birth of great works, despite the importance of the events.[2] Only the talents of journalists or polemicists, of diplomats or policemen were then revealed. It is not a matter of chance that the great expansion of the press dates back to this period, which was so inauspicious to the arts: to 1789. One must add that dictatorship, which frequently accompanies or follows those troubled times — the dictatorship of a Napoléon or a Clémenceau — definitively deadens every impulse toward personal creativity, letting only an official and conventional art subsist, an art represented, e.g., by the works of Bosio during the period of the Empire style or by the patriotic poems of Richepin and Rostand in 1914. A minimum of material freedom and freedom

[2] In painting, e.g., David's cold and sad production can not be compared to those of Watteau and Latour, who were despised by certain revolutionaries because of their political indifference.

of the mind, the possibility of a certain disinterested attitude are needed for the flowering of works of art — freedoms indispensible to the true artist.

* * * * * *

These conditions, I fear, are not fully understood by part of the younger generations. As they see it, the artist who wants to disregard the ambient material conditions of time and place and who takes his stand *sub specie aeternitatis*, on the level of the absolute, of eternity, is the victim of a vain idealism. It is impossible, they say, to seek beauty or truth in themselves, for their own sake. Every scholar, every writer, these young people assert, is indissolubly linked to a given society; he works either *for* or *against* it. The pretence of disinterest is but a bourgeois illusion. Hence, the artist ought to suppress all screens that intervene between his self and social life. There exists no longer any difference in *nature* between intellectual work and manual labor. The latter, which for the past 150 years has not ceased daily to become more rehabilitated, tends to turn, at present, for the younger generations, into the quasi-symbolic, quasi-sacred form of all labor. Proust who, on the contrary, only considers the artist's activity as partaking of a particular essence, like a sort of free, spontaneous and gratuitous game (which is only later controlled by our voluntary intelligence) appears an idler in the eyes of today's young people, i.e., he represents a type that seems to have practically disappeared, that dates back to the days of symbolism and of art for art's sake, like a sort of troglodyte. And this unoccupied, sick, morbid man spends the better part of his days in an attempt to resurrect the past, in what he himself calls embarking on *A la recherche du*

371

temps perdu. Indeed, how much "time lost," to the thinking of these youths! And even worse: this rich bourgeois considers all ordinary tasks of man as inferior, negligible, without interest.[3]

In fact, however, one must concede that there exists a basic difference in *kind* between intellectual and manual labor. Doubtless, there are all sorts of degrees between these two extreme forms of human activity, and one passes from one to the other, as in biology, from the vegetable kingdom to the animal level. All the same, it is nonetheless true that, on one hand, the *purely* mechanical and specialized worker at the assembly line is rivetted to a monotonous and fastidious task which separates him from the end-product of his labor, taking away from him any understanding for, and any interest in it, while, on the other hand, labors of creation, of free invention and of research, already those of the mechanic, more so those of the engineer, and still more so, those of the scholar and the artist, are sometimes accompanied by sublime joys. Man should strive to lessen as much as possible the mechanical side of his work which demeans and stupefies him, to develop, on the contrary, the role of free invention, of research, which is the very aim of life...[4]

Thus, youth fails to comprehend the value of the disinterested attitude in art. If Proust scrutinizes the past, he does so, not to enjoy it as a pleasure taken in his own consciousness, but in order better to understand, in order

[3] These criticisms were mainly formulated by young people at a number of writer's conferences.

[4] A minimum of the mechanical, of course, remains necessary to the extent that it relieves — like certain acquired habits — the life of the intellect.

to clarify his feelings in the light of his intelligence. In other words, all of Proust's work, this extraordinary work of analysis, has knowledge as its only goal; knowledge which, for the author, is inseparable from art. There is perhaps no more beautiful, more noble activity than that of man in the pursuit of knowing himself and of knowing the world around him.

But today the existence of a gratuitous, disinterested activity of the mind is negated or misunderstood; *pure* knowledge, knowledge for itself, is neglected and despised by the majority of young people. A *cultured* person is considered by many of them — curious paradox! — as someone who must, above all, serve the State and be capable of devoting himself to collective society. This affirmation, it is true, is defensible to the extent that the sense of fraternal solidarity, while moving into the foreground, can contribute to the diffusion of a new culture, to its changing contents. On the other hand — and thence comes the real danger — there is an entire faction of young people declaring that a relatively uncultured, but physically healthy individual, an ignoramus who has adopted a certain nationalistic exaltation, is more useful to the community than a puny, selfish person of genius. It is not impossible that a robust exemplar of the former type could, in fact, be useful, but never as an artist. Art, and in particular literature, could not thrive on such concepts. History has seen, e.g. in Sparta, societies of this nature: will our civilization, influenced by a part of the new generations, adopt similar forms, which may perhaps bring us material and social progress, but which will not leave any more traces and will no more enrich the common fund of humankind than did Lycurgus' ancient city? Did not art, and poetry in particular, since the 19th century, choosing the road of hermeticism, enter an impasse, and is not Proust's work a terminal point rather than a point of departure? It is possible that we are bound to take steps backward (in literature, only history and the reporter's prose keeping their standing) so that eventually a new impetus of artistic creation can be reborn...

* * * * * *

Considering Proust's work from certain particular viewpoints, one notices the almost fundamental opposition between the author and contemporary youth, especially in their differing concepts of love. In Proust, as we have seen, passion takes the form of physical desire, but of desire thwarted by circumstances; passion soon turns into an anxious need which overflows the carnal exterior of the beloved, who in a certain way serves in the end as a mere support for the lover's imaginings. Hence, Proust's lengthy analyses of jealousy.

These analyses tend to confuse today's young reader. Who could devote so much time to love and its psychological complications? The flirtations, the feints, the estrangements, the reconciliations, the passions which disappear at the height of their fulfillment, only to be reborn as soon as they are threatened by obstacles: all these contradictions are considered superfluous, vain, embarrassing by our contemporary youth.

Yet, there is nothing as unreal as the denial of passion. Passion not only exists, it enriches the individual; it multiplies him, renewing his interest in life, associating, precisely in Proust's case, love with nature, travels, painting, music. Passion is also the basis of the couple, and thereby, at least ideally, the basis of the family: nothing makes children happier than to see their parents love one another, says Bertrand Russell.[5]

It may be added that there is perhaps not a single aspect of Proust's work, down to his fundamental pessimism, that does not disconcert the contemporary reader. At certain moments, Proust appears to be a sort of quasi-Buddhist Schopenhauerian: for him, the introduction of "evil" into life consists in "time" in which we are immersed; time incessantly transforms and dulls the world, while we in vain aspire to fasten on to some stable point. But the world continues to evolve, indifferent to our longing for an element of permanence in it, indifferent to our desire to feel our consciousness swathed in lasting tenderness. Surrounded by inferior characters and one or two friends, Proust became more and more lonely during the last years of his life, clinging to art as the sole buoy of salvation in the midst of the perpetual and universal renewal of all things. Art alone enabled him to endure his illness: he did not even hesitate to prolong his suffering, in order better to seize the essence of emotions, the ultimate goal of his work. We have seen that, on his sickbed, ill, nervous, having lost all illusions, his only thought — as long as he remained lucid — went to the addition of observations to this or that passage in his book, or to the inclusion of a new metaphor in a sentence. One might say that, from the last moments of his life, there emerges the image of a *hero*, certainly of a singular character, who, weak in willpower and constantly drifting through worldly pleasures, had to appeal to all sources of his energy, to an exceptional concentration of his innermost being, in order to be able to work.

[5] Cf. Bertrand Russell, *Marriage and Morals*, a remarkably level-headed and audacious work where the author envisages a renewal of the family, founded upon the parents' sexual passion.

True, today's young man has a thoroughly different concept of a hero; he sees him as someone physically healthy, disciplined and capable above all of sacrificing his personality to a collectivity: that man collaborates, joyously and with infinite hope, in the construction of a new society. There is nothing more vivifying, nothing more seductive than such a creative optimism which is needed whenever the individual devotes himself to an enterprise that entirely belongs to the domain of practical life.

However, Proustian pessimism is no less fertile, where a different type of action is concerned: namely action turned towards pure knowledge.

Heroes are not only leaders, administrators, "shock troops" of the working class, builders of factories or civic communities, great legislators. The life of an artist can also be heroic, as illustrated by Proust's biography, even reduced, if necessary − which would not be difficult − to *images d'Epinal.*

Thus Proust is right when he claims that he has properly served his country: he could only do his service as a writer, and the writer, as he defines him, can only be useful to his country "on condition that, at the moment when he studies the laws of art, he thinks of nothing else − not even of the fatherland − than of the truth that lies before him."

* * * * * *

We have closed the author's books again. And we have had the impression, even more strongly than before, that they are, like all great works, timeless.

Doubtless, they take place in that 19th century which, without worrying much about the moral consequences of the general materialistic development, dedicated itself to

376

the freedom of knowledge. Proust himself belongs to the last generations of writers of that century, who, in elevating literature to a summit, have sought salvation by way of art.

At present, in the imbalance brought on by the catastrophe of the economic depression,[6] a new era is rising while, simultaneously, new morals seem to be born. Would we witness the birth of a different type of works if a different society could be built with people who live in the fullness of their will? Architecture, with its ties to collective life, might perhaps come to flourish. But literary movements would be dealt a setback, no doubt, at least at the beginning of that period...

Let us go a step further: imagine an ideal society where there would no longer be any social classes, any police, any army, any mass production labor. There would then be no *raison d'être* for the artist. In the complacent optimism that would prevail, he would no longer naturally create works detached from his personality: every individual would become a creator and, simultaneously, his own sympathetic disciple. The possibility exists that a nation in perfect health would no longer produce artists and no longer feel the need to find artistic emotions through their mediation, since everyone would adhere completely to a daily pattern of action; everyone would be so totally aware at every instant, in every attitude, that never again would he call upon his memory, his imagination, use metaphors. But people fully aware at every moment, no matter what the circumstances, would in truth be gods.

September 2, 1935

[6] Sign of our times: here, peasants die of starvation while elsewhere governments or landowners voluntarily set fire to heaps of wheat.

3. REMARKS ON THE LAST MONTHS OF
PROUST'S LIFE

When a great artist creates his oeuvre, he gives it his most precious best. His correspondence can be little more than a document.

Proust's letters which I have just read add only a few minute anecdotes to literary history.[1] Their interest derives from the writer's character traits, on which they are focussed.

A novelist's correspondence never reveals someone unknown. But as the author was constrained to submit in his work to certain laws of his art, his letters — gross magnifying glasses — stress and often exaggerate the characteristic marks of his genius. Hence, his flaws become apparent and help us to understand how, in gaining mastery over them, he has turned them into his most genuine gifts. In a similar way, pathology often provides insights into the phenomena of normal life.

* * * * * *

What I noted, above all, in these few letters is the writer's manner of letting himself be guided by associations of ideas. When Proust speaks in his novel of a ray of sunlight or of the sales cry of a news vendor in the street, he insists on communicating to us all the other thoughts and feelings which occupied his mind at that same moment.

[1] As a matter of fact, I have written the following pages after having read the few letters which Marcel Proust had addressed to M. Paul Brach, during the last months of his life.

This spontaneous tendency of his intelligence, in fact, became a method in his work. If he does not resist the desire to empty the entire contents of a memory, he nonetheless disciplines it; if he moves away from his point of departure, he does not fail to come back to it, with all his will power: thus he succeeds in evoking the object in its full "density," in its complexity and its depth. On the contrary, in his correspondence, where there is not the slightest preoccupation with composition, associations of ideas unfold from one another, all on the surface. He has his chauffeur deliver a letter. And this letter brings back memories of a *soirée* at *Le Boeuf sur le Toit* and the "well roasted" chicken he had eaten: "And this chicken under the roof (*sous le toit*) made me think of Sem," he writes, "and of a nocturnal automobile ride with him." Then, as the links which hold the ideas together become ever more lax, this ride (or is it the *soirée* at the *Boeuf*?) evokes a scene in an insane asylum near Dijon, "which you know perhaps because of the sublime sculptural entrance which fronts it, and which is named by a preventive title, because it dates actually back to the 16th century: Moses' well." This entire passage seems to me comparable to those curious examples, given by certain English philosophers as types of absurd associations of ideas: a plate of biscuits, for instance, immediately suggests Joan of Arc, because the biscuits are arranged like the faggots of a stake in certain *images d'Epinal.*

No doubt, the singular character of Proust's letters gives us better insights into his creative efforts. This surrender of the mind to a chain of ideas and this perpetual distraction are constantly repeated in his immense correspondence; it is because of this that he succeeds in varying it, in filling it full of surprises. But in the letters which

I have just read, I have found, besides, a desperate tone, an avowal of distress — rapidly overcome, however, which hitherto I had not encountered...

* * * * * *

These letters were written in July and August 1922. In November, Proust died. They are some of his last notes. They bear witness to his intelligence, ever avid for new facts, curious like a famished stomach; he speaks of his friends whom he finds it increasingly difficult to meet; he worries about Montesquiou's posthumous attacks in his *Memoirs*: he takes pleasure in observing Céleste's and Odilon's reactions, gives the latter a course in the history of France; he is amused by a thousand trivia; he incessantly reminds his friend of the funny abbreviations and the secret formulae they had agreed on in their last conversations, never forgetting those that can provide the greatest pleasure. In the midst of his sadness, he maintains a continually spirited style, by means of which he seeks to prove more than his customary courtesy: a friendly thoughtfulness that would never slacken. At the same time, and despite his asthma attacks, his cough, his failing eyesight about which he complains, his fatigue and his irremediable boredom, he courageously attempts to proofread *Sodome et Gomorrhe*; he remains the artist he always wanted to be, sensitive to the magic of fame which is beginning to reward him now that he is almost no longer able to savor it.

During the last months which precede his death, he has arrived, by way of an imperceptible progress, at a sort of separation from life. His stark anguish is apparent in relation to his everyday routine and the material organization of his day's activities, which have become totally chaotic.

It is no doubt his asthma which had led him into an impasse. Asthmatics suffer less from their choking oppression during the night. Proust went to bed later and later. Soon he would stay awake all night long. Going to bed at dawn, he would often suffer from insomnia. To avoid the drama of tossing about on his pillow, where one vainly seeks a merciful respite, he took sleep-inducing drugs. Little fairy phials that he so lovingly evoked, magic phials that would dispense rest with a few drops. But miracles demand sacrifices in return. Since the effects of sleeping drugs extend into the following day, into the waking state, they must be counteracted with caffeine. Forcing nature entails calling for her revenge. Little by little, Proust had reached a point were he was living artificially. Maintained in a state of excitation by tonics, he no longer felt tired. After 24 or 36 hours of consecutive wakefulness, he went to bed again by a decree of his will, having actually lost the habit of spontaneously going to bed at night. He had to rationalize the situation: body and mind, he reasoned, must relax after a certain period of activity, and this is the moment for me to rest. He would not be able to rise if, before going to sleep, he had not ordered Céleste to enter his room the next day at 11 p.m. (e.g., one hour before a friend's visit). In fact, there was no reason for what he still called his nights to end by themselves (since they had no natural beginning). He had destroyed in himself that kind of instinct we have for sleep: but it is not with impunity that one escapes any reflex action. He stood now completely outside the social settings that provide a rhythm for our gestures. He had a sense of pure inner existence, flowing indefinitely, disconnected from all outside collective movements. And this explains the vertigo produced by certain very simple sentences in his letters: "Since I cannot stay in bed for so many days, I decided to go out *today*, Tuesday (*yesterday*), for on days when I go out, I stay out all night long"...etc.) or again, "I had myself awakened on purpose (something that I should never do). The result was such a momentous change of hours, that, deceived, as if by [long] summer days..." These unimportant phrases resound, however, like certain banal but heart-rending words: "Mother," "Dear God," murmured so plaintively by those whom one suddenly reminds of sorrows that are still quite alive.

Today, yesterday, evening, morning, weeks, seasons: he had ended in a total disordering of the flux of his consciousness, like Rimbaud's systematic disordering of his senses. But the 20-year-old poet had voluntarily chosen this sacred disorder, which leads, as he says, to madness. On the other hand, the novelist, this novelist of "the past lost and recaptured," doubtless was destined, against his will, to fall victim to time.

In his terrible isolation, without regular points of reference, the questions of the great problems of life are perpetually raised again, and they are the source of an infinite distress. I recall with what panicky terror one of my friends spoke to me of a hide-away he had found in the countryside, a property undisclosed to his family. The first day, very tired, he had stayed in bed all day long; the next day, he hesitated to get up, not seeing any good reason that could incite him to stir. The following day, he was lost: on the horizon, he looked in vain for the smallest reason to get dressed, to make the slightest effort. Does not conventional wisdom teach that one is better off seated than standing, and lying down than seated? Absolute despair. One does not even envisage suicide, because suicide would still be a homage to life. And it is sufficient to be deprived, be it only for an instant, of the unconscious habits which sustain our wretched existence, and immediately we are faced with the eternal question: what is the good of living? And since man has not yet found a satisfactory answer, he has no decisive motivation capable of inciting him to break out of his inertia.

If we act, we do so because we are guided day by day by insignificant immediate rationalizations. When they disappear, all our motions come to a halt. This explains why a person rarely worries about the course his life might take beyond the current year. I have never heard anyone saying: Five years from now, I shall leave France and travel around the world, or, ten years from now, I shall give up writing. Only those who have conquered time could thus face the future, if their Pyrrhic victory would not be transformed for them into intolerable pains. Proust's legendary visits at 2:00 a.m., the remainder of his worldly life, pursued under such extraordinary conditions, have given rise to many a strange anecdote. But every one of his inadequate actions was the result of a series of extremely distressing efforts or feelings. There was, first, a physical malaise: "Whenever I stay in bed too long, I perspire so profusely that I have to change my nightshirt...every quarter of an hour, and consequently, I catch a chill..." Then, the impossibility of accomplishing, by himself, the routine gestures of existence. This marvellously intelligent man had become a sort of big and heavy manikin in practical life, barely manageable even by himself, and who had to be shaved by a barber, and dressed by Céleste. If Céleste is not with him, he writes, "It is 2:00 in the afternoon, Wednesday, and I have not yet taken off my hat and my overcoat..." This amiable apparent nonchalance, at which his friends smiled with sympathy as though it were a benign infirmity, on the contrary concealed an extreme sensitivity, an utter lassitude. To understand this feeling, it suffices

383

to imagine those moments which we have all experienced at least once, when after a night of dissolute pleasures, one comes home exhausted, nauseated, and, still fully dressed, suddenly plumps down on the bed, crushing it. Unable to make the slightest movement, one is nonetheless kept from falling asleep by the desire to take off his collar and over-coat. In vain does his imagination offer fortunes to the ideal valet who would tuck him, without any effort on his part, between the warm sheets of a marvellous bed. In vain one invents a perfect mechanism which, triggered by his pure thought, would lower on him an immense cutting blade, precise enough just to cut off his clothes and relieve him of them, like certain machines which husk seeds. But brusquely, one wakes up a little later, atrociously sickened and in a crumpled tuxedo. "I think with horror about my life," wrote Proust.

There is, however, still another type of suffering in this existence which perpetually unfolds as though above a void: it is a feeling of unmotivated fear. The only real fear. It recalls to my mind the anguish which sometimes seized me, when, working for instance from evening to morning, I had irremediably passed the hour when one can still go to bed at night. Here is the morning twilight, rising like remorse. Didn't I leap in a dreadful bound over a whole night, violate my sacred sleep, break a law of nature? A superstitious fear leads me to the obsession: Will I ever recover the rest which my prolonged nervous excitement has in fact put to flight? It is a mad man's panic, like the one which may seize us at the thought of "the mysteries of those infinite spaces".

Yet, this fear is entirely terrestrial. It can emanate from a dangerous way of living, from a life gnawed by the void. Proust had never experienced metaphysical fear. He

384

had simply understood that the frightful vertigo that was deepening under him could not last much longer, that it had led him close to death — a death he awaited with tranquillity. The earth turns. It is day. It is night, says Genesis. Man adapts the rhythm of his movements to the motions of the planet he inhabits. Proust, doubtless, had adapted his activity to the oscillations of a far away star. He was no longer truly a son of this earth; he had ceased to lead "a life," that normal life characterized by regular alternations which were alien to him. No longer being in life, he knew that death was very close at hand.

He felt no regrets about the road he had taken, because it had in fact detached him from everything. "In the interval [between my childhood and today] is placed a whole world of pleasures and sufferings, and I no longer know how to hold the pen which I took up again too late." The prospect of beginning his existence all over again, or, in fact, any other existence, seemed to him the worst of punishments, hell, the only true hell that frightened him. In *Le Temps retrouvé*, he writes that the possibility of experiencing a new amorous passion with all it entails in the way of abrupt movements, of unrest, anxieties, tormenting jealousies, would appear to him as the most severe punishment that could be inflicted upon him. Doubtless, sexual desire still tortured him and the satisfaction he afforded it could only add a sombre sadness to his state of mind. It is true that there remained for him the faithful friendship of his old companions and of his new admirers: but that feeling of urgency which vainly seeks an absolute in the intellectual excitement of conversation, led him to write: "In the end, it's all very well, one thinks of people and gets along easily without them." Or again, in the following letter, "When I depart, I will never come back: good

385

riddance for my friends." Finally, art, the supreme value and his real goal, seems to have been surpassed by him in the course of this last period of his life. In those days measuring fifty hours, in those endless nights which he would suddenly interrupt, in this exceptional existence, his work seemed trivial to him. Art appeared to him little more than the expression of the suffering and ills he had known, and which it was futile to relive. In the end, the only pain he had not experienced was anguish about a beyond. I know few men who have faced death with so much affective indifference regarding the after-life and who were as tired of life as he was. This prevailing lassitude did not otherwise keep his generous intelligence from passionately scrutinizing a thousand superficial problems; a scrutiny to which he gave all he had, up to the last moment. But the very moment after these labors, he would fall back into a state of mind which fairly closely resembles that of the Buddhist in his quest for progressive detachment from all passions. At that time, he had conceived the idea of death as deliverance. Since his first attack of influenza, caught in the beginning of the winter of 1922, he did not want to be treated; he put up no resistence to the natural course of the illness. "Complications" set in and caused his death in November...

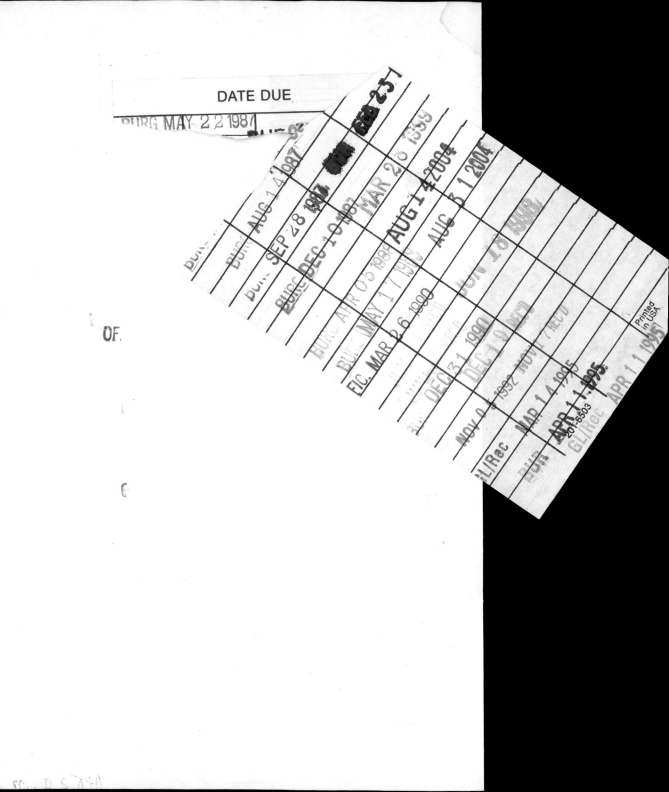